Come Now,
Let Us Argue It Out

Anthropology of Contemporary North America

Come Now, Let Us Argue It Out

Counter-Conduct and LGBTQ
Evangelical Activism

Jon Burrow-Branine

University of Nebraska Press | Lincoln

Library of Congress Cataloging-in-Publication Data
Names: Burrow-Branine, Jon, author.
Title: Come now, let us argue it out: counter-conduct and LGBTQ evangelical activism / Jon Burrow-Branine.
Description: Lincoln: University of Nebraska Press, [2021] | Series: Anthropology of contemporary North America | Includes bibliographical references and index.
Identifiers: LCCN 2021005237
ISBN 9781496224200 (hardback)
ISBN 9781496228192 (paperback)
ISBN 9781496228710 (epub)
ISBN 9781496228727 (pdf)
Subjects: LCSH: Christian sexual minorities—Religious life. | Christian sexual minorities—United States.
Classification: LCC BV4596.G38 B88 2021 | DDC 261.8/357660973—dc23
LC record available at https://lccn.loc.gov/2021005237

Set in Charter ITC Pro by Mikala R. Kolander.

For Jane

Come now, and let us reason together.

—Isaiah 1:18 KJV

Come now, let us argue it out.

—Isaiah 1:18 NRSV

It will always happen that he who is not your ally will urge neutrality upon you, while he who is your ally will urge you to take sides.

—Machiavelli, *The Prince*

My people are destroyed for lack of knowledge.

—Hosea 4:6 NRSV

Always in your stomach and in your skin there was a sort of protest, a feeling that you had been cheated of something that you had a right to.

—George Orwell, *1984*

Go therefore and make disciples of all nations.

—Matthew 28:19 NRSV

An existence can become defending an existence.

—Sara Ahmed, Tweet

Contents

Illustrations

Acknowledgments

I want to thank, first and foremost, all the gracious and inspiring people whom I met during my fieldwork. In addition to the many people who took the time to share their experiences with me at TRP events, I owe a debt of gratitude to TRP's staff and the members of the steering committee. Thanks especially to Paul Creekmore and Matthew Vines for tolerating the presence of a shy and inexperienced ethnographer and making this project possible.

This book is the outgrowth of my doctoral dissertation in the Department of American Studies at the University of Kansas (KU). I was fortunate to have a dissertation committee whose members from the very beginning provided penetrating feedback and encouragement that ultimately helped to bring this book to life. Ben Chappell, Lynn Davidman, Sherrie Tucker, Henry Bial, and Dave Tell—thank you for challenging my thinking on ethnography, power and religion, religion and the body, critical theory, Foucault, the genres and conventions of academic writing, and so much more that informs this book.

Beyond my committee, I am indebted to many others who provided incisive feedback and thoughtful criticism on the numerous drafts of this book. First, I would like to thank both reviewers for the University of Nebraska Press for their kind words and penetrating feedback, which made the book even stronger. I would like to thank audience members and fellow panel discussants for asking tough questions at several academic conferences where I presented early chapter drafts.

The other members of my graduate cohort at KU helped me sharpen the earliest ideas that formed the foundation of this project. Thanks in particular to Justine Greve, Steve Marston, Saoussen Nour, Bobbi Rahder, Katie Vaggalis, and Halimah Williams. Along the way, I also had the honor of learning from many other amazing graduate students, in American studies and elsewhere at KU, but especially Crystal Boson, Finn Boson, and Stephanie Krehbiel. Also a big thank you to Jennifer Hamer, whose seminar in methods in American studies gave me the self-confidence to pursue an ethnographic project.

All through my graduate studies, I also had the great joy of teaching in the Humanities Program at KU. The work funded the bulk of this project, but more important, it also gave me the opportunity to work with and learn from some truly smart and passionate people. Thanks particularly to all my students over the years. It was an honor to have played a role in your development as individuals and informed citizens. All of the Humanities faculty are great, but I would especially like to thank Rick Botkin, Antha Cotten-Spreckelmeyer, Chris Forth, Jenny Heller, Marike Janzen, Sean Seyer, Dale Urie, and Sandi Zimdars-Swartz. The other graduate instructors in the program were similarly inspiring, especially Ashley Acosta-Fox, Amber Beasley, Andrea Clark, Shelly Cline, Marwa Ghazali, Luke Herrington, Terilyn Johnston Huntington, Emily Leck, Ora McWilliams, Brian Moots, Tamara Ricarda Vitale-Keenan, Rachel Schwaller, Damon Talbott, and Heather Yates. I'm grateful for all the stimulating conversations about inclusive pedagogy and the value of a liberal education.

On a hotel elevator at one of TRP's conferences, I had the happy coincidence of meeting Dawne Moon. Despite my rudely interrupting her conversation with someone else on the elevator after I realized who she was, Dawne was eager to talk and invited me to dinner the same evening. I'm incredibly grateful for her generosity and the opportunity to exchange fieldwork stories and share ideas.

I reserve my greatest gratitude for all the family and friends who gave me encouragement and respite throughout this project. Even though I didn't always have the time and energy to reciprocate, an unbelievable number of friends went out of their way to include me in their lives and express interest in my work. At the risk of offending friends (both old friends back in Wichita and new ones in Kansas City) for not mentioning them by name, I want to thank Andy Campbell and Ronnie Felder, and all the fabulous people I've met through them, for being like family to Jane and me.

Finally, I would not have had the flexibility, tenacity, or courage to complete this project without the unwavering support of Jane and her incredible family. I could list almost all of them, but without Gary and Camille in particular this work wouldn't have been possible. Thanks to Ross, Penny, Jax, and Abbey for being the best furry writing companions ever. And to Jane: here we go, you and me.

My apologies to the many people I didn't mention by name. I hope you know how thankful I am. Any errors or omissions are, of course, my own.

Come Now,
Let Us Argue It Out

Introduction

I stood shoulder to shoulder with twenty-two other people in front of a makeshift stage facing an audience of several hundred. It was late on a Thursday evening in November 2015 in a hotel ballroom in downtown Kansas City. We were there for the first day of a three-day conference on lesbian, gay, bisexual, transgender, and queer (LGBTQ) issues in primarily conservative Christian communities, and we had volunteered to participate in a ceremony memorializing the transgender women who had been murdered in the United States that year. The conference organizers designed the ceremony to coincide with the upcoming Transgender Day of Remembrance, an international event held annually on November 20 since 1999 that honors the memory of lives lost to acts of antitransgender violence.[1]

Each of the participants in the Transgender Remembrance ceremony held an 8-by-10-inch photograph of one of the murdered women and a long-stemmed red rose. Most of the photographs came from the women's social media accounts or local LGBTQ news outlets, the only photographs of them the organizers of the remembrance were able to find. On the back of each photograph were a few handwritten notes: the woman's name, her age, and how she died. I held a picture of a Black transgender woman, named Keyshia Blige, who was wearing a white and black, low-cut, sleeveless shirt and a fuchsia flower in her hair. The photograph, which was her Facebook profile picture, was a selfie that Keyshia took with a fuchsia-colored cell phone in front of a mirror in what appears to be a dressing room. The back of the photograph read "Keyshia Blige. Murdered (shot) in Chicago. 33." Later I learned that Keyshia was shot in her car and died while trying to drive herself to a hospital. Unlike most of the other transgender women memorialized in the ceremony, it's not clear whether Keyshia was explicitly targeted for being transgender.[2]

One by one, we held up the photographs and said the women's names. In between each photograph, from the stage behind us, Nicole Garcia—a transgender woman, Latina, and candidate for ordination in the Evangelical Lutheran Church in America (one of the largest mainline Protestant denominations in the United States)—read a short eulogy for each of the women. Each was a pastiche of the women's hopes and struggles, along with recollections by family or friends stitched together from social media profiles and hurried, sometimes unreliable, media accounts of their deaths.

When my turn came, I held up the photograph of Keyshia and made my best attempt to say her name "firmly and with love," as I had been instructed to do earlier that day. "Keyshia J. Blige," Garcia repeated from the stage behind me, "was a Black transgender woman from Naperville, Illinois. She was thirty-three years old and had recently begun transitioning. Keyshia graduated from community college with a degree in accounting and worked for Chase Bank. She posted this proud statement of her identity: 'Ms. Keyshia J. Blige one of the baddest bitches on the land I call it for the big girls.'"[3]

After the final name was read and the final eulogy delivered, the ceremony ended with a moment of silence and a final quiet amen from Garcia. Afterward a few of the volunteers extemporaneously began to turn the makeshift stage into a makeshift altar, laying the photographs and roses in a pile before the stage. I did the same.

This ritual memorializing the lives and deaths of transgender women of color is but one moment in the ongoing, often overlooked conversations among and about LGBTQ people in contemporary evangelicalism.[4] In addition to marking transgender lives as sacred, the ceremony illustrates some of the strategies some LGBTQ Christians are using to challenge mainstream evangelicalism's exclusionary teaching and practices—especially the indifference, ignorance, and enmity—concerning LGBTQ people.[5] Like the broader conversations it reflects, the conference where the Transgender Remembrance took place represents an effort to change conservative evangelicalism from within and to create space for living as both LGBTQ and Christian. Countering conventional narratives about the antagonistic relationship between the evangelical and LGBTQ communities in the wake of the culture wars, the argument in such spaces is that LGBTQ social justice is not only compatible with Christian faith—even conservative Christian faith—but also necessary for living authentically as a Christian and a responsible citizen.

Come Now, Let Us Argue It Out provides a look into a little-known community that challenges taken-for-granted narratives about what it means to be LGBTQ and Christian in the contemporary United States. Based on participant observation fieldwork with a faith-based organization called The Reformation Project (TRP), this book is an ethnography of how some LGBTQ and LGBTQ-supportive Christians negotiate identity and difference and work to create change in often hostile spaces and intractable situations.

TRP is a national nonprofit organization with Kansas roots, working in primarily conservative evangelical Christian communities to change attitudes and teachings regarding LGBTQ people and to promote their full acceptance and inclusion. TRP's strategies include grassroots organizing and theological training, building networks of LGBTQ and ally Christian activists and equipping them with the tools they need to go back to their communities to create change. Their primary mission is to provide an education in theologically conservative, LGBTQ-supportive theology to aid already supportive Christians in their conversations with nonsupportive Christians. Among other activities, TRP's work includes developing educational materials, training community leaders, networking with pastors and other evangelical leaders, organizing educational and dialogue-centered events in local churches, and hosting annual conferences. It's a bottom-up approach to social change and a form of relational organizing. The goal is to influence everyday conservative evangelical attitudes, values, and beliefs through relationship building at the grassroots level to create a foundation for broad social and institutional change. While this book narrates the strategies and conversations specific to TRP's efforts to foster change, I also use TRP as a window into a broader conversation currently under way in some corners of evangelicalism where what it means to be a Christian and LGBTQ is an object of concern.[6]

I tell two broad stories about the struggles and aspirations of the LGBTQ and LGBTQ-supportive Christians I met during my fieldwork. My primary argument is that the individuals organized around and motivated by LGBTQ inclusion in conservative evangelical communities can be understood as constituting a community of counter-conduct. "Counter-conduct" is a concept proposed by the philosopher and historian Michel Foucault in 1978 to describe practices and movements of resistance and refusal that can arise in regimes of power and control, as the ritual described previously illustrates.[7]

As I learned, the LGBTQ and LGBTQ-supportive Christians I met were theoretically and rhetorically adept at creating and parsing genres and scripts in the pursuit of making space for living as LGBTQ and Christian in conservative Christian spaces. Through careful description of rhetorical and embodied performances, I document everyday moments of agency and resistance that result in new politics, ethics, and ways of being as individuals in this community navigate the exclusionary politics of mainstream evangelical institutions, culture, and theology.

The second broad story I tell is about the politics of inclusion and representation in LGBTQ Christian activism in evangelicalism. At the same time that activists wrestled with the exclusionary theological and institutional habits of evangelicalism, they also had an ongoing conversation about their own assumptions about what it means to be LGBTQ and a Christian. As such, I also tell a story about how those I met grappled with the internal politics of advocating for LGBTQ inclusion in evangelical spaces—whose interests were being served, whose needs were being met, and who was being included and excluded.

TRP and Entering the Field

I first learned of TRP the same way as did many of those with whom I spoke during my fieldwork: by watching a viral YouTube video called "The Gay Debate: The Bible and Homosexuality."[8] The unembellished video, filmed and posted in 2012, shows the then twenty-one-year-old Matthew Vines delivering an hour-long presentation at a church in Wichita, Kansas. Vines, who introduced himself as gay and Christian, outlines a biblical argument in support of gay people and same-sex relationships that's designed to resonate with a conservative evangelical audience who views the Christian Bible as God-inspired and authoritative. At the time I was researching Andrew Sullivan, a writer, political pundit, and gay Catholic, and his now retired blog, *The Dish*, for another project in which I was examining the role of sexuality and the body in shaping the shifting boundaries between the religious and the secular in American culture.[9] In a post titled "The Next Generation Speaks," Sullivan had embedded a link to Vines's video with an excerpt of an endorsement by the writer and gay activist Dan Savage.[10]

I was immediately as interested in the circulation and reception of the video as I was in its content. In particular, I was interested in how Vines and his arguments were appropriated to both confirm *and* challenge conventional narratives about the relationship between being gay and being Christian in contemporary American culture. Commentators—whether in the conservative Christian or mainstream media—generally interpreted the popularity of Vines's video as a sign of the waning influence of conservative evangelicalism and so-called traditional Christian values in the United States, although they disagreed about whether this waning influence should be celebrated or lamented.

Many commentators also emphasized Vines's Kansas roots. In recent decades the state's religious and political reputation has come to be associated with aggressively conservative politicians (like Sam Brownback and Kris Kobach), Christian fundamentalist groups (like Westboro Baptist Church and their "God Hates Fags" campaigns), and Kansas's role as a laboratory for insights into national political trends—as illustrated by books like Thomas Frank's *What's the Matter with Kansas?*[11] In any case, by situating himself *within* conservative evangelicalism, Vines's self-identity and arguments also raised important questions about what it means to be Christian and gay and who gets to decide.[12]

After the YouTube video went viral, Vines followed up on its success over the next two years by publishing a book on similar themes and announcing his new nonprofit organization, TRP.[13] TRP is a "Bible-based, Christian grassroots organization," as it's described on the organization's website and in promotional materials, with a mission of "promot[ing] inclusion of LGBTQ people by reforming church teaching on sexual orientation and gender identity."[14] In early 2014, while I was researching a field site suitable for my interests in the intersections of conservative evangelical and LGBTQ social movements, I learned that TRP would be organizing a conference later that year in Washington DC, so I made the trip from Kansas to do some exploratory fieldwork and begin the process of gaining access to the community. The conference brought together more than two hundred LGBTQ and ally Christians for education and training on how to make a biblical case for LGBTQ inclusion and to explore ideas for how to organize for change in their own faith communities. It also provided a space for participants to talk about the shared joys and difficulties of identifying as LGBTQ or LGBTQ-supportive and Christian.

On the second day of the conference, I introduced myself to Matthew Vines and Max Kuecker, a white straight man around the age of thirty who at the time was TRP's national field organizer, and expressed my interest in doing fieldwork with the organization. I also met Paul Creekmore, who was a participant in TRP's inaugural multiple-month leadership-development training program in early 2013. After completing the program, Paul continued to work with TRP as a volunteer organizer, among other things chairing the steering committee responsible for planning TRP's regional training conference in Kansas City in November 2015.[15] Paul happened to be facilitating a breakout session to which I was assigned at the Washington DC conference, and I learned from his name tag that he, like me, was from Kansas City. When the session was over, I struck up a conversation with Paul and made a note in my fieldnote journal to contact him when I returned home. A few months later, after a couple more conversations by email and in person, Paul graciously invited me to serve as the administrator for the Kansas City conference steering committee.

Conversations

This book draws on and contributes to ongoing scholarly conversations at the crossroads of gender and sexuality studies and American religious studies while using the methods of critical ethnography. Scholarship on the identities, communities, and lived experiences of LGBTQ Americans has broadened our understanding of the lived experience, diversity, variability, politics, and cultural specificity of gender and sexuality in the United States. This book is inspired by analytical frameworks in this interdisciplinary field of research that are interested in the relationships among gender, sexuality, and power—both in the sense of how gender and sexuality are sites for the negotiation of power relationships and how power is itself productive of regimes of gender and sexuality. As John D'Emilio and Estelle Freedman summarize in *Intimate Matters*, the history of sexuality in the United States is less a linear progression from repression to freedom than "a tangle of power relations that constantly reconstruct sexual norms."[16]

This body of scholarship is broadly informed by postmodern and poststructuralist theories of the social construction of identity. Such theories of identity formation view identity not as given or essential but as socially constructed, enmeshed in power relations, and enacted through everyday discourse and practices.[17] Moreover, inspired by feminist theories of intersectionality, another primary concern in this field has been to understand how sexuality and gender intersect and work in tandem with each other and with other categories of social identity such as class, race, and nationality.[18]

Despite these insights, religion as an analytical framework continues to be conspicuously absent from this literature or, if present, typecast in familiar roles.[19] As several scholars working in this area have observed, this literature often positions LGBTQ people as outsiders to American religious—especially conservative Christian—history while at the same time writing religion out of LGBTQ history.[20] In 2012, for example, D'Emilio and Freedman, in the afterword of the third edition of *Intimate Matters*, reflected that the lack of sustained engagement with religion is still one of the notable lacunas of the field, suggesting that scholars should turn "to further explorations of the role of spirituality and organized religion in the sexual history of America, a subject that remains understudied despite the continuing power of religious values to shape both sexual meanings and political contests over sexuality."[21]

Jasbir Puar attributes the lack of robust engagements with religion in theories of sexuality and queerness in part to what she calls "queer secularity," an assumption that queerness and legitimate queer identity and politics belong in the secular category of the religious-secular binary. For instance, queer secularity sometimes assumes that queer agency and resistance require a transgression of religious norms: "Queer secularity demands a particular transgression of norms, religious norms that are understood to otherwise bind that subject to an especially egregious interdictory religious frame. The queer agential subject can only ever be fathomed outside the norming constrictions of religion, conflating agency and resistance."[22] Thus religion is viewed as "*always already pathological*," which fails to account for ways in which the "establishment and observation of religion itself" may be a "mode of political or social criticism, dissent, or resistance."[23] Janet Jakobsen makes a similar point while also calling attention to some of the stakes of ignoring religion: "The traditional view of religious repression underwrites a form of gay politics that appears to be necessarily secularizing, an appearance that has been extensively exploited by the political Right. . . . It seems one cannot be both gay and religious, a disjunction that is belied by the lives of many gay persons and that splits gay rights movements from progressive religious movements that might provide crucial alliances."[24]

Building on the insights of these and other scholars working at the intersections of religion, gender, and sexuality, I move religion to the center of the tangle of power relations that continually shape and reshape gender and sexual identities, norms, values, and politics.[25] I am interested in how religion fashions gender and sexuality, how gender and sexuality function as sites for the production of religious values and meanings, and how power is negotiated through the intersecting discourses of religion, gender, and sexuality.

To provide a fuller account of the role of religion in the lives of LGBTQ people, a recent interdisciplinary body of scholarship has focused on the religious and spiritual lives of LGBTQ people in general and LGBTQ Christians in particular.[26] It is important that this scholarship charts a way forward for thinking about religion in relation to LGBTQ social justice that goes beyond antagonisms, repression, and conflict while also emphasizing everyday moments of agency and resistance.[27] At the same time, studies that put specifically conservative evangelicalism and LGBTQ issues into conversation have mainly focused on either the antagonistic relationship between the Christian Right and LGBTQ social movements or the practices and institutions that help gay Christians reconcile cognitive dissonance between their faith and sexuality.[28] And despite recent and important contributions to the history of LGBTQ activism in Christian traditions, this scholarship tends to overlook recent LGBTQ Christian identity work and activism under way in evangelical spaces.[29] Part of my effort, therefore, is to intervene in settled narratives that evangelicalism is incompatible with LGBTQ people, gender and sexual diversity, or even strategic moments of resistance and subversion.[30] By focusing on LGBTQ Christian activism in evangelicalism, I show how these discourses and practices are productive of both evangelical and LGBTQ identities.

Perennial conversations in the field of American religious studies on the contemporary articulation of religion and politics also inform this book. However, instead of viewing religion and politics as distinct and competing yet overlapping spheres of human experience, I contribute to a scholarly project that conceptualizes religion as a contested object and political practice.[31] I draw on a few different conceptual threads in this scholarship. As a mode of political practice, this body of work suggests, religion is intimately related to—that is, conditions and is conditioned by—other political and body regimes. In fact, religious traditions might productively be understood as historically specific regimes of body practices.[32] Some, therefore, have called attention to the training, negotiation, and practices of the body that are central to the production and maintenance of religious experience, identity, and community.[33]

Finally, these theorizations of religion open the possibility of connecting everyday religious practices to political regimes and, even more fundamentally, tracking the everyday production of what counts as "religion" and "politics." As Mitchell Dean has noted, "Contemporary political struggles and spirituality are far more intimately connected than the narrative of a liberal art of government built on the tolerance of a privatized religious belief can allow."[34] Dean goes on to suggest, therefore, that "we could analyse religion in terms of the practices of training which constitute forms of asceticism or self-government, and how this self-government is linked to political government, to relations with others and to members of one's own community, and the obligations that all this imposes."[35] Bringing these insights together, this book asks how religion and politics are negotiated and produced through the everyday embodied and discursive practices of LGBTQ Christians in conservative evangelicalism.

TRP can be situated in the history of LGBTQ Christian organizing and activism at the intersection of LGBTQ social movements and the restructuring of religion and politics in the United States since the 1950s. As documented by the sociologist of religion Robert Wuthnow, the economy of American religious and political life was redistributed over the last half of the twentieth century.[36] The vast economic, institutional, social, and demographic changes put in motion by World War II resulted in a decline in the importance of denominationalism and the rise of antitraditionalism that have continued to characterize Protestantism through today.[37] The size and influence of the mainline Protestant denominations that had dominated American religious life up until the war contracted, more conservative religious denominations and parachurch organizations emerged in their place, and an increasing polarization between "liberal" and "conservative" Christians organized around sociopolitical issues and disagreements over the proper role of religion in the public sphere came to the fore.[38]

The latter half of the twentieth century also saw a resurgence of politically engaged evangelicals and conservative Christian activism in American political life. This new brand of evangelical conservatism—part of, as some scholars have referred to the movement, the broader Christian Right, a coalition of white conservative evangelicals and other like-minded Christians—represented a renewed commitment to organized political activism and a desire to marry conservative religion and conservative politics.[39] Some scholars use "Christian fundamentalism" as a way to think about and distinguish politically motivated conservative Christians from evangelicalism more broadly. George Marsden, for example, defines Christian fundamentalism as "militantly anti-modernist Protestant evangelicalism" and, famously, a fundamentalist as "an evangelical who is angry about something."[40] By contrast to evangelicalism, which historically has been capable of moderating and accommodating to a pluralistic society, Christian fundamentalists before the 1940s were more isolationist in their attempts to achieve doctrinal purity; they tended to be more withdrawn from society, unwilling to moderate, and eager to abolish separations between church and state in local communities.

A distinguishing feature of Christian fundamentalism since the 1970s is the engagement in national mainstream politics.[41] This deep investment in secular culture and national politics took a circuitous route. Evangelicals busied themselves from the 1930s through the 1960s "building alternative social networks and religious and educational institutions as shields from the cultural influences of the outside world."[42] This work reflected a desire to build a coalition of white conservative evangelicals across denominations, while maintaining a commitment to doctrinal purity and suspicion of mainstream culture, as a response to the increasing social isolationism of Christian fundamentalists. These new parachurch organizations—for example, the National Association of Evangelicals, Fundamentalist Churches of America, and the Fundamentalist Baptist Fellowship—laid the intellectual and organizational groundwork, perhaps ironically as Tina Fetner observes, for the emergence of the Christian Right's grassroots political activism and entrance into local and national politics in the 1970s.[43]

Moreover, while its roots can be traced to the anxieties of white conservative Protestant segregationists in the first half of the twentieth century, the postwar Christian Right coalesced around and was motivated by opposition to the emergence of the lesbian and gay social movements (in addition to abortion and other social issues).[44] What Didi Herman calls the "antigay genre" of the Christian Right—a deluge of magazine articles, opinion editorials, books, films, Bible study guides, and sermons—began, in the late 1960s, lamenting and politicizing the perceived existential threat that "the homosexual" and "the gay agenda" posed to evangelicalism and, by extension, the nation-state.[45] Grassroots activists and organized campaigns relied on this rhetoric to reassert cultural hegemony and to galvanize opposition to lesbian and gay movement demands for equal rights. Mark Jordan argues that these early campaigns functioned as laboratories for the Christian Right, "in which it learned the usefulness of homosexuality as a wedge issue for both churchly and secular politics—or rather the fusion of the two."[46] And as Fetner suggests, it was this early antigay activism that brought "evangelical Christians into secular politics."[47]

The broad contours of the new Christian Right began to take shape during the 1980s and early 1990s. A network of conservative parachurch organizations, special interest groups, and think tanks—the Religious Roundtable, the Heritage Foundation, Jerry Falwell's Moral Majority, James Dobson's Focus on the Family and Family Research Council, to name a few—implemented a fine-tuned approach to organizing local activism behind issues ranging from women's rights, sex education, and lesbian and gay rights.[48] Inspired by the successes of these organizations, leaders of the Christian Right, with the help of Pat Robertson's Christian Coalition, began pursuing a more direct political approach, seeking to take over the Republican Party by running religious conservatives for elected office and installing them in party leadership.[49] By the 1992 presidential nominating conventions, the Republican Party included as platform planks opposition to antidiscrimination protections for gay people, same-sex marriage, and gays in the military. On the opening night of the Republican National Convention, in what later came to be known as the "Culture Wars Speech," Pat Buchanan articulated a vision of the new conservative religious-political orthodoxy that included pitting "homosexual rights" and other social issues as existential threats to "a nation that we still call God's country."[50]

Beyond the organized campaigns of the Christian Right and the politicization of homosexuality in local and national politics, gay marriage and the ordination of lesbians and gay men similarly erupted as divisive issues in local congregations and most of the mainline denominations beginning in the early 1970s. In the years that followed, the "homosexual issue" led to the splitting of denominations and the formation of new nondenominational churches and parachurch alliances.[51]

Several consequences of the restructuring of American religion and the rise of the Christian Right's anti-LGBTQ rhetoric and activism have endured. For one, this history resulted in "new modes of religious identification," wherein to be authentically Christian meant to hold "conservative" positions on women's reproductive rights, LGBTQ rights, and a range of other sociopolitical issues.[52] In part due to the portrayal of LGBTQ people and organizations as antireligious and anti-American, the Christian Right's politicization of homosexuality also perpetuates the assumption that Christian and LGBTQ identities are mutually exclusive.[53] Such antigay activism, Jordan notes, "succeeded in polarizing the rhetorical field between gay and

Christian. . . . You must speak as gay or Christian, you must *be* militantly gay or fervently Christian."[54]

Meanwhile, religion also increasingly became a wedge issue among and within some of the early lesbian and gay activist organizations.[55] The disagreement over movement tactics between the homophile and gay liberation organizations before and after the 1969 Stonewall uprising in New York City was a central moment in this history. Whereas the "homophile movement," Jordan writes, "was an uneasy coalition of religious and antireligious groups, comprising antireligious Marxists or Communists, religiously indifferent socialists, and religiously motivated activists," after Stonewall more "antireligious or nonreligious groups gained greater control over politically effective representation of lesbian and gay history."[56] So while homophile organizations often sought to work with sympathetic religious leaders and communities, gay liberation organizations like the Gay Liberation Front viewed homophile efforts as overly accommodationist, arguing instead for a greater disruption of societal norms and the institutions of power, including churches, that perpetuate them. Moreover, some lesbian and gay organizations, especially during the Gay Liberation Era, increasingly adopted the "us versus them" language of a threatened minority over consensus-based approaches that emphasized shared values of justice and equality.[57] As a result, lesbian and gay liberation increasingly came to mean also liberation from religion, and Christianity itself came to be seen as an entrenched enemy of LGBTQ social justice.[58]

But to focus only on such antagonisms fails to account for a similarly long history of LGBTQ people's and LGBTQ-supportive Christians' advocacy of LGBTQ social equality with and within Christian communities.[59] There are two divergent yet entangled expressions of this LGBTQ Christian organizing. On the one hand is the formation of LGBTQ Christian churches and parachurch organizations seeking to meet the spiritual and social needs of LGBTQ people. On the other are organizations agitating for LGBTQ social equality either in individual church communities and denominations or in society more generally.

Perhaps best known among the former is the Metropolitan Community Church (MCC), an international Protestant Christian denomination founded by Troy Perry, an excommunicated Pentecostal pastor and gay man.[60] From the start Perry's goal was to create a Christian church that would not only "serve the religious and spiritual needs of the homosexual community" but also be inclusive of people from any faith tradition.[61] In this way Perry imagined a community that would transcend the exclusionary politics of both sexuality and religion. Perry led the first service of what became MCC in his living room in Huntington Park, California, on October 6, 1968. By 1970 MCC had become the largest gay organization in the United States.[62]

Early members of Perry's church disagreed somewhat over how involved they should be in the broader lesbian and gay social movements. While some wanted to keep church and politics separate, Perry was involved in local homophile organizations when he founded MCC, later collaborated with the Gay Liberation Front, and began performing same-sex marriage ceremonies in 1970 as a form of protest. MCC, at moments in its early years, was known as a central agitator in southern California gay activism.[63] Even though Perry did not set out to establish a "gay church," MCC has come to represent a separatist approach to LGBTQ Christian organizing, creating separate spaces to celebrate gender and sexual diversity and to meet the spiritual and social needs of LGBTQ people.[64]

If MCC has come to represent a separatist model of LGBTQ Christian organizing, there is also a rich history of lesbian and gay organizations, faith-based parachurch organizations, and denominational organizations working with and within religious communities to bring about social change. For some of the homophile organizations of the 1950s and 1960s, for example, the work of social uplift and support for the lesbian and gay community was not only political but also spiritual. Often this required working with local churches and religious leaders. Among other strategies, organizations kept lists of sympathetic clergy and welcoming churches, conducted surveys to better understand the religious convictions and spiritual lives of lesbians and gay men, frequently ran religious and spiritual interest stories in their publications, and brainstormed ways to field requests for religious counseling.[65]

Finally, during the same time that the various Protestant denominations began codifying rules against gay marriage and ordination, organized efforts were under way to promote tolerance and social justice for lesbians and gay men in those very same denominations. The United Church of Christ (UCC) Gay Caucus, formed in 1972, was perhaps the earliest of such organizations advocating for lesbian and gay issues in a mainline Protestant denomination.[66] Shortly after, similar organizations emerged in the other mainline denominations, and by the early 2000s there were more than fifty LGBTQ Christian organizations in the United States representing every major Christian denomination. There have also been a handful of organizations that, like TRP, work primarily within conservative or evangelical Christian traditions, including Evangelicals Concerned, Soulforce, The Marin Foundation, and the Gay Christian Network (GCN).[67] While these and other parachurch organizations differ somewhat in aims and strategies, generally they either work to organize outreach ministries to LGBTQ people or seek to agitate for change in particular denominations or churches. The latter might include advocating for doctrinal changes, organizing public education campaigns and annual meetings, sponsoring Bible study and support groups, and, at times, using direct action.[68]

Evangelicalism, Activism, and Counter-Conduct

While sharing in this broader history of LGBTQ Christian activism and organizing, TRP is also informed by, and engages in conversations with, those who primarily identify with the tradition of evangelicalism. In this community, "affirming" and "nonaffirming" are perhaps the most common terms for describing the differences among Christians on LGBTQ issues and to identify the target of reform: roughly "affirming Christians" view the lives, intimate relationships, and faith of LGBTQ people as compatible with Christian tradition and Scripture; "nonaffirming Christians" do not. The language of "affirming" and "nonaffirming" effectively organizes all Christians, no matter their denomination or church affiliation, around this single issue.

The language of "affirming" and "nonaffirming" dates at least to the various mainline denominational LGBT organizations of the 1980s; these would sometimes use the language of welcoming or open and affirming to describe the goal of their activism. "Affirming" and "nonaffirming" were later popularized in the evangelical community by the evangelical theologian Stanley Grenz. According to Grenz, "affirming" in the Baptist tradition of welcoming and affirming churches, from which he borrows the language, meant both ministering to lesbians and gay men and sanctioning same-sex sexual practices. Grenz argued that evangelical churches should "welcome" gay people but not "affirm" same-sex relationships.[69]

The word "affirm" has at least three popular meanings: to make an affirmative public declaration, to offer support or encouragement, and to describe an experience that gives life meaning (as in "life-affirming"). The LGBTQ and LGBTQ-supportive Christians with whom I spoke seemed at times to mean all three aspects when using the language of affirming. To be fully affirming means to take a public position when the lives and dignity of LGBTQ people are at stake, to provide services and support to LGBTQ church members, and to recognize that accepting one's sexuality or gender identity is a life-affirming act. In this way "affirming" has a resonance with allyship.

However, to follow my interlocutors' lead and use this language myself would miss the broader field of conversations and concerns I encountered during my fieldwork. Although the people with whom I spoke affiliated themselves with a range of Christian traditions and not everyone would identify as an evangelical—in fact some explicitly rejected this term as part of the politics of identification—I situate much of what follows in the ongoing contests in the United States over who and what is evangelical and who gets to decide. A self-described movement of social and spiritual reform, TRP activists and participants seek more broadly to reform conservative evangelicalism—or, as it was often simply called, the "conservative Church"—seen by those I met as one of the last bastions of opposition to the acceptance and inclusion of LGBTQ people in Christian communities and American society more generally.[70] As I discuss in the chapters that follow, while LGBTQ social equality is one of the primary things that bring this community together, broader critiques of the regressive politics of conservative evangelicalism and the Christian Right, a disillusionment with the culture wars, and a reclamation project of what it means to be evangelical and compassionate fellow citizens were also defining features of this community.

Where and how to draw the boundaries of evangelicalism is a matter of much debate among scholars of religion. In general, religious studies scholars view evangelicalism as a movement within Protestant Christianity defined by a high regard for Scripture, a belief in personal salvation through the death and resurrection of Jesus, an emphasis on conversion or being born again, and a conviction that one's faith should influence one's private and public life.[71] Following critical theorists of religion, I define "evangelicalism" as a contested discursive and embodied tradition, an assemblage of inherited language and embodied practices with a history.[72] Throughout this book I use "conservative evangelicalism" and the "Christian Right" to refer more narrowly to the organized political activism and informal coalitions of predominantly white evangelical Christians, churches, and parachurch organizations organized around and motivated by socially conservative issues; I use "evangelicalism" to refer more broadly to a contested discursive tradition and "evangelicals"—who span the spectrum from liberal to conservative—to refer to those who participate in that tradition.[73]

To call TRP an activist organization is not to distance it from everyday evangelical identity and practice but to stitch it into traditions of activism and organizing that are central features of evangelicalism. As John Fletcher underscores in *Preaching to Convert*, the various evangelism and conversion outreach strategies that modern American evangelicals have developed are forms of highly successful activism: "Evangelicals are by nature performance activists. . . . Despite wide variation and internal disagreements, evangelicals unite in defining themselves—explicitly, eponymously—by their mission to go out into the world and make disciples."[74]

It would also be a mistake to conflate the activist ethic of evangelicalism with the organizations and grassroots activism of the Christian Right. With the polarizing narrative of the culture wars and the Christian Right's disproportionate influence in defining evangelicalism, it's commonplace to view evangelical Christians as a cohesive voting bloc that can be activated in support of conservative sociopolitical issues. In reality, though, the politics of evangelicals are far from monolithic.[75] Evangelicalism is not *a priori* conservative, nor should it be conflated with the Christian Right.

The evangelical activist ethic, or the "expression of the gospel in effort," is simply a conviction that personal faith should influence and direct one's private and public life.[76] Some evangelicals, even some who would otherwise be considered "conservative," are less motivated by the campaigns of the evangelical culture warriors than by social justice work as an expression of their faith, organizing instead around issues such as poverty, immigration, environmentalism, human trafficking, homelessness, and LGBTQ rights. Broadly speaking, the difference among evangelicals regarding the relationship between personal faith and public action is a difference between those who emphasize the need for individual transformation and those, following in the tradition of the Social Gospel, who stress the need to reform systems of oppression.[77] Thus scholars of evangelicalism have proposed various labels—for example, progressive evangelicalism, socially engaged evangelicals, postevangelicalism, new evangelicalism—in an attempt to describe evangelicals who are more disillusioned with conservative evangelicalism and consider social reform an expression of evangelical identity.[78]

At the same time, such categories—affirming, conservative, progressive, socially engaged, postevangelical—fail to capture the range of affiliations, tensions, and conflicts that shape LGBTQ Christian activism. Does being LGBTQ or an "affirming Christian" automatically make one "liberal"? Can one identify as a "liberal" Christian but support "conservative" sexual ethics? Are "progressive" critiques of gender and sexual politics only understood as such when articulated by "secular" organizations or actors? Do "conservative" readings of Scripture necessitate opposition to LGBTQ social justice?

To characterize TRP as an activist organization also has its limitations. While I find a framework of organizing and activism helpful for describing TRP's work, in part because the organization itself uses such language, it's important to note that such terms are contested. Some of those with whom I spoke happily called themselves activists and used language drawn from activist culture to describe their Christian identity and work. Others, similar to what Omri Elisha found in his study of socially engaged evangelicals, distanced themselves from being called activists or describing their work as activism. Sometimes this was because they view their work as more intermittent; for others it was due to the fact that activism is often associated with progressivism and secularism in conservative evangelical discourse.[79]

That said, listening closely to TRP activists who embrace the language and culture of activism helps us to think of LGBTQ and evangelical activism beyond the narrow constraints of the secular-religious or conservative-liberal binaries. As Jonathan Coley has argued in his study of LGBT organizing on Christian college and university campuses, studying organizations like TRP expands our understanding of forms of activism, the people who are drawn to such organizations, and the reasons they are often ignored by scholars of social movements. Whereas direct action might be more readily understood as a form of activism, TRP activists and participants might also express activism in value- or solidarity-based terms and through collective educational action or building safe communities.[80] Either way—and this could be said of evangelicalism more generally—the lines between ministry and activism were often blurred in the community that I studied. As I discuss in the chapters that follow, the work of LGBTQ social justice in evangelical spaces is not only political but also social and spiritual.

The LGBTQ and ally Christians I met through my fieldwork with TRP—and the broader conversations in evangelicalism into which they provide a window—can be better understood as constituting a community of counter-conduct. As noted previously, Foucault introduced the concept of counter-conduct as a way to think about movements of resistance that arise within regimes of power.[81] Foucault first landed on the notion of "conduct" as a way to describe both the object of power and the techniques and practices through which individuals are made, and make themselves, subject to power: "Conduct is the activity of conducting, of conduction if you like, but it is equally the way in which one conducts oneself, lets oneself be conducted, is conducted, and finally, in which one behaves as an effect of a form of conduct."[82] Specifically Foucault developed his notion of "conduct" while analyzing the totalizing Christian institutions of the Middle Ages, a "highly specific form of power with the object of conducting [people]" that he called "pastoral power."[83]

Sometimes, movements of "refusal, revolts, and forms of resistance" arise not outside but within specific regimes of power.[84] Foucault called these movements of counter-conduct. "They are movements," he argued, "whose objective is a different form of conduct, that is to say: wanting to be conducted differently, by other leaders and other shepherds, towards other objectives and forms of salvation, and through other procedures and methods"; in other words, they "seek . . . to escape direction by others and to define the way for each to conduct himself."[85] I submit that the struggles in evangelicalism concerning LGBTQ social justice are more than doctrinal disagreements: they are struggles over conduct—over how one is conducted and conducts oneself as LGBTQ and Christian—with counter-conduct creating the potential for new ethical and political realities and ways of being.[86]

Thinking of TRP activists and participants as a community of counter-conduct helps to address some of the conceptual problems, reflected also in the scholarly conversations discussed previously, that arose during my fieldwork. First, it enables the study of a community of resistance that was often dispersed and heterogeneous.[87] The community I studied was defined less in terms of a particular location or shared identity than by an object of reform: the exclusionary politics and normative values of conservative evangelical Christianity. In addition to a critique of mainstream evangelicalism's ongoing role in the production and protection of normative gender and sexuality, activists and participants at TRP's conferences also incorporated critiques of evangelicalism's historical and contemporary complicity with whiteness, nationalism, and (to a lesser extent) capitalism. In their efforts to transform an evangelical sexual and gender ideology that insists LGBTQ people do not have rights to their own bodies and to rehumanize LGBTQ people after decades of antigay activism and rhetoric, they also sought to reform evangelical practice, identity, and community to make these generally more equitable and inclusive.

A community of counter-conduct also calls attention to the interconnectedness between movements of resistance and the regimes of power they arise within. Rather than portraying LGBTQ Christians as outsiders to normative evangelicalism, it positions them as participants in the ongoing negotiation and contestation, hegemony and counter-hegemony, of evangelicalism. It lays bare the shared practices and discourses that are "continually re-utilized, re-implanted, and taken up again in one or another direction."[88] The shared practices and discourses also include the struggle to define religion and politics and their demarcation. To pay attention to LGBTQ Christian activism in conservative Christian spaces therefore is to attend to how religion and politics or ministry and activism are demarcated and deployed in everyday spaces and practices.

Finally, rather than portraying actors as being only accommodationist to systems of oppression or reactionary to them, a community of counter-conduct also emphasizes the agency of those who resist and the productiveness of resistance. Counter-conduct shares a family resemblance to what Foucault calls "reverse discourse" in that counter-conduct also relies on the rhetorical genres and assumptions of dominant narratives and, as such, can reproduce the very narratives that it's seeking to transcend.[89] Two of these narratives include homonormativity and the cultural authority of white evangelical identity, both of which the LGBTQ conservative Christian movement has a complicated relationship with, a topic I come back to throughout the book.

However, counter-conduct enables a more robust reassessment of resistance that goes beyond the power-resistance binary—a theme that many scholars thought was lacking in Foucault's rethinking of power.[90] As Arnold Davidson underscores, one of the benefits of rethinking the relationship between how power works and how it is resisted as a relationship between conduct and counter-conduct is that "counter-conduct . . . goes beyond the purely negative act of disobedience" by relocating resistance as "something 'as inventive, as mobile, as productive' as power itself."[91]

The potential fruit of counter-conduct is the expansion of the range of what is possible politically and ethically in regimes of power. At the same time, in my discussion of LGBTQ Christian activism as a community of counter-conduct, I also strive not to paper over disagreements and conflicts in these movements of resistance and change. As I discuss in the following chapters, activists and participants often disagree over movement politics and tactics and worry at times about their complicity in reproducing systems of oppression.

Setting and Methods

The stories I tell and arguments I make throughout this book are based on participant observation fieldwork with TRP over a twelve-month period beginning in November 2014. In keeping with the anthropological conviction that one must take part in communities to understand them, I sought to become a participant in conservative LGBTQ Christian culture. I had conversations with LGBTQ and LGBTQ-supportive Christians. I read their books and visited their online communities. I went to the places where they fellowshipped or gathered to witness.[92] I tried to understand the world as they saw it by focusing on the problems with which they were preoccupied. In short, I sought to participate in the everyday places and practices those in this community found meaningful.

I gained behind-the-scenes access to TRP through my work as the administrator for the steering committee tasked with organizing TRP's regional training conference in Kansas City in November 2015. As the administrator, I was primarily responsible for organizing, scheduling, and keeping minutes at the monthly meetings and facilitating communications between TRP staff and members of the committee. In addition, I accompanied members of the steering committee and TRP staff to other Kansas City–area locations and events, including church services, a launch party for the Kansas City conference, and an informational table at Kansas City PrideFest. I also attended three of TRP's three-day-long regional training conferences: an inaugural training conference in Washington DC in November 2014; a conference in Atlanta in June 2015; and the Kansas City conference in November 2015.

As such, I had the opportunity to speak to and learn from a diverse group of people in this area of social justice work, from TRP full-time staff and volunteers to other long-time activists working with similar organizations to novices getting involved in social justice work for the very first time. Although I conducted nine semistructured, in-depth interviews—ranging from half an hour to more than two hours in length, all of which I recorded and transcribed—with members of the steering committee and others I met during my research, most of what follows draws on my participation in this community and on more informal interviews and passing conversations with individuals I met at TRP conferences and elsewhere.

The membership of the TRP steering committee fluctuated some over the months, ranging from ten to fifteen members, and in the later stages of planning it also included Matthew Vines and his small team of full-time organizers and support staff.[93] The committee members were all white; all cisgender but one; and included about six gay men, seven straight women, and two straight men. Most of the members, who ranged from about twenty to ninety years of age, would also be considered middle class; they included (among others) an electrical engineer, a lawyer, a public relations professional, several female pastors, a retired male pastor, an events coordinator for a local nonprofit, and several full-time activists and volunteers associated with other organizations. They also were all Protestant, and many of them were members of or affiliated with three large Kansas City–area moderate to conservative-leaning Methodist or Presbyterian churches. At the time of my fieldwork, the main TRP staff, all in their twenties or early thirties, included Vines, who self-identified as white, cisgender, and gay; a white cisgender straight man; and three women of color, one of whom identified as lesbian and the other two as straight allies.[94]

The conference attendees were quite diverse in some ways and less so in others. Although it's difficult to generalize, conference goers included an even mix of straight and gay participants, with probably more gay men than lesbians and at least a few who might identify as queer, bisexual, intersex, or questioning. A vast majority of the participants were white, although a few people who might identify as Black, Hispanic, Latina/o, Asian American, and other categories of race and ethnicity also attended the conferences. The participants were also mainly cisgender, although I did speak to a few conference attendees and speakers who identified as either gender nonconforming, transgender, or genderqueer.

In my experience most of the conference attendees came from either nondenominational evangelical church communities or a church affiliated with one of the various mainline Protestant traditions, including Presbyterian, Methodist, Episcopal, Baptist, Evangelical Lutheran, and others. Like members of the steering committee, conference attendees at all three conferences might be considered mostly middle class, although there was undoubtedly a range in economic backgrounds and access to income and wealth. At minimum they were individuals who could afford the registration fee, other related travel expenses, and the flexibility to attend a conference at the end of a work week.[95] They were (to identify a few) seminary and university students, accountants, pastors and church staff, musicians, artists, activists, teachers, and parents. The conference speakers similarly represented a diverse range of faith, racial, sexual, and gender identities. Some were affiliated with TRP through previous training; others were pastors and other individuals of some notoriety in the evangelical community; still others were affiliated with other activist organizations or nonprofits.[96]

Despite the fairly diverse participants, it could also be said that the conversations among and about LGBTQ Christians in this particular community often assumed and reflected the subject position and interests of mainly white middle-class cisgender gay people; this dynamic was further complicated by their attempts to foster change in a tradition whose institutional and theological habits are white, straight, and male. As I note several times throughout this book, both issues proved to be points of contention as individuals wrestled with the politics of inclusion and representation.

To situate TRP in a broader field of conversations, I supplemented the fieldwork by immersing myself in a range of other cultural production in contemporary evangelicalism made by, for, or about LGBTQ Christians—from blogs and online communities to magazine and newspaper articles to theological treatises and spiritual autobiographies. Such resources are talked about endlessly in the spaces where evangelicals congregate: at church on Sunday mornings, in small Bible study groups, in coffee shops, on social media. Evangelicals often identify fellow travelers by referencing which books they are currently reading in their small groups or on their own, much like academics might drop a reference to the latest theoretical intervention as evidence of their insider status and to position themselves in a discursive community.

Some of the books that are being read, and the genre of evangelical self-help and spiritual advice literature more generally, have a similar function to those that Foucault calls "prescriptive" or "practical" texts. Foucault defines prescriptive texts as those "written for the purpose of offering rules, opinions, and advice on how to behave as one should: 'practical' texts, which are themselves objects of a 'practice' in that they [are] designed to be read, learned, reflected upon, and tested out, and they [are] intended to constitute the eventual framework of everyday conduct."[97] Many of the texts I read ended chapters with discussion questions or general advice for conduct and self-government, often with the intent of being meditated upon and discussed in the context of Bible study groups.

My approach to fieldwork and the ethnography that follows were informed by the methods and sensibilities of critical ethnography, which, as Jim Thomas suggests, "is conventional ethnography with a political purpose."[98] My understanding of critical ethnography includes two main commitments: on the one hand, critical ethnographers are concerned with connecting everyday practices and discourses to critical-theoretical questions and the scrutiny of political regimes; on the other, critical ethnography also implies a commitment to participating in a shared project of realizing social change and challenging systems of oppression. In other words, "critical ethnography begins with an ethical responsibility to address processes of unfairness or injustice within a particular *lived* domain."[99]

Questions of representation and reflexivity inevitably arise in the practice of ethnography. As a number of feminist, queer, and of color anthropologists have argued, an ethnographer must be attuned to the processes of othering and flattening that take place in studying and representing "cultures." Throughout my aim is not to present a homogenous, static culture but to emphasize the "particular," leaving in tension contradictions in everyday practice and discourse, internal disagreements and competing desires, incoherence and disappointments.[100]

I also viewed my fieldwork as a practice of immersion, an embodied practice and open-ended process wherein knowledge is produced in conversation between the people I encountered—as well as the materials, practices, and ideas they found meaningful—and me.[101] As such, my subject position—my politics, personal history, and identity—was necessarily an inherent part of the research. In fact, my subject position as a researcher and individual with a personal history was unavoidable during my fieldwork: as I sought to understand through conversation, participation, and observation what was meaningful for those I met, I was continually made aware that my own meaning-making practices and politics were under investigation as well. My interlocutors, for the most part, did not compartmentalize or bracket off my life experiences and personal beliefs; instead they folded them into their own practices of self-representation. My position as a particular person—beyond but including my status as a researcher—mattered to them and shaped our conversations.

It's not uncommon in ethnographic research for people to be somewhat ambivalent about an ethnographer who seeks entry into their community. This is especially true in situations where a marked power differential between the ethnographer and the community exists, including groups who have been historically marginalized and oppressed. As many of the stories I tell in the following chapters illustrate, the pain of rejection runs deep after coming out as, or otherwise being suspected of being, lesbian, gay, bisexual, transgender, queer, or even questioning in conservative evangelical communities. I heard stories about mothers scared to divulge to their small group that they have a gay child for fear they would be shunned; about people being denied or losing leadership positions in their faith communities after coming out; about people being told they are not fit to serve in childcare or youth services because they might molest children or convert them to a "gay lifestyle"; about children being told, and in turn convincing themselves, they are simply "confused" about their sexual orientation or gender identity and risk eternal damnation if they can't figure it out. Beyond the rhetorical violence and shame, LGBTQ Christians also often face accusations of being divisive in their efforts to create more inclusive faith communities, an issue that I discuss in chapter 1.

So it's not surprising that there was often a probing of my intentions—sometimes subtle, sometimes more direct. The first time I met with Paul Creekmore to discuss fieldwork with the steering committee, for example, he began our conversation by asking about my interests in TRP and what brought me to this topic. I responded by telling him my interests were both academic and personal. While I thought TRP would make a good field site for exploring my questions about the negotiation of politics and identity in conservative Christian spaces, I also told Paul that I was critical of the rhetoric and politics of the Christian Right, which I view as damaging and hypocritical. Where some conservative evangelical Christians, citing Scripture and Christian tradition in justification, see discrimination as a legitimate expression of their religious liberty, I see the opposite: people reading contemporary politics and meanings into the Bible and Christian tradition, weaponizing the Bible to justify and protect social and material conditions. My hope, I told Paul, was to do a small part in disrupting settled narratives that enable "traditional Christian values" to be leveraged in struggles over religious and LGBTQ rights and freedoms. Paul replied that he was glad to hear this. He wanted to be sure that my interests went beyond the academic; he wanted to know my politics and where I stood on this issue.

When the topic came up in other conversations, I tried to be candid and clear about my own values and politics. Even though I strongly support social and political equality for LGBTQ people and am mostly supportive of TRP's mission and work, I also had reservations about, and at times sharply opposed, some of TRP's official positions and other issues I encountered during my fieldwork. But for the most part, my moral convictions—a commitment to diversity, equality, fairness— aligned with the people I met, making my experience as a researcher somewhat different from other ethnographers working in evangelical contexts, wherein their politics were in more direct conflict.[102]

In addition to trying to determine my politics and motives, people endeavored to locate other aspects of my subject position in relation to their own. In particular, they wanted to know about my sexuality, my church background, or where I might be in my own "faith and sexuality journey." The first time I met Matthew Vines, for instance, he asked, pointedly, after noticing my wedding ring, "Are you married to a boy or a girl?" "A girl," I replied. Other people raised this subject by asking whether I had children or identified as a "gay Christian" or "LGBT."

However, most people seemed less interested in knowing my sexuality than my faith, and this in some ways contributed most to my feelings of being an outsider in this community. I sought to be transparent about my convictions when the issue arose, primarily because I felt not to do so would be dishonest and betray trust. My self-identification usually went something like this: "I grew up in a Pentecostal church and even at one point played with the idea of going into some form of ministry, but I no longer consider myself to be a Christian for a variety of reasons." On more than one occasion, after the issue of faith came up, I noticed that a person who had previously been eager to talk would try to find a way out of the conversation. This also made my work on the steering committee a little precarious. Shortly after joining, I gained access to an instructional manual for volunteer organizers of T R P's regional training conferences. According to the manual, steering committee members should be Christians who hold a high view of Scripture and have a strong personal sexual ethic.

Thankfully, Paul and I had discussed my not identifying as a Christian at our first meeting before he invited me to join the steering committee, and it was never an issue. Nor did it matter when the subject came up with other members of the committee. Throughout my fieldwork members of the steering committee were always receptive and welcoming, supportive of my research, and gracious with their time. Moreover, most people I encountered didn't seem to care all that much; instead they seemed genuinely glad to talk to someone who was interested in and empathetic to their experiences.

Unlike some other ethnographers working in evangelical spaces, I never got the impression that I was viewed as a subject to be converted.[103] On a few occasions I was invited to church, but such invitations came up only in the context of my sharing with people what I felt was gained and lost when I shed my Christian faith. On another occasion an individual invited me to read the Bible with them, but I interpreted this as more of an effort to establish a relationship than an attempt to save me. More often I was merely folded into their self-narratives about God working in their individual lives or faith communities or in society more generally.[104] In any case the focus of this community was less on saving the unsaved than on saving the church from itself: to mend the damage of the culture wars; to reclaim evangelicalism from people like Mike Pence and Jerry Falwell Jr.; and to convert fellow Christians into allies and empathic people attuned to the experiences and lives of L G B T Q people.

Perhaps my biggest challenge working with the steering committee was figuring out how to navigate my dual roles as a researcher and volunteer and even "activist." As the months went by, my contribution expanded to tasks beyond taking minutes and scheduling meetings, such as researching Kansas City–area L G B T Q community organizations and L G B T Q-supportive churches and parachurch organizations; helping staff the informational table at Kansas City PrideFest; contributing ideas to conference planning; participating in the Transgender Remembrance described previously. Over time it seemed that the other volunteers began to regard me less as a researcher than a fellow laborer in "the LGBTQ Christian movement."

However, I sometimes worried about being an ineffectual volunteer. In the months leading up to the Kansas City conference, for example, each member of the steering committee was asked to provide a list of ten contacts as part of a mapping campaign to achieve turnout goals.[105] For practical reasons I was unable to participate. While the other members of the steering committee were active in their church communities and knew many people who might benefit from a Bible-based conference on LGBTQ issues in Christianity, I struggled to identify anyone in my own circle of friends who would be interested in participating.

In addition, my position as a religious outsider required a bit of distance, not because I maintain some notion of objectivity in research—in fact, I view scholarship and teaching as a particular mode of activism and political work—but because while I might share in TRP's commitment to LGBTQ social justice, I do not share in its mission of "advancing the Kingdom." Thus I felt compelled to avoid passing as a Christian or speaking on behalf of the organization. One such occasion occurred when the steering committee organized an effort to advertise the conference at Kansas City PrideFest in June 2015. I volunteered to help set up the informational table and provide support as needed, thinking it would be a productive opportunity to observe TRP's strategies for reaching out to and understand its relationship with the LGBTQ community. On one of the several trips from the exhibitors' tent to the parking lot to pick up supplies, I expressed to another volunteer my reservations about speaking on behalf of TRP should someone ask me for information. However, he quickly dismissed my concerns and remarked that I probably knew more about TRP and its message than the other volunteers who were there. We spent the hot, muggy, midsummer afternoon and late into the evening passing out flyers and water bottles, the labels of which we had carefully peeled off and replaced with stickers of TRP's logo of a dove and olive branch against a rainbow background. It was awkward at first, but by the end of the evening, I had the basic pitch down: "Have you heard of The Reformation Project before? No? Well, The Reformation Project is a national organization seeking to transform conservative Christian teaching on sexual orientation and gender identity, and we do that by training people how to have more effective conversations in their own church contexts. There's a conference in Kansas City later this year, if you're interested."

Although I no longer share the same convictions, the time spent when I was younger cultivating the sort of evangelical sensorium described by Tanya Luhrmann, as well as my academic background in religious and biblical studies, proved to be a useful bridge at times to understanding aspects of the lived religion and relationship to Scripture that I encountered.[106] At the same time, there was much I needed to learn: What do people engaged in these conversations mean by "grace?" What does it mean to "cultivate a heart" for something? What do "reconciliation" and "not breaking fellowship" mean to them?

Chapter Overview

Chapter 1, "Grace-Filled Conversations and Public Things," is about the community-making exercises that are central to conservative LGBTQ Christian counter-conduct. More broadly it explores the relationship between politics and religion in LGBTQ Christian activism in evangelical spaces. I examine the discourses and practices through which LGBTQ and LGBTQ-supportive Christians in this community negotiate contested issues and seek to create change while working within and against the normative politics of conservative evangelicalism. To do so I draw on Bruno Latour's rethinking of politics as "making things public" in conversation with Nancy Fraser's concept of subaltern counterpublics and Thomas Rochon's critical communities to analyze how individuals attempt to make things public that are normally rejected as "political."[107] I show how discourses of reconciliation, fellowship, generous spaciousness, and grace function as rationales and discursive spaces to imagine community, negotiate politics, register dissent, and foster change.

Chapter 2, "The Problem of Scripture," turns to the role and social life of the sacred text in conservative LGBTQ Christian activism. It discusses TRP's attempt to reclaim Scripture from the abuses of conservative evangelicalism and to assert the right for people to identify as both Bible-believing Christians and LGBTQ or LGBTQ-supportive. I introduce TRP's core reformation message and strategy of recruiting, training, and coordinating a cadre of people to disseminate the message, a strategy that scholars of social movements call social movement schools.[108] In telling the story of returning to Scripture as a mode of counter-conduct, I also tell a larger story about the role of Scripture in fashioning the self, policing community boundaries, justifying rules of inclusion and exclusion, and doing the messy political work of determining who and what is a Christian. Throughout I show how the authority and sacredness of Scripture are actively maintained through conflict—what might be understood as a tension between delegitimizing and *re*legitimizing Scripture—and how some activists and participants wrestle with the politics and consequences of trying to create space for LGBTQ people in conservative Christian communities by reaffirming the authority of Scripture.

The remaining three chapters broaden the discussion—in three separate but related directions—to the attempt to build communities that are inclusive while wrestling with both the exclusionary politics of conservative evangelicalism and assumptions in LGBTQ Christian activism itself about what it means to be LGBTQ and Christian. Chapter 3, "The Sexual Self and Spiritual Health," is about the relationship between the sexual body and spiritual health in this community of counter-conduct. Central to this chapter is a discussion of what I call "reconciliation narratives," a genre of storytelling wherein individuals narrate how they came to accept—or continue to wrestle with—being both Christian and gay. I argue that reconciliation narratives are a shared practice central to the production of gay Christian identity and community in conservative Christian spaces. I finish the chapter with a discussion of how some participants in these conversations wrestle with the potential consequences of trying to make room in conservative Christian spaces for gay people and their intimate relationships without a broader reassessment of evangelical sexuality and sexual ethics.

Chapter 4, "Transgender Figures and Trans Inclusion," turns to aspects of gender, in particular conversations about how to be truly trans-inclusive in LGBTQ Christian activism. The first part of the chapter is an examination of "transgender" as a rhetorical figure in recent evangelical discourse. I show how some conservative evangelical thinkers draw liberally from the Christian Right's late-twentieth-century toolkit of antigay activism and rhetoric to rationalize and justify opposition to social equality and protections for transgender people. I argue that this "transgender rhetorical figure" is put to work not only in the construction and maintenance of the gender binary but also in struggles over democratic citizenship, the nation-state, and evangelical cultural hegemony. Referring to the conversations I encountered during my fieldwork, I turn next to a discussion of how, despite sincere efforts, transgender issues tend to be either an afterthought in conservative LGBTQ Christian activism or conflated with the politics and interests of lesbians and gay men. I finish the chapter with a discussion of some of the strategies that some transgender and ally Christians use to create space and compassion for transgender and gender-nonconforming people in conservative Christian spaces.

Chapter 5, "Academies of Racial Justice," describes how TRP, in response to a series of events that took place in the United States over the twelve months of my fieldwork, increasingly began to incorporate a critique of racial violence and oppression into its training conferences. I focus on a workshop called the "Academy for Racial Justice" that TRP developed for and introduced at its conference in Atlanta in June 2015 and that was designed to help participants make a connection between racial and LGBTQ social justice. Drawing on Sara Ahmed's "affective economies" and Alison Landsberg's "prosthetic memories," I show how activists put the body and affect to work in an attempt to cultivate an ethical orientation rooted in suffering and shared vulnerability.[109]

In the conclusion I return to the framework of counter-conduct to elaborate on LGBTQ Christian activism in evangelicalism as an everyday negotiation of democratic possibilities. I reflect upon how thinking about the negotiation of gender, sexual, and religious identities as a relationship between conduct and counter-conduct reveals an enduring feature of contemporary evangelicalism—that is, the tension between conservative evangelicalism's authoritarian tendencies and its ideals of self-transformation and individual freedom and responsibility. I conclude with some comments about the perils and promises of the activism that I studied, the relationship between identity and belief, and what other concerned citizens might learn from TRP's strategy of relational organizing and attempts to reason with its fellow Christians.

1   Grace-Filled Conversations and Public Things

On a mild Thursday evening in November 2014, I took a seat in a wooden pew lined with crimson cushions in the dimly lighted National City Christian Church in Washington D C. The green-domed neoclassical tower of the church rises 160 feet above the northwest end of Thomas Circle, a mile northeast of the White House and National Mall up Vermont Avenue. I was there with more than three hundred others gathered for TRP's inaugural regional training conference. The opening evening featured, as many conferences do, a keynote address from a leader and innovator in the community, although the rest of the evening's liturgy blurred the lines between a conference and the theatrics of a contemporary evangelical church service.

A small band of seven or eight called the audience to worship and invited us to join them in a chorus of "Welcome to This Circle." The audience members eagerly stood to sing along, some raising their hands and swaying to the rhythm of the music. I sensed palpable enthusiasm in the room. After an opening prayer, choruses of "Be Thou My Vision" and "Come Thou Fount," and a reading of Isaiah 40:26–31, Allyson Robinson—a white woman in her late thirties or early forties, wearing dark-rimmed glasses, a gray-brown blazer over a white shirt, and straight bangs with shoulder-length blonde hair—came to the pulpit to deliver the keynote address. Just a few months earlier, the title of a video on MSNBC's website suggested that Robinson was "the most radical preacher in America," presumably because of her disruption of multiple categories of normative identity and politics.[1] Robinson is a West Point graduate, former U.S. Army captain, ordained Baptist pastor, LGBTQ rights activist and former employee of the Human Rights Campaign, married to a woman, a mother of four children, and a transgender woman. At the time of the conference Robinson was serving as the transitional pastor for Calvary Baptist Church, also in Washington DC.

"So much of the work of our wilderness days," Robinson observed, "has been *political* work, if you'll excuse the use of such language in this sacred space." Robinson's keynote—she called it a sermon—was titled "The Three Great Temptations of the Affirming Church."[2] The sermon was an allegorical reading of the temptation of Christ, upon which Robinson mapped the politics and lived experiences of contemporary LGBTQ Christians.[3] In her rendering LGBTQ people have been in exile—like a coerced fast—from Christian communities and mainstream culture more generally, but now that the "culture war" was "coming to a close," their "time in the wilderness [was] almost over." Now LGBTQ Christians faced a test: they must decide what kind of a church and community the "affirming church" would be.[4]

The first test LGBTQ Christians faced, Robinson argued, was the "temptation to self-reliance." "Why would I participate," Robinson asked on behalf of other LGBTQ Christians, "in a denomination that still refuses to acknowledge" the lives, relationships, and faith of LGBTQ people? "Why not leave [the churches and denominations] behind?" she asked. The pressing issue for LGBTQ Christians, Robinson elaborated, was whether they should "abandon the churches" and "create for [themselves] new churches and new denominations to sustain [them]" or resolve to stay and seek to be voices for change, especially in more conservative churches. While she praised those who, with courage, found or established separate spiritual homes and communities that would support their spiritual and social lives, Robinson suggested that LGBTQ Christians now were called to "compassion, to reconciliation, and to unity. God's words call us to self-sacrifice rather than self-reliance."

The second test is the "temptation to power." Even though LGBTQ people now "have a President who speaks our name and members of Congress who speak at our banquets and council members and school board members who speak on our behalf," Robinson continued, the LGBTQ community should "be cautious of political power and very circumspect when it offers us its support."[5] Robinson insisted that LGBTQ Christians shouldn't use positions of power for personal and political gain. They should reject, to be precise, defining and using politics as it's used by the Christian Right: "Our coreligionists turned their churches into organizing units, rallied volunteers for hurtful campaigns, placed petitions opposing our rights and even our safety in the narthex for their parishioners to sign." Even so, Robinson's caution wasn't an outright rejection of the political process but rather a reminder that one should be intentional about one's engagement in politics and the use of political power. The temptation, Robinson argued, was to use newfound political clout to pursue self-interest and personal gain rather than to work on behalf of other social justice issues. The antidote to the former is self-sacrifice. LGBTQ Christian engagement in the political process should be defined by the pursuit of justice everywhere rather than just one's "own issue."

Robinson warned that the "temptation to presumption" is the final test: "We must turn our ears toward our language, our ways of speaking about those who oppose us. When we mock them, deride them, scorn or disparage them, you can be sure that we're being tempted to presumption. When we call them sad but feel no sympathy, when we say they're lost but make no effort to lead them home, we need to check ourselves." To not do so would be to confuse being on the right side of the issue "with being holy." The temptation to presumption, therefore, is a reminder to be conscientious and compassionate when navigating difficult conversations and relationships. For Robinson this means approaching conversations with civility, empathy, an awareness of personal shortcomings, and an interest in the person with whom one is conversing rather than only winning an argument.

Sitting in a church in the city perhaps most identified with power and politics in the American imagination made for an apropos site to reflect upon the relationship between religion and politics in conservative LGBTQ Christian activism. Robinson's remarks captured many of the same pressing concerns and questions I encountered time and again at TRP conferences and throughout my fieldwork more generally: people having conversations about how to have more effective conversations; about the proper response to and use of power; about how community should be conceptualized and managed; about how to realize change in the face of often unyielding opposition; about how to respond to non-affirming Christians who actively question whether LGBTQ Christians are capable of love or participation in Christian community and who subject them to what Dawne Moon and Theresa Tobin have called "sacramental shame"; and about how to maintain relationships with others with whom one deeply disagrees, even with those who would deny one's rights and very existence.[6]

This chapter examines community making as a mode of counter-conduct and the practices through which LGBTQ and LGBTQ-supportive Christians negotiate contested issues and seek to create change while working within and against the constraints of the normative politics of conservative evangelicalism. If normative evangelicalism characterizes LGBTQ identity as incompatible with evangelical Christian faith, systematically excludes LGBTQ people from Christian community, and dismisses critique as "political," the central premise of this chapter is that the formation of conservative LGBTQ Christian community is itself a method of refusing submission to the pastoral authority and institutional and theological habits of evangelicalism.[7]

Robinson's digression, when she invoked the category of the political—"if you'll excuse the use of such language in this sacred space"—rehearses a practice many scholars of the contemporary articulation of religion and politics in the United States have observed: the construction of religious spaces, practices, and discourses as apolitical and their secular counterparts as political. Religion and politics are often understood to be essential and opposing spheres of human experience, consisting of different practices and motives directed toward different ends.

Many evangelicals, including many of those with whom I spoke, draw sharp distinctions between their religious and their political lives (if they acknowledge they have such a life). For them "politics" means something like either professional politics—a category that includes politicians and other political actors, governmental bureaucracy, or political games such as those portrayed in political dramas such as *House of Cards*—or a situation in which one is being unnecessarily contentious or combative or taking unfair advantage. Authentic religion and religious experience, by contrast, should ideally be free of the contaminating effects of "politics." In her ethnography of internal debates about homosexuality in two United Methodist churches, Dawne Moon argues that church members would invoke the category of politics to delegitimize things that threatened to undermine their worldviews.[8] Rather than addressing the content of the criticism, it is a strategy of dismissing the criticism as "political." Thus one of the ways in which the category of politics functions in such spaces is to police the boundaries of acceptable behavior and speech, as well as what counts as authorized religious performance and experience. In my own fieldwork the category of the political was similarly contested. Some tried to distance themselves from being seen as overtly political while Christian or in Christian spaces; others openly embraced the need to speak precisely and honestly about the politics of religious institutions, ritual, or theology.[9]

According to Talal Asad and other scholars of religion, our received wisdom about the essential characteristics of religion and politics is a product of the narrative of secularization, which relegates religion to the private sphere and the secular to the public sphere. However, this distorts from view, Asad argues, that "what many would anachronistically call 'religion' was *always* involved in the world of power" and that, in fact, "the categories of 'politics' and 'religion' turn out to implicate each other more profoundly than we thought."[10] In other words, religion and politics are not separate domains of human experience so much as they are constituted by historically specific, often overlapping, techniques and procedures in the application of and resistance to power.[11]

As such, and despite my interlocutors who would resist such language, I view the work of TRP activists, conference participants, and others working on LGBTQ social justice in evangelical spaces as an effort to *make* this a political issue. I use "politics" in its broader sense to refer to the decision-making process of a group or the way in which ideas, identities, and the norms of communities are negotiated and contested. I'm interested in how LGBTQ and LGBTQ-supportive Christians navigate disputed issues and seek to affect change, especially in the context of conversations where the dismissal of politics is not a mistake but a strategy, wherein a charge of being "political" functions to limit, if not outright silence, critique and rigorous debate.

To understand the production of politics and religion in these everyday spaces, I draw on Bruno Latour's rethinking of politics as "making things public."[12] Latour returns to the ancient notion of politics as *res publica*—meaning "public things" or the affairs of the city-state—in asking what it might mean to make things "public." Latour reminds us, borrowing from Heidegger's discussion of the German *Ding*, that buried in the etymology of the word "thing" is a dual meaning designating both "matter" or "inanimate objects" and "meeting" or "concern": "The *Ding* designates both those who assemble because they are concerned as well as what causes their concerns and divisions."[13] In short, Latour's repositioning of politics as making things public calls attention to the way in which a public is constituted by a contested issue or "matter of concern."

For my purposes thinking about politics as making things public provides at least two important benefits. First, it focuses our attention on the production of politics outside of the "authorized" assemblies of normal political discourse—be they religious or secular political bodies and actors. By contrast, matters of concern "bind all of us in ways that map out a public space profoundly different from what is usually recognized under the label of 'the political.'"[14] Making things public helps us think about the work and spaces of LGBTQ Christian activism as ways in which LGBTQ social justice is made public outside of and despite the authorized assemblies of mainstream evangelicalism.

Second, Latour's notion of making things public is a corrective to thinking of politics as only something that *divides* a public to how a public is formed *because* of a contested issue. In other words, a particular issue or matter of concern "brings people together *because* it divides them."[15] For Latour this allows us to avoid the twin pitfalls of demanding unity at the expense of dissent or disunity at the expense of common ground; the hope is to imagine a democracy with "fewer claims to unity, less belief in disunity."[16]

It was evident during my fieldwork that TRP activists and participants sought to tread this fine line between unity and disunity. But instead of seeing politics as something that necessarily caused division and therefore should be avoided at all costs, they sought to imagine a community and discourse wherein disagreement would be deeply valued as something that brought people together and, in the end, made for a stronger and more inclusive community. A motivating concern was the desire to move LGBTQ Christians from the world of "objects" to be debated in evangelical discourse to matters of concern. This chapter tells part of this story about *how* people assemble around this matter of concern and seek to make their lives, and the issues that matter to them, public.[17]

In what follows I explore how the assemblies that I studied function as sites to practice new languages and rules of engagement for imagining more inclusive communities and ways of being in conservative evangelicalism. I argue that TRP conferences, along with the other sites I examine in this chapter, can be understood as critical communities with the explicit goal of making public what's normally rejected as political. In particular I focus on how discourses of fellowship, reconciliation, generous spaciousness, grace, and the like function as discursive spaces to imagine community and foster change. These varied attempts of making things public are ways in which those working toward LGBTQ equality in conservative evangelicalism negotiate politics, imagine community, organize for change, and register dissent. They are productive sites where participants learn *how* to be political and are actively engaged in the project of determining what constitutes Christian community and acceptable political discourse.

Reconciliation and Not Breaking Fellowship

As I discussed in the introduction, TRP is but one organization in a decades-long history of LGBTQ Christian parachurch and denominational organizations. While TRP seeks to "reach people in the pews" in primarily conservative evangelical communities through grassroots organizing and public education, other organizations have focused their attention on working within the institutional and political structures of particular denominations. The latter approaches to activism and community building are sometimes conceptualized through the language of reconciliation. One of the more influential organizations using the strategy of reconciliation is the Reconciling Ministries Network (RMN), the unofficial LGBTQ organization of the United Method Church.[18] I spoke with many people during my fieldwork who were familiar with the organization's reconciliation process, whether currently attending a "Reconciling Church" or having gone through the reconciliation process in their home church or small group.

I introduce the reconciliation process here because of the overlap in strategies and discourses between organizations like RMN and TRP.

At the same time, the institutional and organizational rules that govern churches that are part of mainline denominations, such as the United Methodist Church (UMC), differ from the more amorphous, ambiguous rules that govern those more loosely affiliated churches that describe themselves as evangelical or nondenominational. As such, although speakers and participants at TRP conferences did sometimes use the language of reconciliation to describe the means and ends of LGBTQ social justice work in conservative Christian communities, they also talked about "not breaking fellowship," a distinction to which I return later.

The UMC is a mainline Protestant denomination that was established in 1968 after the merger of the Methodist Church (USA) and the Evangelical Brethren Church, both denominations that were remnants of earlier Methodist movements in the United States.[19] Like the other mainline denominations, the UMC tends to be viewed as politically and theologically moderate, although individual churches in the denomination span the spectrum from conservative- to liberal-leaning.[20]

In some ways it could be said that the modern UMC grew up with the LGBTQ rights movements. In 1972 in Atlanta at General Conference, the top legislative body that meets every four years and is responsible for doctrine and government, the "homosexual issue" erupted as a major point of disagreement. Delegates disagreed over the status of gay people in the denomination and how to formulate a public response to the growing visibility of the lesbian and gay rights movement after Stonewall. After a heated floor debate, the assembly voted to add language that declared "the practice of homosexuality . . . incompatible with Christian teaching" to the "Social Principles" section of *The Book of Discipline of the United Methodist Church* (or *The Discipline*, as it's commonly known).[21] Over subsequent General Conferences a majority reaffirmed the language on homosexuality, and in the 1996 revision of *The Discipline*, the denomination added language that restricts UMC churches and pastors from hosting or performing same-sex marriage ceremonies. During this time activist organizations like Good News and Transforming Congregations were influential in lobbying for conservative positions on LGBTQ issues both at General Conference and through local chapters at churches and seminaries.[22]

In response to the statement on homosexuality being added to *The Discipline*, Gene Leggett and Rick Huskey, along with a few other openly gay Methodist clergy, formed the United Methodist Gay Caucus in 1975 to advocate for gay women and men at the 1976 General Conference.[23] The mission of the organization, later renamed Affirmation: United Methodists for Lesbian/Gay Concerns, included "[pursuing] policies and processes that support full participation by lesbian, gay, bisexual and transgendered people in all areas and levels of the United Methodist Church" and "[empowering] people to undertake works of inclusion and justice where they are" by "[providing] theological foundations and socio-cultural insights leading the church to respond to God's call to be fully inclusive."[24]

In the early 1980s Affirmation introduced the Reconciliation Churches Program with the goal of shepherding individual churches through the process of becoming LGBT-inclusive, insofar as they were able within the constraints of the denomination.[25] Affirmation leaders chose the language of reconciliation to reflect what they saw as the need for "reconciliation" between the LGBT community and the denomination, and they used the More Light Program of the Presbyterian Church (USA) as a model.[26]

The reconciliation process is a form of community-based organizing and activism wherein members of a community—in this case a congregation—mobilize a constituency to achieve specific goals and to create systemic change. Although the actual implementation of the reconciliation process varies across church communities, RMN provides an overall strategy and resources to help with it. The reconciliation process is not limited to congregations; any church-related community can pursue reconciliation, including other groups in or outside of a traditional congregation, such as Bible study groups or campus ministries. It is not uncommon, for example, for a small group to become reconciling without the consent, support, or perhaps even knowledge of church leadership or the rest of the congregation.

RMN's materials suggest that the process should ideally begin with a small group of five to ten people in a particular church community "who are already inclusive in heart."[27] This initial core group meets to share ideas, initiates a master plan for community-wide reconciliation, and reaches out to other "reconciling-friendly people" in the congregation through one-to-one visits. Eventually, depending on the idiosyncrasies of the reconciliation process in a community, the core group is replaced by a publicly recognized committee. The committee conducts internal research to better understand the institutional and power structures of the congregation and to map out spheres of influence. It also plans and facilitates educational meetings, discussion groups, and Bible-study sessions on the topic. Eventually the issue is put to a community-wide vote. If the congregation or group votes in favor of reconciliation, the community then declares itself a "reconciling congregation," a declaration that RMN emphasizes should be unambiguously public and visible.[28]

In her study of similar reconciliation or dialogue groups, Dawne Moon suggests that what often makes them useful is that "dialogue groups endeavor to avoid politics, focusing on giving each participant the time and space to 'tell their story,' speaking 'from their hearts.' In doing so, they give participants the opportunity to humanize each other, to see each other as members of the same moral community."[29] By contrast, "when opponents convene to make policy decisions without the transformation of consciousness that comes from relating to each other . . . the interaction can feel like a war between groups from utterly different moral worlds."[30] Similarly RMN encourages a particular "posture" throughout the reconciliation process for navigating politics, sticking with difficult conversations, and advocating for change. In my reading the posture reflects an attempt to circumvent partisan debate in favor of common ground, personal experience, and emotional response. At the same time, even if reconciliation groups endeavor to avoid politics, they are nevertheless an exercise in making things public, assembling around a matter of concern, and mapping out alternative modes of community making.

A resource called "Building an Inclusive Church," available on RMN's website, illustrates this strategy and posture for making things public.[31] The sixty-page toolkit provides a framework and resources for the reconciliation process, including surveys, assessment materials, discussion guides, literature on conflict resolution, educational material on sexuality and gender identity, a bibliography of resources, and tips for developing effective storytelling and other strategies of persuasion. Throughout the authors emphasize several conversational and persuasion techniques summarized into four "tools": graceful engagement, choosing the right frame, one-to-one visits, and public storytelling. The authors stress that the concept of "graceful engagement" should guide the reconciliation process from the beginning. According to the toolkit, graceful engagement is a "way of practicing holy conversation," a practice that "[avoids] and [does] not value divisive rhetoric or actions." In fact, to embody graceful engagement is to embody what it truly means to be a Christian: "such a posture is what discipleship is all about."

The toolkit provides activities for embodying and practicing this posture of graceful engagement beginning with the first meeting. A worksheet included in the toolkit, for example, instructs participants to begin with silence, prayer, and "breathing deeply and inviting God's presence to be fully felt by all in the room" before discussing and meditating upon "what it means or how it feels to be filled with GRACE." Graceful engagement, the authors emphasize, is not "debate" or imposing opinions "through argument," nor is it "exclusion or outright [condemnation]" or "leaving the church to find a place 'where everyone agrees.'" Instead it is "living together in relationship and compassion"; "fully valuing other people and their beliefs, even when they differ from our own"; "listening more than speaking"; and "meeting people where they are, not where we want them to be." Participants are reminded that graceful engagement is something that must be practiced. The suggested activities include participants' visualizing potential scenarios or conversations where they might practice graceful engagement or rehearse moments through storytelling or visualization when they had an experience characterized by graceful engagement.

This attitude of relational, nonconfrontational dialogue is mirrored in the other tools as well. The focus is on imagining and nurturing a particular type of community, one that is rooted in storytelling and personal experience, relationships over doctrine, and empathy, with a lot of flexibility and openness. For example, the one-to-one visits are thirty- to forty-minute meetings with members of the congregation, preferably in their own homes. It is not the standard political canvassing with talking points or a list of position questions: "One-to-One Visits are an exchange about what is important to each of you, not a session where you work to get the person to do something." One-to-one visits, therefore, make use of "relationship-building" and "relational culture" as a form of organizing. The toolkit stresses the need to move beyond one-size-fits-all approaches to persuasion; instead the primary goal is to establish an authentic connection and cultivate personalized relationships by tailoring the conversation to shared values, interests, and personal experiences and passions.[32]

For many evangelical churches, particularly those not affiliated with mainline denominations, there are no organizations equivalent to, for example, RMN or More Light Presbyterians that are focused on building coalitions of reconciling congregations and advocating for LGBTQ people at the national policymaking bodies of their denominations. This is due in part to differences in ecclesiastical polity or the organizational structure and governance of a church or denomination.[33] Generally the ecclesiastical polities of mainline Protestant denominations tend to be more centralized and hierarchical. They are characterized by regional or national legislative bodies who oversee the policymaking and administration of the denomination and the appointment of leadership in local congregations.

By contrast, many nondenominational evangelical churches have a congregationalist polity, which means that they tend to be more decentralized and self-governed. That is, churches with a congregationalist polity are often autonomous or more loosely affiliated with other congregations and are governed internally by their own members. As Randall Balmer summarizes the principal distinction, "Modern-day evangelicals still subscribe to the rudiments of Luther's theology, although they rejected his ideas about polity and worship as too formal and 'papist.'"[34]

Nevertheless, many evangelical and nondenominational churches do affiliate with other like-minded churches through voluntary associations such as the National Association of Evangelicals and the Southern Baptist Convention.[35] Even if these organizations do not play a direct role in governing local congregations, affiliated groups must assent to a statement of faith to become members, and they can lose access to funds or membership status if they take a position on an issue that runs counter to those organizations' official resolutions or agendas. Such parachurch organizations also function as clearinghouses for determining collective action, from charitable initiatives to efforts to shape public policy. Thus even though evangelical churches ostensibly are responsible for themselves and obey no canon law, such parachurch organizations play a vital role in mobilizing activism and determining the political lines between orthodoxy and heresy.

In addition to differences in ecclesiastical polity, differences among individual denominations regarding their orientation toward the moral order also help explain differences in activism and arguments among LGBTQ religious organizations. As Fuist, Stoll, and Kniss have shown, the denomination with which an LGBTQ organization is affiliated "both constrains and enables the kinds of cultural resources available for the [LGBT organizations] associated with them to construct rhetorical claims."[36] But rather than viewing such organizations through a typical liberal-conservative or mainline-conservative lens, the authors suggest a more heuristic multidimensional framework. One axis represents a denomination's orientation toward moral projects, and the other represents the orientation toward moral authority, with individual denominations falling on a spectrum from individual to collective projects along both axes. For example, more progressive mainline churches tend to view moral authority as an individual project (placing greater emphasis on individual reason and experience than tradition and sacred text) but view moral projects in collective terms (placing greater emphasis on structural change than only personal transformation). By contrast, conservative Christians tend to view moral authority as a collective project and moral projects in terms of reforming people's personal behavior.

As such, LGBTQ organizations that grow out of the former (such as the RMN model described previously) tend to be "more assertive with their questioning of anti-LGBT scriptural interpretations, tend to have an activist mission, and rhetorically concentrate more on reform of the church and protection of LGBT persons as a social group than the identity reconciliation of any one LGBT individual."[37] Organizations associated with the latter tend to be "less direct with their theology, less activist-oriented, and place individual identity reconciliation above reform or structural change in their work."[38] As I show throughout the rest of the book, TRP is emblematic of the heuristic value of this framework while it also adds valuable nuance to it. While shaped by conservative evangelicalism, the organization's explicit activism, direct theological approach, and emphasis on structural in addition to individual change challenges our understanding of conservative LGBTQ Christian activism.[39]

All of this is to say that in place of an organized effort to shepherd individual churches through the process of becoming more inclusive, the LGBTQ-supportive parachurch organizations working in the tradition of evangelicalism—TRP, GCN, The Marin Foundation, Evangelicals Concerned, and others—tend instead to focus more on public education or ministry, such as creating support groups and safe spaces for LGBTQ Christians, than on changing internal church policy or governance. They also play a crucial role in raising awareness and cultivating a sense of LGBTQ Christian community, solidarity, and a common purpose for social action. One might call it pride.

As a form of counter-conduct to the authorized assemblies of normative evangelicalism, TRP conferences provide a space where matters of concern can be voiced and heard and, equally important to TRP conference organizers and participants, spiritual needs can be met. It is, in fact, this aspect of the conferences that seemed to resonate most with participants: the fellowship, the communal worship, the storytelling. Participants at TRP conferences came for the refuge and pride of community but also for the opportunity to take part in the community-building process. These temporary communities provide participants the ability to circumvent traditional authority figures and institutions to gain access to aspects of church life and the sacraments to which they are often systematically and routinely denied: the opportunity to speak from a position of authority; to lead God's people in worship; to join in prayer with people who don't question their sincerity or authenticity; to engage in the decision-making process of a community and the collective project of discerning God's will; and to be coparticipants in defining evangelicalism and what it means to be a Christian.

The communities formed by Christians working within evangelicalism in the pursuit of gender and sexual justice—whether in individual churches, at TRP conferences, in online chatrooms moderated by GCN, or elsewhere—might be thought of as subaltern counterpublics. As defined by Nancy Fraser, these are "parallel discursive arenas where members of subordinated social groups invent and circulate counter-discourses to formulate oppositional interpretations of their identities, interests, and needs."[40] Similarly TRP conferences, as well as the related sites I examine throughout this book, enable individuals to invent, repurpose, reclaim, and rehearse language and scripts in the pursuit of imagining new politics, practices, and ways of being.

Also critical are TRP's efforts to open space in political argument to make it possible to talk about LGBTQ inclusion and equality without their being dismissed out of hand as "liberal" or "progressive." TRP's strategy in this regard, which is the primary focus of the regional training conferences, is to train people to have more productive conversations in their faith communities. A promotion on TRP's website for the Kansas City regional training conference, for example, advertised that "the conference will be a prime networking opportunity for all Christians who want to advance the dignity of LGBT people, especially Christians in non-affirming churches, denominations, or communities who seek to have more loving, fruitful, and informed conversations with non-affirming friends and family members."[41]

In this way TRP conferences can also be thought of as critical communities. As Thomas Rochon suggests, critical communities consist of "small groups of critical thinkers . . . whose experiences, readings, and interactions with each other help them to develop a sense of cultural values that is out of step with the larger society."[42] The critical community thus functions as a space to develop ideas and remake identities, a process that can inspire cultural change through their dissemination to a wider audience, "turning private issue[s] into public" issues.[43] Similarly TRP's conferences are designed to explore biblical and theological arguments that would resonate with conservative evangelicals and to train participants to advocate for LGBTQ inclusion in their own church communities by disseminating those ideas.

In addition to the instruction of ten talking points, to which I return in the next chapter, TRP's conferences also include panels and discussion opportunities for broadening the conversation about sexuality and gender identity in conservative contexts: parents of LGBTQ youth; transgender inclusion; the intersections of race and sexuality; celibacy and singleness, to name a few. And while the conferences place a heavy emphasis on the content of such conversations, there is as much, and perhaps more, of an overall focus on how to engage in more productive ways beyond the substance of a conversation. This issue came up often in small group discussions, in breakout sessions, and in passing conversations outside of conference rooms. Even if they were not the primary focus of presentations, panelists and keynote speakers often detoured into conversation tips as well. In short, TRP conferences function as a laboratory for talking about how to have more useful conversations, how to raise concerns with pastors and fellow church members, and how to sustain difficult relationships.

Many of these conversations about conversations were about how to handle disagreement and dissent. Sometimes this was framed as the desire to "agree to disagree." Instead of consensus, participants strived to create room for disagreement, which was viewed as a more stable foundation for community and change. Those with whom I spoke at TRP conferences told me they were trying to find ways to create space for constructive conversations in situations where "the conversation" is often foreclosed before it ever begins. Often this was conceptualized as "not breaking fellowship." This is how Max Kuecker described the rationale behind TRP's focus on helping people have more productive conversations:

> For most of American culture, we see people shifting from nonaffirming to affirming of LGBT people. . . . One of the sectors of society where that's not the case is the more conservative church. . . . The reason that is the case is because . . . the conservative Christian church, especially churches that hold a high view of Scripture, really look at the Bible as being God-inspired and authoritative, [and] we have a hard time accepting LGBT people because our understanding of Scripture up until recently has been that homosexuality itself is sinful.
>
> So what The Reformation Project is striving to do is to change the nature of that conversation: to provide the resources for people in the pews to have conversations with their peers or pastors to unpack why the Bible does not say that, why the Bible *does* . . . affirm LGBT

people and same-sex relationships. . . . So our aim, by changing the conversation around what the Bible says about homosexuality, is to create some more space for conservative Christians to affirm LGBT people and to include them in all levels of church life.

So that's our primary mission. And the reason that we're looking primarily to be engaging people in the pews, basically a grassroots movement, is that a lot of conservative Christian leaders are scared to death of talking about this topic at all. The landscape is such that [there] is a cultural shift happening that millennials are largely LGBT-affirming, and so they're afraid of losing the next generation of people in their churches if they say things negatively about gay people. On the flip side, they're afraid of losing their funding base, members of their congregation, ordination, invitations to speaking engagements, things like that, if they come out as too affirming or too inclusive. . . . There are many, many, many more who are interested in taking steps in that direction but are afraid of losing their place. . . . And so that's the nature of the landscape that we're in.

So that's what our goal is: so that churches over the next few years, that big congregations and Bible study groups and mentor and discipleship groups or whatever, won't be just antigay—won't just see homosexuality as a sin or that same-sex relationships are a sin—but will shift to saying that there are multiple views that are legitimate interpretations of these verses. And, therein, this is not a matter that we should be breaking fellowship over.[44]

Fellowship signifies a few different things in evangelical discourse. As John Bartkowski explains, "evangelicals foster collective bonds—affectionately dubbed 'fellowship' by the faithful—through an array of social networks: church worship activities; congregational ministry programs for men, women, married couples, youth, and whole families; small-group Bible studies; outreach service programs to the poor, elderly, and imprisoned; and, of course, para-church organizations."[45] So, on the one hand, fellowship refers to special relationships or collective bonds among fellow believers. At the same time, fellowship also refers to the practice of cultivating those relationships. In short, fellowship is part solidarity, part deep hanging out.[46] In the context of LGBTQ Christian activism in this community of counter-conduct, as illustrated in Kuecker's explanation of TRP's strategy, not breaking fellowship refers to the effort to maintain community despite, and perhaps even because of, disagreements over sexual and gender norms and values.

To not break fellowship seems at first like an abstract commitment to the Christian ideal of unity in the body of Christ. On the ground, though, the desire to not break fellowship was more often motivated by the threat of losing or being rejected by loved ones, family members and childhood friends, mentors and pastors. At its most extreme "breaking fellowship" with a person or group is the contemporary evangelical equivalent of excommunication. While maintaining unity is the ideal, some Christians will point to biblical passages such as I Corinthians 5:13 to justify breaking fellowship with church members whom they consider to be continuing to live in sin despite repeated admonishment. In this line of reasoning sometimes church discipline and separation are required so that the offending individual or group will not contaminate the whole community. During my fieldwork I spoke with several people who came to TRP conferences for this very reason—that is, to cope, by being in community with others who have also felt the sting of rejection, with relationships already lost, to learn strategies to have better conversations and to find inspiration to be patient and gracious.

Another reason why not breaking fellowship is such a motivating force in this community is because of charges of divisiveness. The actors concerned with policing the boundaries of so-called orthodox Christian identity and community often charge LGBTQ Christians and LGBTQ Christian organizations with causing division in the church. That is, they rely on a common tactic of limiting critique and dissent: accusing LGBTQ and ally Christians of fomenting division for simply calling attention to divisions that already exist.

One example from my fieldnotes from a steering committee meeting in late June 2015 is especially illustrative of this concern. A few months earlier two of the steering committee members had abruptly resigned from the committee for reasons undisclosed to most of the other members. Peter, a member who stayed in regular contact with the individuals who had left, took a few minutes early in the meeting to update the group about what had happened. Simply put, Peter told us, the former members no longer agreed with TRP's mission. "They heard from some TRP detractors," Peter said, "essentially conservative spies who had been at our conference in DC. Based on what they heard from these people, they came to feel like TRP was a dividing force instead of a reconciling voice. It's rather mysterious, and I wholeheartedly disagree, but in the end that was their rationale for leaving."

We were nearing a short mid-morning break in between Bible-training sessions on the second day of TRP's regional training conference in Atlanta. Before excusing the audience, Max Kuecker took a minute to explain the purpose of the evening caucuses. "In addition to providing tools for making a biblical case for LGBT inclusion," he said, "one of the other primary goals of The Reformation Project is to help you connect with other LGBT-affirming Christians that are motivated around similar issues and concerns."

Kuecker called our attention to a series of large white pieces of paper taped to the wall on our right and extending to the wall behind us. Each contained a proposed caucus topic: Asian Pacific Islander; Black; Latin@; Trans; College; Parents; Baptist; Evangelical Covenant; Methodist; Presbyterian. In addition to the topics already present, blank pages were available for people to propose new caucus topics. Kuecker encouraged everyone to congregate under a topic of choice during the break and make plans for fellowshipping later that evening. The conference program included a few suggestions: "That caucus will decide how they want to spend their time. Do they want to start by fellowshipping over dinner, then settle down to strategize for transformation towards greater LGBTQ inclusion? Or, do they want to begin with a working session, then fellowship over dinner later?"

Over the break people lingered to make small talk, to connect or reconnect, some pulling out cell phones to follow each other on social media. Others stayed in their seats or filtered out to the meeting space outside the ballroom to find a quick coffee or snack. Hoping to catch a speaker who had just left the stage, two people (wearing newly purchased bright yellow T-shirts with the word "Reformer" printed on the back) worked their way up the center aisle against the flow of people leaving the room. Toward the front of the room three young women

1. Caucus topics above the Racial Justice and LGBT Equality Timeline at TRP's regional training conference in Atlanta, June 2015 (see chapter 5 for more information on the timeline and racial justice training). Photo by the author.

gathered in a tight circle and began to pray, one of them leading the prayer and placing her hands on the shoulders of the other two, all their heads bowed. Small groups formed under the caucus topics.

Generous Spaciousness

The type of conversations, practices, and communities imagined by the language of "not breaking fellowship" were sometimes also articulated as "generous spaces" or "generous spaciousness." Wendy VanderWal-Gritter, a white woman and former director of an ex-gay ministry turned gay Christian ally who describes herself as "mainly straight," discusses the concept of generous spaciousness at some length in *Generous Spaciousness*. The book is an account of VanderWal-Gritter's change of heart concerning homosexuality, as well as an attempt to rethink conservative evangelical community through the lives and experiences of gay Christians.[47] In other words, as the tagline on the back cover reads, the book is about "transforming controversy into community." While VanderWal-Gritter's arguments are not without controversy in the community of LGBTQ Christians I studied, they nevertheless illustrate how the language of generous spaciousness was sometimes used to imagine a more inclusive community and define its rules of engagement, to expand political discourse, and to organize practices of the self.[48]

Generous Spaciousness is part memoir, part theology, and part, as Foucault refers to the genre, "practical text."[49] It is also very evangelical, demonstrating characteristics of a genre to which one becomes accustomed after spending time reading books written by and for evangelicals. The text includes several examples of the sort of "attentional learning" described by Tanya Luhrmann in her study of how contemporary evangelicals come to experience God as real through practices of the body.[50] "Attentional learning" is a practice of learning how to read body sensations as evidence of God's presence and direction in one's life. Similarly VanderWal-Gritter writes often about her own embodied experiences of God. For example, she describes sensing God's call for her to go into ministry, going through a "discernment process," hearing the "Spirit whisper" to her during times of indecision, or having moments of "visceral, gut-level angst, crying out to God" during pivotal moments in her spiritual growth.[51]

VanderWal-Gritter opens the book by talking about her experience as the executive director of New Direction Ministries in Canada, an Exodus International–affiliated ex-gay ministry that began in the 1980s.[52] VanderWal-Gritter became New Direction's director in the spring of 2002, and while in the beginning she was committed to Exodus's claim that sexual orientation change is possible, she slowly became disillusioned with the organization. In particular she was frustrated with how the claims of sexual reorientation success promoted by Exodus leaders, often parroted by conservative evangelical writers and leaders, failed to accurately reflect the fact that "radical reorientation at an attraction level is *not* the typical experience," something she knew firsthand from working with lesbians and gay men at New Direction.[53] She at first intended to change the narrative from within but eventually separated from Exodus in 2008 after coming to the conclusion that there needed to be a "reformation in evangelical ministry to gay people."[54] She turned her focus toward creating an environment of "generous spaciousness," including the organization of generous spaciousness small groups and retreats that "[cultivate] places where true dialogue and conversation [can] happen despite disagreements about sexuality."[55]

GCN played a pivotal role in VanderWal-Gritter's and New Direction's transitioning away from the ex-gay model. Justin Lee, a white gay man and the founder of GCN, appeared on the *Dr. Phil* show in 2006 to debate the ex-gay activist David Kyle Foster on the claims of ex-gay ministries and their role in evangelicalism. VanderWal-Gritter describes the exchange: "I was horrified by what I heard. In a nutshell the ex-gay leader proclaimed . . . that everyone could change their orientation and that if this didn't happen it was because the individual didn't try hard enough or have enough faith. After the show aired, on the Exodus leaders' discussion boards, I tentatively asked what others thought of the show. . . . To my utter surprise, no one, even the people I considered to be more moderate, offered any critique of the Exodus leader's comments."[56]

Later VanderWal-Gritter began to attend GCN conferences—she was a guest speaker at the 2014 and 2015 conferences—and discovered "they were modeling a safe place to authentically hold convictions while being relationally present in a supportive, encouraging posture to those who held different convictions."[57] In VanderWal-Gritter's telling, these experiences of the type of community fostered by GCN inspired her to advocate for a broader application of what she came to call a "generous spaciousness" in how evangelicals talk about human sexuality and gay Christians.

VanderWal-Gritter draws on the concept of "generous orthodoxy" for her generous spaciousness, the term with which Hans Wilhelm Frei came to describe his theology.[58] Frei was one of the theologians at the center of the postliberal or narrative theology movement of the late twentieth century, an attempt to move beyond the Enlightenment faith in universal rationality and certainty. In one place Frei described the project as one that "looks for a relation between Christian theology and philosophy that disagrees with a view of certainty and knowledge which liberals and evangelicals hold in common."[59] The sociologist and Frei scholar Jason A. Springs argues that Frei's concept of "generous orthodoxy" is characterized by "the complex tension generated between a scripturally centered orientation and ceaseless interpretive contestation."[60] A generous orthodoxy, Springs continues, "will attune itself to the best insights of various Christian theological traditions" and, moreover, "will reach beyond itself in order to engage the full wealth of resources made available by nontheological interlocutors."[61]

The tension and doubt inherent in the practice of doing theology and scriptural interpretation motivated Frei to disrupt the shared faith in universal rationality. "Generous orthodoxy," while rooted in Christian tradition and Scripture, requires a constant interrogation of one's assumptions, an openness to tension and doubt, and a commitment to an interdisciplinarity that transcends the typical binaries that structure modern thought—liberal and conservative, theology and philosophy, religious and secular. The concept of "generous orthodoxy" was later popularized in evangelicalism by evangelical theologians like Stanley Grenz and Brian McLaren.[62] Both Grenz and McLaren sought to move beyond the liberal/conservative dichotomy that frames much of Christian thought and practice, including the polarization of the culture wars.

VanderWal-Gritter envisions, in what she describes as the posture of generous spaciousness, a similar disruption of categories and a practice of ceaseless self-interrogation; rather than seeking the "right answer or solution," she advocates a "spiritual formation" or "posture" marked by an "openness that is inquisitive, personal, relational, and dependent on the Spirit."[63] Instead of one having to run from doubt and tension, these moments are indulged and celebrated for their transformative potential.

VanderWal-Gritter perhaps offers her clearest definition of "generous spaciousness" through the telling of a story about a celibate gay woman. This particular woman, VanderWal-Gritter writes, "experiences same-sex attraction and is committed to living a chaste, single life" because of her belief that homosexuality is sinful.[64] However, the woman later meets a committed, sexually active lesbian couple who also attends her church. "After the meeting," the woman "felt confused for a time. But then God confirmed to her in a very beautiful and personal way that he wanted to be her husband."[65] In other words, meeting the lesbian couple caused the woman to doubt not only her life of singleness but also her belief that sexually active gay couples are living in sin. Through an encounter with God the woman came to understand, despite her deeply held convictions, that both of their life choices were equally valid. "God had enlarged her heart. She had grown to make room for the gay couples in her church. . . . She has allowed God to teach her and humble her such that she is not an obstacle to the gay couples in her church. This is, I believe, a beautiful example of generous spaciousness."[66]

Disputable Matters

In addition to "not breaking fellowship" and "generous spaciousness," repositioning contested issues as "disputable matters" is another common tactic used by some in evangelical spaces to imagine different politics and communities. For example, Ken Wilson attempts to reposition the "gay issue" as a disputable matter.[67] Wilson, a straight white man who is an evangelical author and pastor of a Vineyard Church in Ann Arbor, Michigan, was a speaker at TRP's regional training conference in Washington DC in November 2014 on a panel titled "Advocating for Inclusion as a Pastor." At the conference and in his book—written as a "confession" to his congregation—Wilson advocates for what he calls a "third way" approach. Drawing on the Apostle Paul's advice in his letter to Christian converts in Rome who were quarreling over dietary restrictions, he suggests that Christians are bound by an obligation to accept and respect one another as fellow Christians even if they disagree in their beliefs, especially in cases where Scripture offers no clear resolution.[68]

This approach has been adopted by a handful of evangelical congregations that have chosen to become Third Way churches, and it has been met by pushback from the conservative evangelical establishment. On February 9, 2014, Danny Cortez, the pastor of New Heart Community Church in Los Angeles, gave a sermon on how he had come to change his mind on homosexuality and how his son later came out to him as gay. (Cortez was also a speaker on the November 2014 panel.) At the end of the sermon Cortez, who is straight and Filipino American, summarized what he hoped his church could become:

> My hope for New Heart is not that you all would agree with me. It's been a sixteen-year journey for me to finally get to where I'm at, and I don't expect anyone to agree with what I believe. I'm not here trying to push my beliefs on you but merely to share with you my journey. And you have every right—I respect whatever you believe. But do we as a church have space for disagreement? Do we as a church, are we as a church, willing to say, "We have different ideas of homosexuality, and therefore can we not judge anyone and accept them into full membership?" Or do we choose to say, "We disagree with you and therefore have no fellowship with you?" Personally, I don't think that's the way of Christ.[69]

In response to the sermon factions in the church began agitating for Cortez's termination. However, after a community-wide vote, the church voted not only to retain Cortez as the head pastor but also to become a Third Way congregation. In September 2014 an executive committee of the Southern Baptist Convention voted out New Heart Community Church for adopting a Third Way perspective. The committee argued that New Heart was no longer a "cooperating church" due to its violation of a bylaw in the Southern Baptist Convention constitution prohibiting affiliated congregations from "act[ing] to affirm, approve or endorse homosexual behavior."[70]

Some months after my fieldwork with TRP had ended, the organization introduced a new series of events called "Elevating the Dialogue on LGBT Inclusion and Understanding in the Church." Somewhat similar to "disputable matters" and the Third Way approach, these events are TRP's attempt to disentangle the LGBT issue from Christian orthodoxy, to foster an environment where Christians can come out as LGBT or voice their support of LGBT people without having their character, sincerity, or faith as Christians called into question.

The events consist of panel discussions with pastors and other influential figures who maintain different views but are willing to have a frank and respectful conversation. In an introductory video that Matthew Vines posted on his Facebook page, he describes how the events grew out of his experience traveling throughout the United States and speaking with nonaffirming pastors and everyday Christians. In these conversations he found that people are often outwardly kind but that the very same people often do not respect his Christian faith and identity as authentic or sincere. The goal, Vines explained, is to elevate the "most respectful nonaffirming voices to create space, to turn down the volume on this conversation, creating space to actually humanize the conversation. [We want to] elevate the dialogue by showing that affirming and nonaffirming Christians can actually be in community together, and that Christians who are LGBT or LGBT-affirming can be respected for the theology they maintain." And while the goal is to bring together Christian leaders from across the theological spectrum, another key element of the events is to include LGBT Christians in the conversation: "We get tired of conversations about LGBT Christians instead of conversations with LGBT Christians."[71] In sum the goal is an attempt to disrupt, by creating space in political argument, the corrosive narrative in conservative evangelicalism that one cannot be both LGBT and Christian or that if one is Christian, one necessarily must be opposed to LGBT social justice.

Judith Butler has argued that "dissent and debate depend upon the inclusion of those who maintain critical views . . . remaining part of a larger public discussion of the value of policies and politics."[72] Those who seek to silence dissent do so, Butler continues, "not only through a series of shaming tactics which have a certain psychological terrorization as their effect, but they work as well by producing what will and will not count as a viable speaking subject and a reasonable opinion within the public domain."[73] This is true also of how some conservative evangelical leaders and thinkers attempt to limit critique: by determining in advance who can speak and the terms of what is debatable or disputable. Often the argument from some conservative evangelicals is that there can be no debate. In response to the Danny Cortez and Third Way controversy, for example, R. Albert Mohler Jr., the president of the Southern Baptist Theological Seminary, flatly objected that "there is no third way" or "middle ground."[74]

Still others seek to control the terms of the debate. This strategy is illustrated by how some conservative Christian writers responded to news that Vines and David Gushee, a leading evangelical ethicist and white, straight ally to LGBTQ Christians, had been invited to speak on a 2015 Q Ideas conference panel featuring Christians who hold differing views on same-sex marriage. What some have referred to as "the Christian TED talks," Q Ideas is a parachurch organization founded by the evangelical author Gabe Lyons that "mobilizes Christians to advance the common good in society."[75] Some conservative evangelical thinkers and activists, such as Eric Teetsel and Owen Strachan, criticized the invitation of Vines and Gushee in that it provided a platform to "sow confusion within the body of believers," saying that while they "relish debate within the Church on a range of issues," not "everything is up for debate."[76]

Writing in a blog post on the conservative-leaning evangelical website *Mere Orthodoxy*, Matthew Lee Anderson, the founder and lead writer of the website, argued that Q Ideas, as well as other "parachurches which sprang up out of our movement," is symptomatic of a trend in evangelicalism wherein conservatives have failed to control the narrative. "If such 'conversations,'" Anderson writes, "were happening in contexts where it was clear our moral convictions were not up for grabs, and we had winsome, cheerful people actually winning the arguments, then Q Ideas wouldn't have a market." Similarly Anderson goes on to suggest that the debate over homosexuality and gay marriage has been stacked in favor of individuals like Gushee and Vines because conservative evangelicals have "abdicated" their authority on sexual morality to the broader culture, claiming that "Evangelicals have been imitating culture for 50 years on sexual ethics." His solution, then, is that conservative evangelicals should control the terms of the debate. Responding to Teetsel and Strachan, Anderson suggests that "it does, in other words, no good for conservatives to suggest that there can be 'no debate' on this question. But it does a world of good for conservatives to own the debate, host it, and set the terms for it. Again, that may not seem 'ideologically neutral' or like a fair fight. But no intellectual engagement ever is that fair, and the arguments for gay marriage aren't very good."[77]

Such attempts to limit or control critique help explain why some advocating for LGBTQ inclusion in evangelical communities are trying to move away from a "debate" framework toward a "conversation" framework, from consensus to disagreement, from certainty to doubt and tension. Even so, these attempts to agree to disagree are not without their critics, even among those who are invested in this issue in conservative Christian contexts. For example, the once-defrocked UMC pastor Frank Schaefer sharply criticized a Third Way–style proposal at the 2016 UMC General Conference because it stopped short of removing the "harmful and discriminatory language" on homosexuality from *The Discipline*.[78] Stigmatizing people with non-normative sexual and gender identities, refusing to acknowledge the freedom of gay church members to love whomever they choose, or denying them church leadership positions perpetuates a form of violence that goes beyond a simple "disagreement." Matthew Vines expressed similar concerns in a 2014 interview with the online magazine Religion Dispatches when describing the pushback against TRP:

> The fact that there is backlash is a prerequisite for starting the conversation, that's not something that I'm concerned about. It's healthy. I'm trying to be as gracious and not to be unintentionally inflammatory. I want to respect people and their motives, even though I strongly disagree with their beliefs.
>
> I don't think we can ultimately agree to disagree because this issue, and nonaffirming beliefs, are very damaging to the lives of LGBT people. It's also a double standard, because most people who hold nonaffirming beliefs are straight and they don't have to live with the consequences of their beliefs. They're asking LGBT people to do something that is vastly harder than they themselves are doing. That sep-

arates LGBT people from God and it's damaging to their dignity and their ability to form relationships.

I don't see much room for compromise, but that doesn't mean that you can't still respect people in their sincerity and their motives.[79]

During the break, I wandered out of the hotel ballroom and into the foyer, where I found two large notepads propped up on easels; they served as a rough-and-ready community bulletin board. The notepads became increasingly cluttered over the two-and-a-half-day conference as attendees left messages looking for dinner companions, offering ride shares to grocery stores or pharmacies, or searching for misplaced program notes. Someone organized a lunch outing to Ebenezer Baptist Church, the childhood church of Martin Luther King Jr. Another person offered their hotel room for a game night late in the evening on Friday, when people returned from fellowshipping with their caucuses.

A man I will call Rick caught my attention to strike up a conversation. He introduced himself as a student at a Disciples of Christ seminary in Texas. Rick, who was white and maybe in his late twenties, told me that he had wrestled with his sexuality for more than ten years but decided to go to seminary anyway in hopes of finding some clarity. He had come to the conference to learn more about affirming theology, saying he didn't have a firm grasp of the biblical arguments. I asked him what he thought about the content, but he didn't seem to have much of an opinion or at least was too timid to talk about it if he did. I asked Rick if he would describe himself as an evangelical. He said the term had too much political baggage for him and preferred identifying just as a Christian.

As the audience was being called back together, I came back into the room to see what caucus topics had been added to those already provided. There were several new ones: Pentecostal; Monogamy/Polyamory; Bisexuality/Pansexuality; Queer theology/Indecent theology; Anglican/Episcopalian; Pastoral care; Mixed-orientation marriage; Challenging church backing for reparative therapy. It struck me that the proposed topics seemed to express a subtle critique of the conference's somewhat narrow focus on conservative Christian theology and committed, monogamous same-sex relationships.

The time between sessions provided an opportunity for people to (as they might say) fellowship. The aisles and hallways in between sessions became spaces for the collaborative work of making things public. These interstices provided time to make new friends, to digest or push back against the conference content, or to speak from one's own experiences. I often jotted down in my fieldnote journal words or phrases I heard as I passed through crowds on my way from one session to another:

Shame

Same-sex attractions

Gender

Challenging conversations

Experience

Grace

God gives us experiences; it's up to us how we handle them

Bisexuality

We have to put ourselves outside of our comfort zones

Of course experience is important

Ministry

I just sat, silently

Deep, emotional things

He needs to stop calling it a "grassroots organization"

Grace-Filled Conversations, Incivility, and Dissent

In this final section I want to pull a little more on a thread that has run through much of this chapter. If one spends any time at all among evangelicals, one will most likely hear a lot about the concept of grace. In the Christian tradition, grace—derived from the Apostle Paul's writings on the Greek concept *charis*, meaning grace but also kindness and life— refers to the condition of receiving or extending undeserved favor. I heard it used in this sense, but I also found that "grace" was put to work as a political rationale for negotiating conversations and relationships.

This was often expressed in the language of having "grace-filled conversations" or "entering relationships with grace."

The critical theorist Giorgio Agamben notes that "grace" differs from "faith" in that the latter describes a relationship of reciprocal obligations. That is, *pistis*—or faith—for Paul meant something like "the unconditional self abandon to the power of another, which obliges the receiver as well."[80] Grace, by contrast, "essentially signifies a gratuitous service, freed from contractual obligations of counterservice and command."[81] In other words, grace signifies the giving of something without condition or without the expectation of anything in return. As such, "grace" differs from Marcel Mauss's "gift" because there's no expectation of reciprocity and exchange.[82] In this way there is something more vulnerable and dangerous about a relationship established on grace instead of faith or reciprocity. Extending grace to another makes one vulnerable because the other person is under no obligation to return the kindness or favor. At the same time, grace is potentially disarming for the receiver in that it's unmerited. Both elements comprise the political rationale of how grace-filled conversations were put to work during my fieldwork.

Grace-filled conversations most often reflected something like one's being civil and hospitable during difficult conversations and relationships, similar to what Vines describes. Empathy and mutual understanding also often accompanied descriptions of grace. In his autobiography, for example, Justin Lee describes grace as "letting the Holy Spirit work through us to show people understanding and love instead of judgment."[83] Elsewhere in the book, Lee describes grace-filled conversations like this: "At the very least, Christians ought to be listening to their gay friends, seeking to understand them, to know their joys and their struggles."[84] At times during my fieldwork "grace" was invoked in advance to push through difficult conversations, to make oneself vulnerable, or to open political space to make concerns public, especially when participants were negotiating uncharted terrain or potential imbalances in power and privilege. For instance, a facilitator prefaced his remarks at a workshop on racial justice at TRP's Atlanta regional training conference in June 2015 by saying, "I'm white and will probably say something wrong today, but I ask that you give grace."[85]

It also became clear, however, that "grace," while potentially establishing a basis for mutual understanding and engagement in civil exchanges among people with different views and experiences, can also function to limit critique. One example of this came during an exchange on microaggressions at the previously mentioned workshop on racial justice. Lucine, a Latina woman who was one of the workshop's facilitators, used her own experience of microaggressions to illustrate the concept. She told a story about being out to lunch with a friend at a Mexican restaurant. The friend told Lucine that she was going to rely on Lucine for help in navigating the menu because, as Lucine said with some humor, "I'm Latina and therefore should have some special knowledge of the language or food or culture." Lucine told us this was an example of a microaggression or "a moment of sometimes unacknowledged racism," despite her friend's not realizing it at the time or intending any harm.

After Lucine finished her story, a middle-aged white man who was participating in the workshop raised his hand and asked, "Since these episodes are often unintentional, should the proper response be to handle the situation with grace?" Rather than chastising the person for ignorance, he suggested, if a person is acting according to grace, perhaps the offended individual should let the slight go. Lucine responded by saying that some issues require a person to be more direct. "People should stop assuming intent is the same as impact," she added. Grace, Lucine explained, shouldn't be used to explain away or excuse bad behavior. Another participant jumped in to say, "I agree. Impact isn't talked about enough. I want to talk to you in grace as an individual, but what people don't understand is that the other five times this same thing has happened to me today makes that very difficult."

A similar exchange occurred during another racial justice workshop at the Kansas City regional training conference in November 2015. The exchange took place during a small group activity called "Family Time," where the workshop participants were split into "affiliation groups"—in this case participants who are LGBTQ and those who are allies—for focused conversation led by the workshop's facilitators. In my affiliation group, the allies, the facilitator began by asking us to provide an example of a time we acted as allies. The discussion quickly turned to grace-filled conversations, which at first were conceptualized as a way wherein people could disagree and offer meaningful dissent without causing division or alienating others. One of the participants, a middle-aged woman and pastor of a Kansas City–area church, began by saying, "In our church, we need to find a way to have a civil discourse about these issues, much like what TRP is attempting to do. How can we have these conversations and be disruptive without alienating people?" Another participant agreed, proposing, "Could we call these conversations 'grace-filled'?"

At the same time, the conversation turned again to the limits of grace-filled conversations. Another of the participants, who was there with her husband, talked about their experience in a small group for parents that was reconciling in a Methodist church that was not: "People in my group are tired of playing nice after forty years of trying to remove hurtful language at General Conference. We as a group struggle and have angst over what the best way is to go about this." Another woman, also a pastor of a local congregation, shared similar frustrations: "I think when it comes to whether to use civil or uncivil discourse, I would say you need both. As a woman who is also clergy, I'm getting more and more pissed that people don't get it." To illustrate, she related a story about going to buy shoes for a funeral and realizing that the clerk helping her could not accept the idea that she was officiating the service; the clerk assumed she could not be a pastor because she was a woman. "The ordination of women has been around for fifty years," she added exasperatedly, "and still there are places and people that won't recognize it. There's a time and place for anger. Sometimes you have to get pissed!"

In some ways the type of grace-filled conversations imagined by those with whom I spoke reflects the "virtue of civility," which American religious history scholar James Calvin Davis argues is a strength of many religious communities. This virtue, Davis explains, is a commitment to "the exercise of patience, integrity, humility, and mutual respect in civil conversation, even (or especially) with those with whom we disagree."[86] However, what often undermines a commitment to civility is that it requires commitment from both sides, and relations of power and privilege can be reproduced even through the transformative process of open dialogue.[87] This is why some of the participants in the Family Time exercise suggested something like what Susan Herbst calls the "*strategic uses* of civility and incivility," and they had the conviction that sometimes "even some incivility can move a policy debate along."[88]

Just like many other activists invested in creating change in their own communities, TRP activists and conference participants often wrestled with the challenges of being seen as either too radical or too conservative in the pursuit of social change. While a commitment to fellowship or reconciliation served as a rationale to stick with relationships through opposition and challenging situations, some of the individuals I encountered understood that playing nice all the time was not going to get the job done. At times people had to be made to feel uncomfortable. Sometimes one must interrupt and be disruptive and step on some toes. There's a time and place for righteous indignation.

What many of those engaged in these conversations might also say is that just because a conversation is contentious, it doesn't mean that it's a failure. Instead the tension itself is productive, or as some of my interlocutors might say, it's a sign of a "holy conversation." In this way fellowship and disruption or civility and incivility are not mutually exclusive. But for disruption to work, the relationship must come first, advocating for change at a deeply intimate level rooted in cultivated relationships.

2   The Problem of Scripture

On July 1, 2015, just days after the U.S. Supreme Court's decision in *Obergefell v. Hodges*, which legalized same-sex marriage, evangelical theologian and pastor Kevin DeYoung published on the Gospel Coalition's website a blog post titled "40 Questions for Christians Now Waving Rainbow Flags."[1] In addition to taking the opportunity to promote his new book on what the Bible teaches about homosexuality, DeYoung's post contains a list of forty questions for Christians who support and celebrate the *Obergefell* decision. The post was shared widely on social media and conservative Christian websites.[2] The underlying assumption of DeYoung's questions is that a rational response would lead any right-thinking and genuinely Bible-believing Christian to the conclusion that proper Christian morality demands opposition to marriage equality. DeYoung writes: "If you consider yourself a Bible-believing Christian, a follower of Jesus whose chief aim is to glorify God and enjoy him forever, there are important questions I hope you will consider before picking up your flag and cheering on the sexual revolution. These questions aren't meant to be snarky or merely rhetorical. They are sincere, if pointed, questions that I hope will cause my brothers and sisters with the new rainbow themed avatars to slow down and think about the flag you're flying."

DeYoung's forty questions tread a familiar path of anxieties, misinformation, homophobia, bad science, and bad theology that has characterized much of the Christian Right's antigay rhetoric over the last several decades. To summarize a few: marriage equality is a slippery slope threatening the moral foundations of American society; Christian influence in the public sphere is in retreat, and the persecution of faithful Christians is on the rise; the LGBTQ community suffers from rampant sexual promiscuity and depravity; children experience social and psychological consequences when raised in same-sex households; America's moral influence on the world stage is in decline.

DeYoung's questions also reenact and reify a relatively recent historical construct: the obviousness and naturalness of heteronormativity in Christian Scripture and tradition. If one recently came to support marriage equality, DeYoung's question two asks, "What Bible verses led you to change your mind?" Question eleven asks: "As you think about the long history of the church and the near universal disapproval of same-sex sexual activity, what do you think you understand about the Bible that Augustine, Aquinas, Calvin, and Luther failed to grasp?" In short, DeYoung protests, one's rainbow-colored social media avatar is at odds with one's claim of also being a Bible-believing Christian.

This chapter is about the role of Scripture in conservative LGBTQ Christian activism. To be clear, this chapter is not about what the Bible does or does not say about non-normative sexual or gender identities or the morality of same-sex sex.[3] Rather it is about what the cultural anthropologist James Bielo calls the "social life of scriptures" or "how Christians conceptualize their scriptures, and what they do with them through various forms of individual and corporate practice."[4] In particular the chapter is about how people live with and put Scripture to work as a mode of counter-conduct in this particular community. As Foucault reminds us, Scripture lends itself to counter-conduct: "In the movements of counter-conduct that develop throughout the Middle Ages, it is precisely the return to the texts, to Scripture, that is used against and to short-circuit, as it were, the pastorate. Because the Scripture is a text that speaks for itself and has no need of the pastoral relay. . . . Reading is a spiritual act that puts the faithful in the presence of God's word and which consequently finds its law and guarantee in this inner illumination."[5] More broadly this chapter is also about Scripture as a contested object of concern in evangelicalism, as well as the central relationship between the self and the sacred text.

The commitment to and belief in the formative nature of the Bible is perhaps one of the most enduring characterizations that people have when they think of evangelicals and evangelicalism.[6] In fact, most definitions of evangelicalism, including the widely used Bebbington quadrilateral, include some element of biblicism.[7] Biblicism, as it's most widely understood, usually implies a belief in the authority of the text over one's private and public life, often including a commitment to a literal interpretation of the "plain sense" of the text, something akin to the bumper-sticker-ready proverb "The Bible said it, I believe it, that settles it."

However, even for Christians who embrace the terms, biblicism and biblical literalism do not adequately capture the complicated and messy reality that is the relationship among the individual, the community, and the text.[8] It's not that biblical literalism necessitates a particular worldview but rather that the maintenance of particular social, political, and material conditions requires something we have come to call biblical literalism. After all, conservative Christians have long had potent techniques for deflecting and reconciling the troubling passages or internal contradictions of Scripture. The familiar claim of "taking the Bible seriously but not literally" is one such technique.

As ethnographers of Bible-reading practices have documented, a subtle interplay of interpreting Scripture through one's experience and experience through Scripture better describes how many evangelicals approach the sacred text.[9] Susan Harding describes this relationship as a "generative" process. Even for those who maintain biblical inerrancy, the practice of reading is wildly creative as readers return to the same passages time and again and discover new meanings. They read the Bible "not as already true, but as always coming true."[10] Scripture is also sometimes experienced, to borrow language from Robert Orsi, as a presence.[11] In other words, many evangelicals do not experience Scripture as a passive text but an encounter with something agentive: the text has the ability to act upon and form an individual. Finally, the text's very sacredness, too, is a collaborative project.[12]

So-called traditional readings of Scripture have offered gay Christians a limited range of options: attempt reparative therapy, submit to lifelong celibacy, or leave the community.[13] As such, gay Christians, especially those raised in conservative Christian families and church communities, often have a conflicted relationship with Scripture. After all, the text at the center of their Christian identity is the same that for decades has been used to justify discrimination and violence, to shame or harass them, or to deny their very existence. Ethnographic studies of the role of Scripture in the lives of gay Christians who have come to accept their sexuality have shown how individuals often must modify their relationship to the Bible to reconcile cognitive dissonance. In some cases this might mean abandoning the belief in the inerrancy of Scripture; in others it might mean emphasizing the Bible's inclusive ethos or message of social justice.[14]

At the heart of the counter-conduct that I studied was an attempt to reclaim Scripture from the abuses of conservative evangelicalism and to assert the right to identify as both a Bible-believing Christian and LGBTQ or LGBTQ-supportive. It's an effort to challenge mainstream evangelicalism's assumption and insistence that gender complementarity and heterosexuality are scriptural commandments. During my fieldwork I observed that people responded in a visceral way to the trauma of traditional evangelical readings of Scripture on LGBTQ matters and the attempt to redirect this viscerality to readings of Scripture that help define what LGBTQ Christian identity might look like in its wake. For some, when they learned for the first time that a biblical case could be made in support of LGBTQ people, it was a revelation. In this chapter I show how TRP activists attempt to share this good news through grassroots organizing and public education, using techniques that scholars of social movements have referred to as social movement schools.

In focusing on the role of Scripture in conservative LGBTQ Christian activism, I also tell a larger story about the role of Scripture in fashioning the self, policing community boundaries, justifying rules of inclusion and exclusion, and doing the messy political work of determining who and what is a Christian. I make two main arguments. First, I show how the authority and sacredness of Scripture are actively maintained through conflict—what might be understood as a tension between delegitimizing and *re*legitimizing Scripture. Second, I show how some activists and participants have wrestled with the politics and consequences of trying to create space for LGBTQ people in conservative Christian spaces by reaffirming the authority of Scripture.

I begin by returning to Scripture to briefly discuss how heteronormativity began to be read into the Bible and Christian tradition over the course of the twentieth century. Next I introduce Matthew Vines's *God and the Gay Christian*, the book that shapes TRP's core message and advocacy work. I then describe TRP's Bible-training strategies, including the leadership-development training and regional training conferences, and I finish with episodes from my fieldwork to illustrate how individuals put Scripture to work as a mode of counter-conduct and negotiate identity and community through their engagement with the sacred text.

The Heterosexual Bible

The word "homosexuals" made its first appearance in an English translation of the Bible in 1946, when a committee of Bible scholars tasked with producing the Revised Standard Version (RSV) combined two obscure Greek nouns into the single word "homosexuals."[15] Over the following decades a handful of other verses took on new meanings as Bible commentaries and interpreters also began reading homosexuality into the text.[16] However, the incorporation of homosexual meanings represented less an objective update to what the original languages meant all along than one stage in a process that unfolded over the twentieth century wherein the Christian Bible began to be read through the lens of heteronormativity.[17] As Heather White argues, "Before the 1940s, the Bible's seemingly plain condemnation of homosexuality was not plain at all."[18] Instead these new meanings are representative of a general "reconfiguring [of] an earlier 'Sodom tradition' into what might be called a new 'homosexuality tradition.'"[19]

Likewise the emerging homosexuality tradition doesn't reflect a universal condemnation of same-sex desire and acts in Christian Scripture and tradition repackaged into new language. Even the "sodomite" in medieval theology is not the same as the modern "homosexual," and to say that individuals understood "sodomy" in the same way that contemporary people understand "homosexuality" is anachronistic.[20] As historians of sex in the ancient and medieval worlds have documented, Christian attitudes toward same-sex desire and acts have always been contested.[21] Thus it is more accurate to think of shifting Christian attitudes toward same-sex desire—as well as sexual desire and the sexual body more generally—as historically specific ways of arranging the sexes and their pleasures, to borrow language from Jonathan Ned Katz.[22]

Foucault famously suggested that "the homosexual" became "a personage, a past, a case history, and a childhood, in addition to being a type of life, a life form, and a morphology, with an indiscreet anatomy and possibly a mysterious physiology" in 1870 with the writings of the German psychiatrist Karl Friedrich Otto Westphal.[23] More recent scholarship attributes the German *Homosexualität* to a Hungarian writer by the name of Karl-Maria Kertbeny in the late 1860s.[24] This "barbarously hybrid" word, as the English physician Havelock Ellis referred to it, is a combination of the Greek prefix *homo*, or "same," and the Latin *sexualis*, meaning "relating to sex."[25] Homosexuality first entered the English language with the 1892 English translation of Richard von Krafft-Ebing's *Psychopathia Sexualis* and was later popularized in the United States with the publication of Havelock Ellis's *Sexual Inversion* in 1897.[26]

Whatever its origin myth, the category of the homosexual—which was used, roughly, to categorize individuals who were thought to have a pathological sexual sensibility—was riddled with contradictions from its beginning in this early psychiatric, psychological, and medical discourse. For example, Kertbeny, in hopes of reforming the Prussian penal code, proposed *Homosexualist* as a "more neutral" alternative to *Urning*, a term used briefly in medical discourse for a "type of individual whose experience could best be described as that of a female soul trapped in a male body."[27] Kertbeny included *Homosexualist* in a taxonomy of other sexual conditions, including monosexuality (masturbation), heterosexuality, and heterogeneity (bestiality).[28] Homosexuality was also mapped onto the term "invert" (proposed by Westphal and described by Foucault), which was used to refer to a condition of "contrary sexual feeling" characterized "less by a type of sexual relations than by a certain quality of sexual sensibility, a certain way of inverting the masculine and feminine in oneself."[29]

Like homosexuality, the term "heterosexuality" also first originated in this medical and therapeutic discourse, not to describe normal sexuality but to describe a sexual pathology that was thought to be a mental condition known as "physical hermaphroditism." According to Katz, "This syndrome assumed that feelings had a biological sex. Heterosexuals experienced so-called male erotic attraction to females *and* so-called female erotic attraction to males. That is, these heterosexuals periodically felt 'inclinations to both sexes.' The hetero in these heterosexuals referred *not* to their interest in *a different sex*, but to their desire for *two different sexes*."[30] Finally, it's also important to understand, as Julian Carter and others have argued, that these emerging typologies of "normal" and "pathological" sexuality shaped and were shaped by discourses of whiteness and masculinity over the course of the twentieth century.[31]

The emerging homosexuality tradition in Christian discourse incorporated these clinical and therapeutic definitions of homosexuality as a pathological condition, "[knitting] together disease theories and religious teaching into an emergent therapeutic orthodoxy."[32] Ironically, rather than fundamentalist or conservative preachers initiating this new orthodoxy, it was liberal Protestant theologians and pastors who "studiously un-muddled the confused category of 'sodomitical sin' and assigned to it a singular same-sex meaning."[33] They did so with the aim of developing pastoral counseling for individuals they saw as having an affliction that required not condemnation but therapeutic support and moral reform. Even though this mid-twentieth-century liberal-Protestant pastoral counseling literature understood homosexuality as a disease that was an obstacle to healthy sexuality and self-actualization, it nevertheless sought to take a nonjudgmental approach.

It was only during the 1950s that a "conservative" Christian teaching concerning homosexuality began to coalesce, in part as a response to the Kinsey Reports, the antihomosexual scapegoating of McCarthyism, and the growing visibility of homophile organizations. From the beginning conservative Christian discourse about homosexuality was remarkably inconsistent, an assemblage of anti-Semitic, nationalist, demonological, disease, therapeutic, and pseudoscientific discourses. One of the primary venues for this new talk about homosexuality was the conservative Christian magazine *Christianity Today*, founded by Billy Graham and other conservative evangelicals in 1956 as a response to the perceived liberal bias of *The Christian Century*, a mainline Protestant journal. Didi Herman points to a 1958 article in *Christianity Today* that associated homosexuality with paganism as the beginning of the Christian Right's preoccupation with homosexuality.[34] Subsequent articles in *Christianity Today* drew on other anxieties in their characterizations of homosexuality, including (among others) an emphasis on the need to protect the purity of a population from contagion, viruses, and infection; linking the "American Sex Crisis" to communism; and suggesting that homosexuality presented a danger to America's youth.

By the late 1960s writers in *Christianity Today* began responding more specifically to the emerging gay and lesbian movements. It is important that the "homosexual" in this discourse was portrayed as not only pathological and contagious but also antagonistic to Christianity. Gay men, in particular, were portrayed as a hybrid of the "Jew" and "atheist"; the discourse drew, on the one hand, on suspicion of Jewish people, who were portrayed as arrogant, pathetic, and greedy, and, on the other hand, suspicion of Communists, who were associated with atheism and anti-Americanism. By the 1970s contributors to *Christianity Today* began to worry that Christianity was under attack by "gay militants" in more publicly visible gay and lesbian organizations. In short, writers in *Christianity Today* depicted the gay movement as "'counter-evangelistic'—as an anti-Christian force, promoting a heresy increasingly sanctioned by the state in the form of decriminalization and the extension of civil rights."[35]

During this time updated versions of English-language translations of the Bible incorporated this preoccupation with homosexuality with all its confusions.[36] As mentioned previously, the first appearance of the word "homosexuals" in an English-language Bible resulted when translators combined the Greek nouns *malakos* and *arsenekoitais* in a list of banished sinners in I Corinthians 6:9–10. The committee who worked on the RSV sought to update the language and reliability of the King James Version (KJV), a widely popular seventeenth-century translation.[37] In this passage in the KJV the same two Greek nouns were rendered much more ambiguously as "effeminate" and "abusers of themselves with mankind" respectively. In the 1971 revision of the RSV the translators abandoned the word "homosexuals" and translated the two Greek nouns into the more general "sexual perverts." Still later, in the New Revised Standard Version (NRSV), a 1989 revision of the RSV, translators revived the medieval "sodomites" when translating *malakos* and *arsenekoitais*.

The English-language translation of the Bible that is perhaps most influential among evangelicals is the New International Version (NIV). Shortly after its publication in 1978 by Zondervan, a conservative evan-

gelical press, the NIV quickly outpaced the KJV and other modern translations to become the best-selling translation among evangelicals.[38] The
NIV was a response to what was perceived to be a liberal bias in other
recent translations, including the more ecumenical RSV.[39] Functioning
under the principle of *nihil obstat*, a certification that a book contains
nothing opposed to doctrinal or moral grounds upon examination, those
who worked on the translation were required to hold a "high view of
Scripture," which included a commitment to biblical inerrancy.

The 1984 NIV translated the Greek nouns in the I Corinthians passage
as "male prostitutes" and "homosexual offenders." However, translators
working on the 2011 revision of the NIV found even the "homosexual
offenders" phrase too ambiguous. Douglas Moo, the chairperson of the
committee that worked on the revision, emphasized that "offenders"
suggested that only certain same-sex sexual acts were wrong, whereas
in his view the original language makes clear that all same-sex sexual
acts are wrong.[40] Therefore, the translators chose a phrase with more
finality and combined *malakos* and *arsenekoitais* into "men who have
sex with men."[41] In a way it could be said that this phrasing reflects the
desire to undercut the strategic essentialism, on which many gay civil
rights arguments are based, by implying that homosexuality is not a
normal and natural variation in human sexuality but a choice one makes.
And even if it is conceded that homosexuality is a benign natural variation, the Bible still declares same-sex sex sinful.

A similar translational tactic has been employed in other passages
and translations as well. For example, Romans 1:26–27, a passage about
God giving his people over to excessive lust, began to be read through
the lens of heteronormativity and used to deny that homosexuality is a
natural variation in human sexuality.[42] The internet-based Conservative
Bible Project, whose objective is to "[provide] a strong framework that
enables a thought-for-thought translation without corruption by liberal
bias," translates verse 26 as: "For this reason God allowed their free will
to lead them into homosexuality: for even their women perverted natural acts into crimes against nature."[43] In the accompanying notes on
the translated passage, the editors wrote that they "emphasized that
God gave people *freedom* to choose, and they misused it to choose
wrongly."[44] That is, the editors explicitly contest homosexuality as bio-

logical, using the language of "free will" to suggest that homosexuality is a choice resulting in "crimes against nature." *The Message*, Eugene H. Peterson's translation of the Bible, calls the very humanity of gay people into question: "Worse followed. Refusing to know God, they soon didn't know how to be human either—women didn't know how to be women, men didn't know how to be men."[45]

The "homosexual issue" among twentieth-century Christian writers has therefore been contested from the beginning. If the new talk about homosexuality began with progressive Christian writers who appropriated the category to challenge the unfair treatment of gay people in light of growing evidence of inborn characteristics, conservative writers followed by portraying homosexuality as the premier sign of the moral and social decay of American society, with one's "position" on the issue increasingly becoming a litmus test for Christian authenticity. All of this talk about homosexuality resulted in the calcification of how homosexuality is still viewed by many conservative evangelicals today, as summarized by Didi Herman: "First, homosexual practice is an incontrovertible sin. Biblical inerrancy demands this conclusion; any other is not truly Christian. Second, homosexuality is a chosen behavior, and not an immutable genetic or psychological trait."[46]

A Return to Scripture

To discuss TRP's Bible-training content and strategies, one must begin with the work of gay evangelical Matthew Vines. As noted in the introduction previously, Vines came to prominence as a rising voice among gay Christians—and in evangelicalism more broadly—with a viral YouTube video of a sixty-seven-minute presentation he gave in early 2012 at College Hill United Methodist Church in Wichita, Kansas.[47] Vines's presentation was a distillation of more than two years of intensive study on homosexuality in the Bible and the Christian tradition. His arguments in the video are a little something borrowed and a little something new; in short, he argues that an earnest reading of Scripture—one that considers its moral trajectory, cultural context, and authorial intent—would lead one to the conclusion that "being gay is not a sin." In less than a year the video had been viewed more than half a million times and translated into over a dozen languages, and by late 2017 it had surpassed a million views.

Early on Vines's presentation garnered the attention of the mainstream media from across the political and social spectrum, including a feature in the *New York Times*, an article in the *Huffington Post*, and an endorsement from Dan Savage in a post on *Slog*, a blog hosted on the website of the Seattle-based alt-weekly *The Stranger*.[48] Many of these commentators invoked Vines and his video as yet another sign of the culture wars coming to an end and the waning influence and soured-regressive politics of conservative evangelicalism. Commentators also tended to attribute Vines's appeal in the video to his youthfulness, intellectual rigor, and emotional appeal.

The presentation emerged from Vines's own experience coming out as gay in a conservative evangelical home and church in Wichita.[49] Vines came out during the fall semester of his sophomore year in 2009 while away at college at Harvard, and while home over the Christmas break, he came out first to his mother and then his father. His father, Monte Vines, was an elder of Eastminster Presbyterian Church, the family's conservative church home in Wichita, and at the time did not accept the reality of homosexuality as an immutable trait and believed the Bible prohibited same-sex sex. Vines's father suggested that the two of them do a joint Bible study, assuming by the end that his son would realize his error and perhaps pursue reparative therapy.[50] Instead of returning to Harvard, except for another brief stint in the fall semester of 2010, Matthew Vines began an autodidactic study of the Bible, including its original languages and Greco-Roman cultural context, and early church writers on sexuality. Six months later, it was not Matthew who had changed his views on homosexuality and the Bible but his dad.

In April 2014 Vines published *God and the Gay Christian*, in which he develops his arguments from the YouTube video. According to Vines, the book is the resource he needed when he was coming out as gay in the context of his conservative evangelical faith and upbringing: "Most of the resources I found were either from a theologically progressive or mainline standpoint. . . . In some cases, the arguments are pretty similar, but [in] other cases they need to be different—and it may be a slight nuance in how you say things but the key fault line in how conservative Evangelicals understand their own theology is how they regard the authority of scripture."[51]

In other words, it had been too easy for conservative evangelicals to reject biblical scholarship supportive of gay people as too "liberal" or "progressive" and by extension non-Christian. Vines's attempt in his book, therefore, is to present a case from another self-identified evangelical Christian using the language and types of evidence that conservative Christians recognize and understand. For him this means maintaining a "high view" of Christian Scripture. Vines writes: "Like most theologically conservative Christians, I hold what is often called a 'high view' of the Bible. That means I believe all of Scripture is inspired by God and authoritative for my life. While some parts of the Bible address cultural norms that do not directly apply to modern societies, all of Scripture is 'useful for teaching, for reproof, for correction, and for training in righteousness' (2 Timothy 3:16–17, NRSV)."[52]

Vines's book, arguments, and public visibility quickly became a flashpoint in the evangelical community. What proved to be perhaps the most controversial point was that Vines claimed Scripture and evangelicalism for his own, striking at the heart of conservative evangelicalism's twentieth-century project of naturalizing heteronormativity. Matthew Vines and his book became the subject of multi-episode podcasts, YouTube videos, sermon and lecture series, lengthy blog posts, and discussions in Bible study classes.

Among those who are critical of Vines's work, the responses run the spectrum from measured and considered to dismissive and patronizing to suggestions that the book is part of a conspiracy. For example, rumors have floated around on message boards and comment sections on evangelical websites that *God and the Gay Christian* is a secret publication in a conspiracy to advance the so-called gay agenda. While the book was published by Convergent Books, a Christian imprint of Crown Publishing Group, another evangelical publisher, WaterBrook Multnomah, was forced to resign its membership in the National Religious Broadcasters simply for being associated as a sister imprint of Convergent Books.[53] Nineteen days after Vines uploaded his YouTube video, a website that bills itself as a "gay Christian watchdog site" published an image of Vines alongside John Boswell with their eyes photoshopped out. The anonymous poster associated both men with a passage in Matthew 15 where Jesus called the Pharisees "blind leaders leading the blind." The poster added, "Vines' rise to attention echoes his youthful predecessor, John Boswell, who traveled this same path only to meet with a tragic death from AIDS at 47." Implied by this association is that other gay Christians advancing a "gay theology" are similarly at risk of not only spiritual death but also premature physical death.[54]

For the most part, though, responses from the Christian Right, even when patronizing, tend not to dismiss Vines's arguments outright but rather take them seriously. On the same day that Vines's book was due to be published, for example, R. Albert Mohler Jr. published a hundred-page "rebuttal" as a free ebook on the Southern Baptist Convention's website.[55] On behalf of the largest Protestant denomination in the United States, Mohler argued that this strategic response to *God and the Gay Christian* was "absolutely necessary" because Vines's claim that homosexuality and same-sex marriage are consistent with a "high view" of Scripture is "exceedingly dangerous."[56]

God and the Gay Christian is representative of a genre, as Mark Jordan describes the category, of "historical studies into the exact contents of Christian teaching on homosexuality and their current implications" that "[return] to public attention at regular intervals."[57] Perhaps the inaugural text in this genre, published in 1955, is a book titled *Homosexuality and the Western Christian Tradition*, by an Anglican clergyman named Derrick Sherwin Bailey. The book grew out of a study of homosexuality conducted by an informal group of doctors and clergyman associated with the Church of England and a pamphlet that emerged from the study authored by Bailey in 1952 called "The Problem of Sexual Inversion." In these works Bailey advocates for the decriminalization in England of consenting homosexual acts on the grounds that homosexuality is an "unalterable condition" that "is morally neutral" and therefore should be "subject to moral judgement no less than those which may take place between man and woman."[58]

Bailey further argues that there is no Christian teaching or tradition regarding homosexuality. The passages in question are concerned with homosexual acts, and neither the biblical authors nor interpreters since understood homosexuality as "a *condition* characterized by an emotional and physico-sexual propensity towards others of the same sex." As Bailey concludes, "The Bible and Christian tradition know nothing of *homo-*

sexuality."[59] Thus Christians are morally required to advocate for decriminalization given the harm caused by fallacious readings of the Bible and Christian tradition. Even though Bailey considered homosexuality pathological and stopped short of celebrating "homosexual love," Jordan considers Bailey "in many ways the patron saint of gay-friendly church history" for his "willingness to challenge established readings of scripture, to reread authoritative theology."[60]

A more widely known and influential example of the genre is John Boswell's *Christianity, Social Tolerance, and Homosexuality*. Unlike Bailey, who wrote from the perspective of a clergyman, Boswell approached the subject as a classicist, medieval historian, and philologist, although Boswell's Catholic faith did inform his work as a scholar. Boswell was also an openly gay man. First published in 1980, *Christianity, Social Tolerance, and Homosexuality* sought to disrupt the assumption that Christians have always believed homosexuality a sin. In what has come to be colloquially referred to as the "Boswell Thesis," Boswell turns on its head the argument that two thousand years of biblical interpretation and church tradition unanimously condemn homosexuality.

Boswell's central argument is that nothing in Christianity's formative years—whether in Scripture, the writings of early Christian theologians, subsequent church tradition, or presumed ascetic reactions against a promiscuous Roman Empire—is incompatible with homosexuality per se. Attitudes regarding same-sex desire were widely contested, variously celebrated or condemned depending upon the social milieu. Instead the intolerance toward same-sex eroticism that emerged during the Middle Ages had more to do with processes of secularization and the "rise of corporate states and institutions with the power and desire to regulate increasingly personal aspects of human life."[61] Christian thinkers later selectively reread Christian Scripture, tradition, and theology to justify this antihomosexual animus. As has been widely discussed, behind Boswell's arguments is an essentialist view of homosexuality as a category of human experience that transcends history and culture, that there were in some sense "gay people" in the ancient world who were in some cases accepted and celebrated, including during Christianity's formative centuries.[62]

In addition to examining the history of Christian teaching on homosexuality, Vines's *God and the Gay Christian* is also an apology—in the sense of the Greek *apologia*—or a defense of being both Christian and gay. In this way *God and the Gay Christian* is also indebted to works like Robert Wood's *Christ and the Homosexual*. An openly gay man, Wood was ordained in the Congregationalist Christian denomination and pastored several churches in and around New York City during the early years of the homophile movements.[63] Appearing in 1960, *Christ and the Homosexual* was the first book published in the United States on the topic of homosexuality and Christianity and also has the distinction of being the first to argue that one could be Christian and openly gay. Unlike Bailey and Boswell, Wood spends little time evaluating arguments about the Bible and Christian tradition; he is more interested in carving out space in Christian community and theology for gay people and same-sex relationships. Assuming the role of a translator, educator, and pastor, Wood sought to correct reductive caricatures of the gay community by introducing his readers to the daily struggles of gay men and to develop a considered theological response. As such, Wood's book stands as an early attempt to articulate the counterargument that gay is not only good but also sacred: in that "homosexuality is the creation of God," same-sex relationships "can be truly sacramental."[64]

Vines's *God and the Gay Christian* covers much of the same ground as Boswell, Bailey, and Wood. Like Boswell and Bailey before him, Vines returns to the Bible and Christian tradition to develop a counterargument to the assumption that Christianity is incompatible with gay people and same-sex relationships. Like Wood, Vines acts as a translator and educator while also defending homosexuality as natural and same-sex relationships as blessed by God. Where Vines's book departs from these earlier works is its intended audience: conservative evangelicals. *God and the Gay Christian* is in many ways an updated and more accessible synthesis of historical-critical biblical scholarship, liberation theology, and the history of sex, but it's written for an evangelical audience.

Vines begins the book by recounting his own experience of coming out as gay in a conservative Christian home and church. The following chapters walk through the biblical arguments and passages that are typically leveraged against gay people in conservative contexts—including gender complementarity, forced celibacy, the sin of Sodom, the "abominations" of the Levitical Code, the "unnatural passions" of

Romans 1, and "those who will not inherit the Kingdom of God" in I Corinthians and I Timothy—summarizing the decades-old work of gay-affirming theologians and Bible scholars like Boswell, Dale Martin, Mark Jordan, and James V. Brownson. The final chapters advance a biblical case for same-sex marriage, offer advice on how churches can support gay Christians, and discuss how gay Christians can take steps toward advocating for change in their own contexts. Throughout the book Vines draws on influential work in LGBTQ and sexuality studies developed by scholars ranging from David Halperin, Kirk Ormand, Marilyn B. Skinner, Jeffrey S. Carnes, and Jeffrey Weeks, interweaving these works with a tradition of Reformed theologians, including John Calvin, Martin Luther, Charles Hodge, and Karl Barth. The primary antagonists throughout the book are leading contemporary thinkers on gender and sexuality in conservative evangelicalism, most notably John Piper, Timothy Keller, Stanley Grenz, Robert Gagnon, and William J. Webb.

While my goal is not to rehash the arguments with which Vines is preoccupied in *God and the Gay Christian*, it is necessary to call attention to the general argument and assumptions of the book to introduce TRP's Bible training and to provide background to specific episodes and concerns that arose during my fieldwork. Vines's primary goal is to convince his readers that they can be sincere Bible-believing Christians and still support the lives and intimate relationships of gay Christians: "My core argument in this book is not simply that some Bible passages have been misinterpreted and others have been given undue weight. My larger argument is this: *Christians who affirm the full authority of Scripture can also affirm committed, monogamous same-sex relationships.*"[65] Vines's argument is a refutation of what has become a standard belief in some corners of evangelicalism; for conservative Christians who have given up on the idea that people can alter their habitual sexual attractions through therapy, prayer, and a strong effort of the will, some will concede the possibility that a person can "be gay" but will still maintain that the Bible condemns same-sex sexual behavior. Thus one cannot be both Christian and a "practicing homosexual." To be faithfully Christian, gay people must either change or resign themselves to lifelong celibacy. Vines's responses to the typical nonaffirming arguments can be roughly summarized as follows:

Nonaffirming Christians: Both the Christian Bible and Christian tradition confirm the naturalness of heterosexuality and unnaturalness of homosexuality.

Vines: The heterosexual/homosexual binary is a modern construct.

Nonaffirming Christians: The Bible has numerous clear prohibitions against same-sex sexual acts.

Vines: The Bible's prohibitions regarding same-sex sex are either prohibitions against excessive desire or were intended to regulate normative gender roles. In such cases it's more instructive to understand why the Bible says what it says on these topics rather than what it says.

Nonaffirming Christians: Christians who experience same-sex sexual desire should seek to change or choose to be celibate.

Vines: Compulsory celibacy: "functionally, it's castration."[66]

Nonaffirming Christians: Gender complementarianism is an indisputable lesson of Scripture.

Vines: Gender complementarianism is rooted in patriarchy, and to use gender complementarianism as a rationale for opposing gay Christian identity one must also accept the patriarchal framework.

Nonaffirming Christians: The Bible's clear message on gender complementarianism is the rationale and foundation for traditional marriage.

Vines: Marriage is not about gender but about commitment and self-giving, and "two men or two women can fulfill that purpose as well as a man and a woman can."[67]

In short what Vines sets out to defend is the sacred and moral worth of same-sex couples and sex but subject to the same sexual ethics to which heterosexual couples are subject in evangelicalism. Vines pauses to acknowledge his commitment to this sexual ethic several times in the book: "At an early age, I committed myself to abstinence until marriage.

That didn't change just because I was gay. I wanted to honor my body as a temple of the Holy Spirit."[68] In this way Vines is not making a moral argument for gay people or gay couples generally but for same-sex relationships of a particular kind—namely, "committed, monogamous same-sex relationships." As Vines described his ask for the evangelical community during a Bible-training session at the Atlanta conference (and as I recorded in my fieldnotes): "TRP is asking churches to affirm same-sex sex in the context of marriage. But we recognize that lots of people don't find that compelling. Those people are welcome to disagree here, to push back on that. This is a generous space."

Vines at times constructs his arguments concerning the compatibility of gay people and committed, monogamous gay couples with the Christian Bible and tradition by exclusion. When working with passages from the Old Testament, for example, Vines often uses a framework of supersessionism. Supersessionism is a doctrine that maintains that the Judeo-Christian god established a new covenant—hence "New Testament"—with humanity through the life and death of Jesus, thereby replacing or fulfilling the Mosaic covenant.[69] Under the new covenant Christians are no longer bound by the old law revealed in what Christians refer to as the Old Testament. Vines frames his discussion of Leviticus 18:22 and 20:13, for example, by suggesting that a Christian's "freedom from the law . . . is rooted in the saving, reconciling work of Jesus Christ. The New Testament teaches that Christ *fulfilled* the law."[70]

The doctrine of supersessionism is controversial even among Christians. For example, one person whom I interviewed explained a concern with arguments that rely on supersessionism in this way: "The Hebrew Scriptures are formative for us. They are part of our story. And before we describe them as irrelevant, we need to be very careful. The other thing is that once you go down that path of saying that the Hebrew Scriptures are not relevant to what we're talking about here, you pretty quickly walk onto this thin ice of what I call supersessionism, and that is to say that Judaism itself has been replaced and is an irrelevant faith. And the history of Christianity is stained by century after century of oppression of Judaism." Some theologians and everyday Christians, therefore, reject supersessionism in favor of what is known as "dual-covenant theology." Instead of the Judeo-Christian God revoking the covenant with the Jewish people, Jesus provided Gentiles access to a supplemental covenant.

Not only does Vines construct some of his arguments through a framework of supersessionism, but he also does so through other binaries that can elide relations of power in contemporary evangelicalism: whereas the Old Testament strictures were rooted in patriarchy, Vines argues, a majority of modern Christians are more egalitarian; whereas sex in the ancient world was rooted in power, modern Christians value sex in the context of self-giving relationships.[71]

Finally, even though Vines, early in the book, suggests his argument is inclusive of "lesbian, gay, bisexual, and transgender (LGBT) people," in reality the argument is as narrow as his thesis and the title of the book suggest.[72] Vines mostly limits his arguments to gay people who are Christian, as evident in his use of the language of "gay Christian," arguing that conservative evangelicals must accept the fact that there are already gay Christians in the pews: "The question is not whether gay Christians exist. It's simply 'How will the church respond to them?'"[73] The slippage between this narrow argument and LGBT people more generally is present throughout the book. "Instead of accepting the divide between more progressive Christians who support marriage equality and conservative Christians who oppose it," Vines writes in one place, "this book envisions a future in which *all* Christians come to embrace and affirm their LGBT brothers and sisters—without undermining their commitment to the authority of the Bible."[74]

As this last quote illustrates, the other pressing preoccupation in *God and the Gay Christian* is affirming the full authority or maintaining a high view of Christian Scripture. As I will discuss, I learned that this was a way in which some LGBTQ and LGBTQ-supportive Christians renegotiate their relationship to the text while actively constructing and maintaining its authority and sacredness.

Apologia *and Making Reformers*

Vines announced the formation of TRP in a series of interviews and blog and social media posts in early 2013. He envisioned an organization that would equip "straight, gay, bisexual and transgender Christians who are committed to reform . . . with the tools and training they need to go back to their communities and make lasting changes to beliefs and interpretations that marginalize LGBT people" by putting "them through a Bible boot camp."[75] For the first few years Vines ran the small organization mostly from his parents' home in Wichita, securing private donations and grants to fund the first conferences from organizations like the Gill Foundation and the Arcus Foundation, both nonprofits that support a range of religious and secular organizations working to advance LGBTQ social justice issues. Vines, who relocated to the Kansas City area in late 2015, now runs the organization, throughout the United States and abroad, with the help of a small full-time staff of organizers and a revolving cadre of volunteers, many of whom have undergone training through TRP conferences. TRP positions itself as ecumenical and inclusive of all Christian traditions, but the primary organizing framework is to provide an education in theologically conservative, LGBTQ-affirming theology to aid already affirming Christians in their conversations and relationships with nonaffirming Christians.

Vines was very optimistic at the announcement of the nonprofit in 2013 about the potential for the organization's tactics to create change. "Careful, persistent arguments about those passages," Vines wrote at the time, "have the power to change every Christian church worldwide, no matter how conservative its theology. The mission of The Reformation Project is to train a new generation of Christians to streamline that process and accelerate the demise of homophobia in the church."[76] This commitment to and belief in objective truth and the persuasiveness of the better argument was something I encountered time and again during my fieldwork. The Bible scholar Bart Ehrman notes that this faith in objective truth among evangelical Christians is a product of their being children of the Enlightenment: "When I say that conservative evangelical Christians and fundamentalists are children of the Enlightenment, I mean that more than almost anyone else, thinkers among these groups are committed to 'objective truth.' . . . The reality is that modern Christian apologists stress the importance of objectivity and champion it more than anyone—much more than most other educated people in our world."[77] Similarly many of those I met assumed that Christians who do not support LGBTQ people merely suffer from a lack of knowledge and that through factual, rational conversations one can clear away confusion and misunderstanding and uncover the objective truth.

TRP's strategies of recruiting, training, and helping those who desire to create change in their own contexts also reflect deep commitments in evangelicalism to *apologia* and evangelism, a defense of the faith and an effort to convince interlocutors of a particular truth that requires a response. Much like the activities of the early Christian church dramatized in the New Testament book of the Acts of the Apostles, TRP is modeled on cultivating a core group of disciples who then go out into the world to spread the good news. In TRP's case the aim is to mount a defense of the inclusion and faith of LGBTQ Christians and to convert fellow Christians to LGBTQ allyship. As Jonathan Coley smartly observes, TRP's core strategy of educating and supporting a cadre of activists can be thought of as a social movement school.[78] Scholars of social movements have defined such communities as sites that are intentionally formed for the purpose of educating, mentoring, and coordinating people for social change. Social movement schools can be important sites for changing the consciousness of participants, creating and circulating new knowledge among participants and a wider audience, and fostering social models that can prefigure future social change.[79]

TRP's main methods of apologetic training include intensive leadership-development cohorts and larger three-day regional training conferences. The first leadership-development training program, a three-month "Bible boot camp" (as Vines called it) for about thirty participants, took place in Kansas City in late 2013.[80] Application to the training program included the submission of an essay, letters of recommendation, and an introductory video, and participants had to agree to TRP's statement of faith.[81] Vines told me the leadership-development program was like an online college course. He asks participants to commit to fifteen hours a week during the three-month program, reading between one thousand to fifteen hundred pages of historical and theological scholarship, written from both conservative and progressive perspectives, on gender and sexuality in the Christian tradition. During this time participants engage in weekly online discussion groups of the readings while also working on fund-raising for the culminating multiple-day, in-person conference. Participants are also coached on organizing strategies and how to be effective leaders in their own communities. More recent cohorts also included training on the intersections of racial and LGBTQ social justice in Christian communities.

For the first few leadership-development cohorts Vines used "reformers" to refer to the individuals who completed the training.[82] Reformers who stay active after the program play a significant role in TRP regional training conferences. For example, reformers often serve as facilitators for the Bible-breakout sessions, lead panels and workshops, and chair local steering committees that organize TRP's regional training conferences. The regional training conferences also serve as recruitment tools for future reformers. The leadership-development programs are advertised in conference programs, and interested attendees can attend a question and answer session on "Becoming a Reformer."

At TRP's regional training conferences one is likely to see people sporting brightly colored T-shirts with "Reformer" printed on the back. It is not as ubiquitous as other terms of identification at TRP conferences, but "reformer" nevertheless reflects part of TRP's strategy in addition to how some participants at TRP conferences come to see an aspect of their Christian identity. I spoke with people at conferences who self-identified as reformers. When I asked one individual who participated in the Washington DC leadership-development program whether he identified as an evangelical, for example, he responded after some deliberation by saying, "Maybe right now I might just say, 'I'm a reformer.'"

If the leadership-development training programs are the backbone of TRP's work, the regional training conferences constitute a more streamlined version of the leadership-development training for a bigger audience.[83] Attendance ranged from two to four hundred at the three conferences I attended. Although the regional training conferences also include worship, panel discussions, keynote presentations, and opportunities to fellowship, the centerpiece of the conferences is the instruction and coaching of a series of ten talking points to aid people in their conversations with family and friends about LGBTQ inclusion. Conference attendees receive a glossy program outlining the talking points, which are more or less a condensed version of *God and the Gay Christian* and follow a similar order, use of evidence, and argumentation. The

2. Conference attendees sing hymns and worship songs at TRP's regional training conference in Washington DC, November 2014. Photo by the author.

instruction of the talking points changed slightly over the three conferences I attended, but for the most part it followed a basic structure: Vines introduced the talking points in the main meeting space during multiple-hour morning sessions, followed by afternoon Bible-breakout sessions to rehearse the talking points in small groups. While Vines did a bulk of the instruction, he was often joined, either in person or by video, by reformers or by scholars such as James Brownson and David Gushee.

The format of the Bible instruction usually consisted of first introducing the "nonaffirming message" that individuals often encounter in such conversations, followed by a countering "affirming message" with supporting evidence and main talking points. The first talking point, to provide an example, is a response to the argument that "LGBT-affirming Christians elevate their experience over the authority of Scripture in order to support their views." The talking point, or affirming message, in response to this argument is that "Experience should show good fruit,

3. A version of the talking points on display at Kansas City PrideFest, June 5, 2015. Photo by the author.

not bad fruit." The program reads, "Jesus teaches in the Sermon on the Mount that good trees bear good fruit and bad trees bear bad fruit. He gives a simple test for discerning false prophets (or teachers) from true ones: 'By their fruits you will know them.'"[84] The argument is that one can determine whether an interpretation or teaching based on Scripture is correct by observing whether it causes harm. As David Gushee summarized it at the Atlanta conference, "Clearly, traditionalist or nonaffirming or noninclusive beliefs about same-sex relationships and transgender identity do contribute to bad fruit in LGBT people's lives" in terms of, he suggested, family rejection and an increased likelihood of attempted suicide, depression, and drug use.

While the talking points specifically address the handful of passages that some interpret as condemning same-sex sexual acts, much of the effort involves simply trying to convince others that the subject overall is worth rethinking and that one can have a change of mind without abandoning one's commitment to Scripture. To question one's interpretation of these passages, it was explained to me, is to question one's faith. That is, if a person admits they are wrong about this one issue, what else might they be wrong about? So the response often is to double-down, to draw a firmer line. Vines spoke to these concerns before beginning the Bible instruction at the Atlanta conference:

> Typically, depending on where someone is at in this conversation, you don't want to just jump in and be like, "Let's talk about Romans 1. Let's talk about," you know, "Leviticus or something." Because if they don't even believe that there are legitimate or important reasons to look at these texts more carefully, then your conversation is less likely to be productive. [But] there's no one good cookie-cutter way to approach this conversation at all; people can come at this from a hundred different backgrounds and perspectives. You'll know best based on your relationship with someone how to engage that.

It was the final afternoon of the Atlanta regional training conference. I meandered my way through the bright hallways in search of the room where my assigned Bible-breakout group was to meet. Like the day before, I learned from the tiny handwritten number scrawled on my conference name tag that I would be participating in breakout group number three that afternoon. Just before one thirty, I slipped into the room and joined the other participants quietly waiting for the session to begin. Our group had dwindled from twenty-five the day before to twelve. As it tends to go with conferences, enthusiasm had seemed to wane a little after a few long days.

On my way to the room, I walked through the hotel's coffee and pastry shop where conference attendees often gathered during breaks. Several small groups huddled around low coffee tables, and I recognized a group of four or five young women as fellow conference attendees. As I passed by, one of the women detached herself from the group and joined me on my way to the breakout session. "They coming?" I asked. From the bit of conversation I overheard, it seemed like the group was debating whether to attend their Bible breakout. "I hope so," she responded. "It's too important to skip."

Practicing Scripture

Following the morning sessions of Bible training, TRP conference attendees were organized into smaller groups—five and ten groups, depending on the conference—to meet in separate rooms to put the talking points to work. The Bible-breakout sessions were designed to provide an opportunity to practice and discuss the content presented during the morning sessions. Here is how Devin, a thirty-something participant in TRP's 2015 leadership-development program in Washington DC, introduced the purpose of the Bible breakouts while facilitating a Friday afternoon session at the Atlanta conference:

> The goal for today is to help you to be equipped, to know what you're saying, to help you practice having conversations for full inclusion—all of us—in the Kingdom of God. It's not every day that you have the opportunity to practice having theological debates, so try to take advantage of this opportunity. In my experience, probably 25 percent or so of people you won't be able to engage in this conversation. But the other 75 percent, you can. These are people who have an exploratory heart.
>
> I want you to think of this room as a safe space to practice having these conversations. It's okay to mess up. I expect you to get it wrong and to stutter. But just because it's safe doesn't mean it's comfortable. After all, Christianity doesn't mean "safety." Jesus's suffering makes this clear.

The format of the Bible breakouts varied from conference to conference and room to room but generally followed a think-pair-share method. At some of the breakouts there was more of an emphasis on role playing, where we were asked to assume affirming and nonaffirming roles in our discussions. We were provided a series of discussion prompts, usually common nonaffirming claims, and were tasked with discussing possible responses in groups of four to six before sharing with the entire room.[85]

People varied widely in their beliefs about the meaning and significance of Scripture, as well as what the Bible might or might not say about LGBTQ people or queer forms of sexual desire. Even Devin, who had gone through the leadership-development training and was moderating our Bible-breakout session, was still exploring the issue. When I spoke with him later the next day, he told me he was still working out the relationship among his faith, sexuality, and the Bible. He was hesitant to describe himself as gay at the time, instead saying, "Right now, I'm about 70 percent affirming," although when I saw him again at the Kansas City conference five months later, he simply introduced himself as a "gay Christian."

I would venture to guess that most of the people I met in the Bible-breakout sessions were not well versed in the subtleties of or debates over biblical interpretive methods. For example, disputes over historical-grammatical methods versus historical-critical methods never came up in our conversations. Nevertheless, for someone who has taught historical-critical methodology and the Hebrew and Christian Scriptures to undergraduate students, I was often impressed with the participants' knowledge of the Bible and its historical context. Some were quite aware of the nuances of biblical interpretation and unafraid to acknowledge that the ancient words were deeply conditioned by their cultural milieu. What they seemed to share was a commitment to understanding this issue (whether personally or intellectually), a faith in the text as formative and meaningful for their everyday lives, and a shared experience of living in these conversations and with the sacred text.

Even though the Bible breakouts were intended to be a space to rehearse the talking points covered during the morning sessions, like practicing scales on an instrument, the conversations expanded to dwell on or attempt to resolve contradictions, to fumble in the dark, to express dissent, to share sometimes raw emotions, and to reaffirm the sacredness of the text.

An exchange at the Bible-breakout session in Atlanta illustrates some of the participants' frustrations with these types of conversations, which they implied often tended not to accomplish much. As I was told, such conversations often reflected less reasoned debate than defensiveness and entrenchment. In this exchange, Osborn, who was in his thirties, white, gay, and a certified public accountant from a nearby town in Georgia, played the role of a nonaffirming Christian in conversation with Linus, a college-aged, white, gay man who was the most reserved and timid of our group, playing the role of an affirming Christian. Linus's task was to challenge the argument that marriage in the Bible is rooted in gender complementarity or the idea that men and women are natural and complementary halves.[86] Linus tried first a strategy presented during the morning presentation of the talking points. He tried to press Osborn to define more precisely what he meant by "gender complementarianism." Osborn, following Devin's encouragement that participants use actual nonaffirming arguments they've encountered in previous conversations, responded by saying that men and women have "complementary sex organs" and that a "gay couple can't produce children."

> LINUS: What about those married couples who can't reproduce? Are they not married then? Are they no longer a man or a woman?
>
> OSBORN: Well, don't you believe in miracles? Even if a particular couple can't reproduce, at least it's still physically possible.
>
> LINUS: If it takes a miracle, couldn't you say the same thing for gay couples?
>
> OSBORN: But for men and women, even if they can't bear children, at least it's normal for most of them. You can't say the same thing about gay couples.

At this point in the conversation, Linus became flustered and didn't know how to continue. Shane, another participant in our small group, jumped in to encourage him: "Keep going! Challenge this guy!"

> LINUS: Okay, so it's one thing to say that miracles *might* happen, but it's another thing to recognize that they don't *seem* to happen. Can you give me an example of a miracle?
>
> OSBORN: It was possible for Sarah. Don't you think God can do miracles today?
>
> LINUS: It depends on your understanding of miracles and if they still happen today. There's a debate about this; maybe miracles don't happen anymore. If you believe so strongly in miracles, do you also believe it's possible for God to change a gay person's sexuality?
>
> OSBORN: Yes.

LINUS: That doesn't seem to be the case.

OSBORN: Well, maybe they should keep praying until the miracle happens.

LINUS: [turning to the rest of our small group in frustration] I don't know how to respond to that.

It was common for participants to voice their frustrations with the hurtful and damaging things they heard while having these conversations in their everyday lives. Later in the same session, for example, another participant protested, "I often hear people say that Paul was talking about AIDS in Romans 1." At a Bible-breakout session at the Kansas City conference, someone else said, "I've had people tell me that my being gay is the result of the Fall and that any suffering I experience from having to wrestle with my same-sex attractions is insignificant, that suffering is part of my life as a Christian. How do you even begin to respond to this?"

While Bible-breakout participants often relied on information presented during the morning Bible-training sessions, it was also common for people to try different tactics in their responses to the prompts. After a role-playing exercise on affirming and nonaffirming responses to Romans 1 stalled during the Bible breakout in Atlanta, our group turned to a general discussion of the passage. Shane, a white gay man in his fifties who was the most animated of our group, seemed troubled that our conversation had stalled and tried another approach by discussing his understanding of this passage. "Look at what it actually says," Shane said, reading the verses from his iPhone: "'For this reason God gave them up to degrading passions. Their women exchanged natural intercourse for unnatural, and in the same way also the men, giving up natural intercourse with women, were consumed with passion for one another. Men committed shameless acts with men and received in their own persons the due penalty for their error. And since they did not see fit to acknowledge God, God gave them up to a debased mind and to things that should not be done. They were filled with every kind of wickedness.'"[87] Shane paused and looked at us. "I don't see myself here," he said. "I'm not an idol worshiper; I'm a Christian. These things don't describe me and my experience. I don't feel shame. I'm not wicked. It is not *natural* for me to be attracted to women."

Through my participation in the Bible-breakout sessions I was constantly reminded of the weight and stakes of these conversations. An exchange I had with Penny during and after a Bible-breakout session at the Kansas City conference is but one example. Penny was a white woman in her midforties working as a high school music teacher in New York City, although she had grown up in what she characterized as a *"very conservative"* Christian home in Kansas. Before coming to the conference, Penny had not been to church for quite some time. She had only recently come out, telling our group, "I didn't come out until later in life because I considered myself a born-again Christian and didn't think being gay was okay. I still struggle with it." Another of her concerns was her conservative father and stepmother. Both, as Penny described them, were elderly and very opposed to her sexuality. In fact, her father had a brother who is gay, and the family no longer speaks to him. She was worried the same thing was happening to her.

After the session ended, I asked Penny what brought her to the conference. I wanted to know whether she had come to learn new ways to communicate with her parents or whether it was a desire to reconcile her own sexuality with her faith. "It's a little bit of both," she said. She went on to say how she was struggling with whether to keep trying to talk to her parents. Penny became emotional as she continued, but she also seemed to take comfort in our conversation. "My father might be a bit more open about it, but my stepmother is simple and doesn't have much of an education. She instigates most of the problems and rejects my sexuality without much thought." All the while, Penny told me, "I still struggle with my sexuality, with wondering if it's okay."

Another common theme of the breakouts was that participants would use the opportunity to talk about the nature of Scripture and to reaffirm its sacredness. For example, one participant at the Kansas City conference, a straight white woman in her late twenties, made the point, "For me, it's important to read Scripture through Jesus." She clarified: "Even in places where Scripture is challenging—where things like rape or slavery go unchallenged—it's important to place the character and meaning of Jesus's life, death, and resurrection above—I mean, he provides the necessary context for—those passages."

This concern over the authority of Scripture came up again later during the same Bible-breakout session. Our group was given three questions to discuss under the broad area of "tradition": (1) How did ancient societies view same-sex behavior? (2) Were the biblical authors ignorant or wrong? (3) Why weren't equal-status relationships accepted? Emmy, a tattooed pastor in her late twenties or early thirties who is white, straight, and recently divorced, took the first turn:

> As for the second question, I would challenge the language of "ignorant or wrong." To me that's far too simple. It's not that the biblical authors were ignorant or wrong; they were just trying to do their best with the knowledge they had at the time. Like Jesus never intended the church to be a patriarchy. He wanted to move the church forward toward greater equality. Look at Paul in First Corinthians. When we read his statements about women through our modern values, they seem backward and unfair. But Paul's comments about women at the time were actually quite progressive. I think they were just doing the best they could at the time.

Carmine, a middle-aged, white, transgender woman, followed up by saying, "For me the Bible is a living document. You can read a passage a hundred times before it makes sense. When I don't understand a passage, I just stick with it and trust that God will help me understand it."

The Bible-breakout sessions often concluded with a few minutes of group reactions and prayer. Participants described the experience as "overwhelming," "informative," "fun," and "awkward." Many of the takeaways reflected less on content than on engagement strategies. "One of the people in our group always began statements with, 'I hear and understand what you're saying,'" a participant said. "We thought this calm perspective and empathetic approach was very disarming and effective." Someone else agreed: "It often seems important just to remind the other person that we both agree the Bible is important." Another person raised the necessity of tailoring one's approach to the individual conversation: "How the conversation goes depends on the person. If it's an intellectual person, you might approach it that way; if it's a scriptural person, perhaps another." "It's okay to stumble," another person said. "It's okay to mispronounce the Hebrew." Another participant added, "Sometimes it's important to just ask questions."

Devin brought the session to a close by reminding us that this process was a journey and offered to pray over us to move us forward. He bowed his head and prayed, "May the Spirit come and speak on your behalf in these difficult conversations."

Negotiating Scripture

Beyond the Bible-breakout sessions I also encountered conversations elsewhere at TRP conferences wherein individuals were engaged in an ongoing negotiation of the authority and sacredness of the Bible. An exchange between Matthew Vines and Shae Washington, a reformer from TRP's Washington DC leadership-development training program in 2015, illustrates this preoccupation; it also illustrates the tension inherent in being compelled to use Scripture to justify or explain one's experience and even one's very existence.

The exchange took place during a Friday morning Bible-training session at the Kansas City conference, during which Vines was introducing the first talking point, a response to those who accuse LGBTQ Christians of elevating their experience above Scripture. Washington introduced herself to the audience as a queer Black woman who had grown up in a conservative evangelical church in the Washington DC area. Coming out as queer in her childhood church home, Washington told the audience, "hasn't been an easy road." Nevertheless, she and her partner still attend the church, trying to create change from within. Washington described the role of Scripture during her process of coming out as follows:

> [After coming out] I felt this profound peace. At the time, I didn't yet have the biblical knowledge, but I just knew. I told my friends that God gave me peace and told me to come out of the closet. Some of them told me to show them where it says it's okay to be gay in the Bible. I was devastated. I wanted them to take me seriously, but they didn't.
>
> I had the same issue with my family. I still didn't have a firm biblical case, only my experience. I headed home for Easter, scared, not wanting it to be 'the Easter that Shae came out.' My family was actu-

ally very receptive. My brother asked me what this meant for my relationship with God. I just told him I had peace with it, and that God was affirming me.

Vines then asked Washington how she now responds to people when they accuse her of elevating her experience above Scripture. "Most non-affirming Christians," Washington joked, "when they find out I'm gay, give a little nod and smile while slowly backing away." She continued: "For people who know me, they have grown on this issue based on seeing me live my life and hearing me talk about God. It's important to talk about my experience. My church has been on a journey on this issue. There are yearly discussions on the topic of homosexuality, for example. One time, I was at this executive meeting, and I thought I failed because I wasn't able to present the biblical case. But later I found out that it was actually my story that did the most work. They needed to see the live flesh-and-blood person."

Vines followed up by making a similar point. In his response he also sought to delegitimize readings of Scripture that lead to abuse and to instead construct the text as inherently just:

> I also didn't have a strong grasp of the biblical case when I was coming out, but I felt at the time that I didn't *need* to fully understand the biblical case in order to be passionate and fully affirming. It's much like how I don't fully understand the passages about slavery. This is a complex, ancient document. Even if I don't know how to make a biblical case against slavery given the plain meaning of the texts, I still have *faith* that you can. I have no doubts whatsoever that I can say that slavery is immoral and wrong, even if the Bible seems to approve of it.
>
> So when someone asks me about what Paul says about being gay, my response is that I don't need to know the Greek to be passionate and vocal about this issue. I don't need to know every Greek term. It's a faith issue. I want to encourage people not to be afraid to speak up, even if they don't have a firm grasp of the biblical case. It's not that you don't believe in the Bible; it's because you have faith in the Bible and its message of freedom.

Vines returned to this point often during Bible-training sessions, encouraging participants to ask not *what* the Bible says but *why* it says it. I learned that this was but one strategy of reproducing Scripture as an authoritative text, above and beyond individual passages that might lend themselves to problematic interpretations. A concluding statement from Washington was even more direct: "The issue is that people are dying. This is completely anti-Jesus to me."

Vines similarly attempts in *God and the Gay Christian* to reclaim Scripture for gay Christian identity and certain same-sex relationships while at the same time trying to avoid undermining the legitimacy of Scripture. Behind his argument is the assumption that the Bible is a just and inclusive text. For example, during a discussion of the Levitical prohibitions against same-sex sexual acts, which he points out have less to do with prohibiting homosexuality than policing normative gender roles that are rooted in patriarchy, Vines pauses to clarify: "But far from being a reason to view Scripture as outdated or sexist, the Bible itself is what points us toward a path where patriarchy is no more."[88] Elsewhere in the book, in light of the omnipresence and apparent approval in the Bible of slavery and patriarchy, Vines argues that "both hierarchies will fade away in Christ, and Jesus calls us to make that a reality now. Scripture lays the groundwork for a redemptive reordering of gender relations in God's kingdom."[89]

Vines developed this latter idea about the "redemptive" nature of the text in greater detail at all three of the conferences I attended. One of the ways in which he made this case was by repurposing a concept popularized by the conservative evangelical theologian William J. Webb called the "redemptive-movement hermeneutic."[90] A "hermeneutic" is an interpretive framework applied to Scripture, especially pertaining to questions of how to apply Scripture to contemporary issues, not dissimilar from the way legal scholars debate the merits of textualism, constructionism, or originalism when it comes to interpreting the U.S. Constitution. Throughout my fieldwork I heard people use the word "hermeneutic" colloquially to refer to the process of reconciling the Bible's internal contradictions or the dissonance between their lived experience and authoritative interpretations of the text. A hermeneutic in this discourse, therefore, can be thought of as a technique or practice through which individuals constitute the self in relationship to the text and other people.[91]

Webb introduces and describes the redemptive-movement hermeneutic in *Slaves, Women and Homosexuals*. Webb summarizes the interpretive dilemma as follows: "Our mandate is to figure out which statements from the Bible in their 'on the page' wording you and I should continue to follow in our contemporary setting. In order to do this we must determine whether we should apply a particular biblical statement in the exact form articulated on the page or whether we should apply only some expression of its underlying principle(s)."[92] Webb outlines several criteria for the redemptive-movement hermeneutic as a response to this predicament, but the "redemptive movement" and "multilevel ethic" criteria are most relevant to my discussion. To suss out how one should apply passages in Scripture to contemporary ethical and political issues, one must look to the "movement" of Scripture in relation to its surrounding cultural context or within the text itself.

For Webb this test enables the reader to distinguish between moral preoccupations that are particular to the cultural context of Scripture versus morals that transcend culture and history—that is, to use his terminology, to distinguish between "cultural values" and "Kingdom values."[93] Slavery, women, and "homosexuals" are his case studies. Regarding slavery, Webb argues that while slavery in the ancient world was ubiquitous, including among the ancient Hebrews, the movement of Scripture is away from the widespread "abuses" of slavery in the Greco-Roman world toward "better conditions and fewer abuses" in Scripture and Hebrew culture.[94] Similarly regarding women, Webb argues there is a movement within Scripture from the Old Testament to the New Testament toward greater equality. Webb argues that whereas the movement of Scripture both within the text and in relation to the surrounding culture tends toward better treatment of slaves and women, concerning "homosexuals," it is more restrictive. Thus "The comparative outcome is this: *the homosexual texts are in a different category than the women and slavery texts*. The former are almost entirely transcultural in nature, while the latter are heavily bound by culture."[95]

It is telling that Webb, at the end of his book, turns to internecine feuds in contemporary conservative evangelicalism, largely in response to evangelical feminists, over gender roles. In particular Webb expands on an influential edited volume called *Recovering Biblical Manhood and Womanhood: A Response to Evangelical Feminism*.[96] The various contributors argue that essential (biological, psychological, spiritual) differences exist between men and women that make patriarchy natural. Webb presents the issue as a rift between those who interpret gender roles through the lens of "ultra-soft patriarchy" and those who do so through the lens of "complementary egalitarianism." The former maintain that women—by nature and confirmed in Scripture—are naturally subject to men's authority; the latter maintain that men and women are by nature equal but play different yet complementary roles in marital relationships and public life. Webb suggests "the 'complementary egalitarianism' position proposed in [his] book is very close to the position of 'ultra-soft patriarchy with a redemptive-movement hermeneutic.'"[97] Webb's conclusions regarding "homosexuals," therefore, function to support what seem to be his more pressing aim: to claim a position of gender egalitarianism while at the same time relegitimizing—and blunting the edges of—patriarchy.

Even though Vines rejects Webb's conclusions on homosexuality, he repurposes the redemptive-movement hermeneutic to argue that within Scripture is a moral trajectory toward greater inclusivity of women and people with non-normative sexual or gender identities. At the Atlanta regional training conference, for example, Vines used the redemptive-movement framework to circumvent issues of patriarchy, misogyny, and slavery in the text. This issue came up during a Bible-training session while he was introducing the seventh talking point, which addresses the same Levitical prohibitions mentioned previously. As part of his response to the passage, Vines emphasizes that the prohibitions are rooted in misogyny: they are prohibitions against a man's asserting misplaced dominance over another man or a woman's assuming a position of dominance over another woman, a relationship of dominance-submission reserved for the male-female relationship. As such, the prohibitions have little or nothing to do with modern understandings of sexual orientation or same-sex sexual desire.

Again Vines paused to respond to imaginary interlocutors who might accuse him, and others who make similar arguments, of rejecting the authority of Scripture by suggesting the biblical authors were operating with misogynistic assumptions. Those who seek to limit critique seem to think that naming patriarchy and misogyny is a greater sin than using the text to justify contemporary inequalities. Vines's response was as follows:

> Some people will say, "Well, you're just saying the biblical authors were rankly misogynistic," and that we just need to set that aside. I think that there is a more helpful understanding of that, though . . . . It's the idea of finding the redemptive spirit in the text, the redemptive movement in the text. No, women are not treated equally in the Old Testament law—they simply are not and in some really significant ways. . . . At the same time, [there is an] egalitarian trajectory within Scripture, which does not erase some of the things we see but can offer us a lens for how we might see Scripture moving in a bigger-picture way. [Also, even though] we don't see an eradication of slavery or an eradication of the male/female hierarchy, we do see here a blueprint of the Kingdom of God. . . .
>
> If these hierarchies will ultimately be overcome and swept away in Christ, then Christians not only have license but are exhorted to be living into the fullness of that. That is a biblical basis for abolitionism. It's not a basis solely in exegesis of the text. There is no compelling biblical argument against slavery that's grounded solely in exegesis. But, fortunately, biblical interpretation has never been solely about exegesis to begin with. If you also bring in this question of hermeneutics and of redemptive movement, then you have a legitimate biblical argument against slavery.

Like Emmy and Carmine at the Bible-breakout sessions described previously, Vines reaffirmed the authority of Scripture by constructing the text as having an overall message of justice, freedom, and inclusivity. It reminded me of New Testament scholar Dale Martin's argument: "Any interpretation of Scripture that hurts people, oppresses people, or destroys people cannot be the right interpretation, no matter how traditional, historical, or exegetically respectable."[98] During my fieldwork I came to understand this as a way to undermine the use of Scripture as a justification for oppression and exclusion while at the same time reaffirming the sacredness of the text. It also positions the divergent, unbalanced experience of violence as a normative framework for interpreting Scripture and Christian conduct, a topic to which I return in the remaining chapters.

Paul Creekmore expressed similar concerns about the tension between his embodied experience and the sacred text when we met for an interview in the early spring of 2015 in Kansas City. (As noted in the introduction, Paul was one of TRP's original reformers who later chaired the steering committee for the Kansas City regional training conference.) Paul had just come from work and, as usual, was neatly dressed in a dark-colored, fitted polo shirt and slacks. As Paul had told me on a previous occasion, he works during the day as an electrical engineer to pay the bills and spends his evenings doing the "real work" of being a reformer. I'll tell more of Paul's story in the next chapter, but for now I would like to focus on how Paul's description of how he came to reconcile his sexuality with his faith illustrates a delicate interplay between the experience of the body and Scripture.

The Bible has played a significant role in Paul's story but especially one night when he frantically searched for answers for what to do about his emerging same-sex desires, which seemed to contradict everything he had been taught about human nature and the Bible. Paul told me that he had lived most of his early life in "a really stunning state of denial" when it came to his sexuality. It was only during his first years of college that he "started to recognize, started to wonder if [he] might be this thing that people called 'gay.'" Paul attended a few different churches—a nondenominational church, an Evangelical Free church, and an American Baptist church—during his childhood in Wichita, Kansas, and at one point his father even served as a part-time pastor at one of the churches. Growing up in a conservative Christian home and church, Paul admitted he knew almost nothing about, or at least had a very biased view against, what it meant to be gay:

> Part of what tripped me up was that it was impossible for me to be gay because I was a Christian, and I would never do that because it was a choice. And I obviously wasn't going to make that choice to be like that. So there was this great impossibility in my mind that I had

to get over, and I suppose [chuckling] it was really my involvement in theater in high school and college that exposed me to other gay people that probably helped me realize—slowly, *very* slowly—that I was wrong about that conception. I suppose it got to the point where I couldn't deny it any more, and that I really did have these attractions whether I wanted them or not.

Once Paul admitted to himself that he might be gay, his first instinct was to resign himself to a life of celibacy: "So as someone brought up in the Christian faith and with a . . . generally traditional, conservative sexual ethic, my very first reaction was, 'Okay, I am this way, but I can't act on it. I cannot be sexually active. If I'm a gay man, that means I have to be celibate.'"

Paul lived this way for the next several years until he turned to the internet in the early days of online dating websites in hopes of finding other people like himself. It's important to note here that during our conversation Paul was aware of how his words could be used against him. One of the more common tactics among conservative evangelicals who attempt to police the boundaries of evangelical gender and sexuality is to charge individuals who challenge authoritative narratives of putting their experience above Scripture or, worse, of using Scripture to justify a "gay lifestyle." Paul initially passed over a part of his story until I asked him to elaborate on what he meant when he said he took "a leap of faith" to find other gay Christians.

> JON: Sorry to interrupt you. You said it was "a leap of faith." Specifically was there anything that changed with you that went along with that?
> PAUL: If the recording could see the smile on my face.
> JON: [Laughing.]
> PAUL: Oh yes. [Hesitating.] I glossed over this on purpose because it's a whole story in and of itself. But now that you've explicitly asked, it is worth telling because there are a lot of people who have the same story. I've shared this story with too many people who say, "Wow, that's what happened to me too."
> JON: I'd love to hear it.

PAUL: This is again one of those points that more conservative Christians will jump on . . . because it is a story of personal experience. There's a number of things I could say about the legitimacy of personal experience, but . . .

It was toward the end of college, and Paul had an overwhelming sense of "absolute emptiness" and "loneliness." He longed to find someone to whom he could relate:

But I started thinking, "I need to find another gay Christian. I really need to find other people like me." And [chuckling] somehow the only avenue available to me that I stumbled across was a dating website. And I realized that you could say that you were a man looking for other men, and I noticed that some of those people had a key word in their profile that was "Christian." So this was my opening; this was my avenue into finding other people like myself. As bad of an idea as it may seem in hindsight, that was it; that was the way I could possibly find someone else who was like me.

Soon Paul met a guy on the website and found himself "suddenly very, very much infatuated":

PAUL: I came to a point where I had to say, "I really just can't do this because I believe that it's wrong." And I had to cut him off. But then I had this absolute crisis. Like, what if I just gave up the best thing in the world that was ever going to happen to me? And I was forced to, really for the very first time, actually ask myself the question, "Why do I believe this? Why do I believe that same-sex relationships are categorically sinful?" . . . So what that resulted in was probably the most genuine, honest, pleading night with God that I've ever had.
JON: What was that process like?
PAUL: It was a combination of me sort of frantically trying to suddenly research all of this online, with my Bible in my lap, reading different opinions, different articles, and an awful lot of prayer, very, very honest prayer.

And honestly, through all of it, I was begging God *not* to tell me that it would be okay to go ahead with this relationship because I knew . . . that was the scariest thing out of all of it. What if I had been wrong all this time and if I did change my mind? As far as I was concerned, the consequences in my life could be huge. I would be rejected by the church. For all I knew, I could be rejected by my family and by all of my friends. I could lose everything—absolutely everything—for all I knew.

So I wanted to save my safe place, what I thought was a safer place, of, I don't know, being more conservative I suppose, not acting as opposed to acting. That seemed like that was safer. It turns out that's not the case. But [at first] I did not find my answers in the Bible or online. I found a lot of conflicting information.

Paul never pursued a relationship with the guy he met online, in part because they lived in different states, but it was through this experience that Paul began to question his "conservative" understanding of Scripture and sexuality. Not too long after this experience, Paul discovered GCN after typing the words "gay Christian" into the search box on Google, and he finally found a community of other gay Christians. It was during this time that he started to question, not the authority of Scripture, but the injustice of its being used to justify oppression or to condemn certain people to a life of loneliness and despair:

I just came to a point where, regardless of all the biblical questions, there's no way in good conscience that I could tell somebody that the accepting and affirming of homosexual orientation was a bad thing, was in some way sinful, when every ounce of evidence I had (and as I got to know other gay Christians, this story played out over and over and over and over again, exactly the same sort of experience as I was having) [demonstrated] that life was in despair and smashed and wilted and withering up until that point that all of these [gay Christians] finally accepted their orientation and life started to flourish. I just can't look at anything and anywhere—even if it's in the Bible—

and say to someone that they're living the wrong choice. I couldn't drive someone back to that broken state that I knew so well.

So it started there, and later on . . . I finally found the Gay Christian Network. And it was really in going to my first conference held by that organization, meeting a bunch of gay Christians, and then going to Justin Lee's workshop on "Side A Theology in 90 Minutes," where I finally said, "Oh wow, there really *is* a biblical case for affirming same-sex relationships."[99] And that's when the intellectual part sort of started to backfill for me, and I realized, "Oh, there really is a reason that I've taken these steps."

A little later in our conversation, Paul came back to his observation on the relationship between the Bible and his embodied experience. He suggested that he's still willing to abandon his desire to one day have a meaningful intimate relationship with another man if that's what the Bible truly demands. He also took the opportunity to again deflect accusations that he is putting his own experience above Scripture:

The truth does not scare me. If the truth of the matter really were that same-sex relationships between homosexually attracted people were sinful, that would be because it is somehow harmful to us. That's the way God's morality works. That is the teaching of the Bible. That's not scary to me because . . . if that really is the truth with a capital 'T' in the world, that's going to be better for me whether I understand it now or not. So I really don't fear the possibility of somehow finding out that I'm wrong.

It's not just about finding arguments in favor of my stance. [Laughing.] I would be really surprised if I ever had to change my mind on this; the overwhelming majority of evidence is in favor of the position I hold now. But that's just worth saying for the record that this isn't just about finding arguments that are [in support of my stance] because of course I get this from people all the time: "You're just looking for what you want to see."

Paul's story, like several others in this chapter, illustrates an ever-present tension in living and struggling with the sacred text in conservative LGBTQ Christian activism. In the very process of reaffirming the authority of the text, one runs the risk of reauthorizing the text's authority to define rules of inclusion and exclusion. As Janet Jakobsen and Ann Pellegrini argue, "Turning to what the Bible 'really' says about homosexuality reasserts the cultural authority of the Bible and the political pronouncements of its interpreters."[100] In other words, at the same time that individuals are attempting to destabilize authoritative uses of Scripture that lead to violence and oppression, they are reproducing a cultural authority of the Bible that lends itself to abuse.

The experience-Scripture binary further complicates this dynamic. As we have seen throughout this chapter, those who attempt to police LGBTQ Christians often use the argument that LGBTQ Christians are guilty of placing their embodied experience above the authority of Scripture. Yet as Tanya Luhrmann documents in her ethnography of evangelical practices of the body, rather than an either-or relationship, a subtle interplay of reading Scripture through one's experience and experience through Scripture better describes how many evangelicals, no matter their sexual orientation or gender identity, practice their relationship to Scripture.[101] It is a process that, if done correctly, is inherently unsettled and unsettling, as those with whom I spoke during my fieldwork emphasized time and again. However, when leveraged as a binary, it makes for a potent disciplinary mechanism, and the charge of placing one's experience above Scripture functions to strip one of the authority to speak.

3   The Sexual Self and Spiritual Health

The play *Next Fall* dramatizes the fraught relationship between being gay and being Christian—and in particular being a gay Christian—in contemporary American culture.[1] It tells the story of Luke, a gay man and Christian in his midtwenties who is dying in a hospital room after a catastrophic car accident and of his being trapped between a family who rejects his sexuality and a partner, Adam, who rejects his Christian faith. The play flashes back and forth between Adam (who is older than Luke and an ardent atheist) and Luke's relationship over the previous five years and the New York City hospital waiting room where Adam is anxiously waiting with his best friend Holly, Luke's friend Brandon, and Luke's divorced parents, Butch and Arlene. The significance of the title is revealed about halfway through the play. Before the accident Luke—who had kept his sexuality hidden from his conservative Christian parents, much like he had kept his Christian faith hidden from Adam when they first met—promised Adam he would come out to his family "next fall."

In the flashbacks we learn that Luke, despite being in a relationship and living with Adam, still feels his sexuality is in some way sinful, and Luke atones for it by praying after sex. Over time Adam becomes increasingly incredulous about Luke's habit and fear of coming out to his family. Adam raises his frustrations with Luke's friend Brandon in the hospital waiting room:

> ADAM: The praying after sex. (*A beat.*) That's the one little quirk I'm still having a hard time with. (*Another beat. . . .*) It's just something that's really been bugging me lately. . . . It just sort of makes everything feel a little tainted somehow. I mean, how am I gonna feel loved for real with, you know, all that in the way?[2]

Like Luke, Brandon is also a gay Christian. Brandon tells Adam he's uncomfortable with Adam and Luke's relationship, not necessarily because of the sex but because the relationship has turned into something more:

> BRANDON: I've been struggling with this stuff my whole life. When I met Luke, it was like, finally someone who understood. Finally someone I felt safe with. But somewhere along the line things started to shift. When you two were just hooking up, it was one thing, but when it turned into something, well, more. . . . Look, I understand the need to act on the urges, believe me, but to choose the lifestyle? To live like it was . . . right, I guess? Well, that's where we go our separate ways.
>
> ADAM: So, you're saying there was a line and, at a certain point, Luke crossed it?
>
> BRANDON: Moved it.
>
> ADAM: So, it's okay to do . . . whatever it is you do . . . but when it comes to actually loving, that's where the line's drawn?
>
> BRANDON: My line.
>
> ADAM: At love? You draw your line at love, Brandon? Loving is too much of a sin?[3]

Before they go their separate ways, Brandon strains to put the relationship between Luke's faith and sexuality into perspective for Adam:

> BRANDON: I don't know if this helps any, but . . . he chose you, Adam. When he moved the line. That's got to have cost him, you know? And maybe praying after sex is the price he has to pay.[4]

By the end of the play the conflict between conservative Christianity and queer secularism remains in tension.[5] Luke dies without ever coming out to his family, and Adam remains skeptical of Luke's faith. Nevertheless, as a commentary on the overdetermined and overwrought directive to be either authentically gay or authentically Christian in contemporary American culture, *Next Fall* illustrates many of the tensions, conversations, and lingering questions I encountered during my field-work. How do people negotiate a profound sense of being caught between two worlds? What constitutes or sanctions meaningful sex and sexuality? How do people negotiate the relationship between their sexual body and their spiritual health? What does it mean to identify as a gay Christian in conservative Christian spaces?

This chapter is about the relationship between the sexual body and spiritual health in the community of gay Christians with whom I inter-acted during my fieldwork.[6] Many of the conversations at TRP confer-ences, and other spaces where what it means to be a gay Christian is an object of concern, are about the meaning and significance of the sexual body in relationship to Christian identity and belief.

Of course the link between the sexual body and spiritual health is not limited to the conservative gay Christian experience. As a body of schol-arship has documented, in evangelicalism more broadly the sexual body serves as a site of spiritual battles over questions of salvation, obedience, and truth.[7] However, narratives that portray evangelicalism as only repressive of sex and sexual desire fail to account for the full range of evangelicalism's participation in the general production and accumu-lation of discourse about sex. Indeed as Amy DeRogatis argues in *Saving Sex*, "Evangelicals cannot stop talking about sex."[8] "Contrary to popular stereotypes that characterize conservative Christians as sexually repressed," DeRogatis writes, "evangelicals did not turn away from the sexual liberation movement begun in the 1960s, they simply made it their own."[9] As such, Foucault's famous challenge to the "repressive hypothesis" could be extended to much of the conventional wisdom about evangelicalism and sex as well.[10] What rituals and discourses like purity balls, marriage counseling groups, evangelical sex manuals, and even ex-gay ministries share—in addition to their role in regulating normative gender and sexuality in evangelicalism—is their role as spaces for thinking about and acting upon the sexual body in pursuit of spiri-tual health. They illustrate the deep conviction that sexuality and sal-vation are linked and that sexual (im)purity has not only private but also public consequences.

As I mentioned in chapter 2, the contemporary configuration of evan-gelical sexual morality provides relatively few options for thinking about the relationship between same-sex desire and spiritual health; because narratives of gender complementarity demand that homosexual orientation cannot exist as part of God's natural order, same-sex desire alternatively is something to be banished and atoned for or tolerated and long-suffered like the Apostle Paul's "thorn in the flesh."[11] At the same time, given the conventional narrative of the gay identity movement as "gradually emancipat[ing] itself from the vestiges of an antihomosexual religious past," it is tempting to view conservative gay Christians as accommodationist or even regressive in their attempts to reconcile their sexuality with so-called traditional Christian values.[12] However, in this chapter I focus on how some gay Christians navigate the exclusionary politics of evangelical sexual ideology and the moments of agency and resistance that emerge in the space between what one is taught about the body and one's experience of the body.

Central to this chapter is an analysis of what I call "reconciliation narratives," a genre of storytelling I encountered throughout my fieldwork wherein individuals narrate how they came to accept (or continue to wrestle with) being both Christian and gay. The reconciliation narratives share common structural features, including a central experience of presence that results in an embodied form of knowledge. As I will argue, these reconciliation narratives function as a strategy for creating space in evangelicalism for gay Christian identity, while at the same time they reveal how what it means to be gay and Christian can resonate differently for individual lesbian and gay Christians. Examining the relationship between the sexual body and spiritual health in this community of counter-conduct illustrates how sexual desire is less something to be repressed than something to be appropriately managed.

I begin with a brief discussion of the ex-gay movement, a matrix of theories about human sexuality and a loose alliance of organizations and ministries that continue to shape how many evangelicals view homosexuality, including often informing how gay people who grow up in conservative Christian churches first come to understand their sexuality and same-sex sexual desires. I then discuss emerging categories for how some gay Christians in conservative spaces parse the relationship between sexual desire and spirituality. Next, I introduce the genre of reconciliation narratives, which I frame as shared practices central to the production of gay Christian identity in the spaces I studied. I finish the chapter with a discussion on how some participants in this corner of LGBTQ Christian activism wrestle with the potential consequences of trying to make room in conservative spaces for gay people and their relationships without a broader reassessment of evangelical sexuality, gender, and sexual ethics.

"Pray the Gay Away"

In October 2014 a Chicago-area blogger named Tim, weighed in on what he perceived to be a growing trend of individuals identifying as gay Christians. "I have same-sex attractions," Tim wrote. "I have for years. But I have never been able to adopt the term 'gay Christian' for myself."[13]

While the distinction might appear trivial to outsiders, for Tim and others like him the distinction could not be more profound. As Eve Kosofsky Sedgwick underscores, terms like "homosexual" and "gay" have distinct histories organizing distinct phenomena and as such perform different, even if related, tasks. On the one hand, such terms are over-determined; on the other, they describe so much that they almost become meaningless.[14] In the context of conservative Christian rhetoric, the word "homosexual," as briefly discussed in chapter 2, is deeply conditioned by a history of talking about a category of (usually) men who—whether because of a pathological condition or lustful excess—desire to have sex with other men. In this discourse the word "homosexual" carries with it an association of filth and sexual excess. For example, Justin Lee, who identifies as a gay Christian, reflects in his autobiography that when he first came out, he realized he didn't like the word "homosexual" because "something about it felt dirty."[15]

Reflecting broader trends in the United States over the last half of the twentieth century, some individuals in conservative evangelical spaces have thus begun to embrace the term "gay" as a positive identity that requires no "cure." Even so, the category of "gay" in the Christian Right's rhetoric still retains remnants of the "homosexual" and "sodomite" that preceded it. According to Mark Jordan, "The 'gay Christian' wants to be a figure of zealous reform and new holiness. But this figure can only speak in the space of the sodomite's retreat."[16] For some gay Christians, even those who come to embrace the term, their initial unease with identifying as gay has been due to the term's being associated with something called the "homosexual lifestyle" in the Christian Right's rhetoric, a phrase used as shorthand for promiscuity, predation, effeminacy, camp, immorality, secularism, and anti-Americanism.

So while the term "gay" is associated in the conservative evangelical imagination with filth and willful rebellion, Tim's unease with identifying as a gay Christian also reflects another belief still widespread in mainstream evangelicalism: while one might experience same-sex attractions, one is not born or created gay.[17] Reflecting the belief that same-sex sexual acts are expressly forbidden in the Bible, many evangelicals believe that homosexuality is either a mental pathology caused by negative factors during childhood or an intentional choice. In the evangelical mythology of human sexuality, homosexuality is not a natural part of God's creation but a reflection of humankind's sinful nature after the Fall. Therefore, like any other sin, the management of a person's same-sex desires, preferably through permanent sexual orientation change, is not only possible but also a prerequisite for living a fulfilled and holy life, perhaps even essential for eternal salvation. As such, to embrace the term "gay" is to embrace same-sex sexual desires as an immutable reality and natural part of God's creation. Some, therefore, choose the language of "same-sex attracted"—or SSA—as an intentional rejection of homosexuality as an inborn trait while leaving the door always open to the possibility of sexual orientation change.

This theory of homosexuality served as a dramatic backdrop to much of the activism I studied during my fieldwork, especially as fueled and amplified by the ex-gay movement.[18] Ex-gay ministries proliferated in the early 1970s as a conservative Christian response to the growing visibility of the various lesbian and gay social movements. Through counseling, spiritual direction, and behavioral therapy techniques, ex-gay ministries and organizations claimed the ability to help individuals eliminate, or at least happily manage, their same-sex sexual desires. Usually such ministries organize or sponsor Bible study groups or live-in residential programs that combine conservative Christian worldviews with techniques reminiscent of the twelve-step principles of Alcoholics Anonymous while drawing on a pseudoscientific field of research known as "conversion therapy" to provide an aura of scientific legitimacy.

Conversion therapy can be traced back to Freudian theories of psychosexual development, although there is some dispute over Freud's actual views regarding the possibility of sexual orientation change.[19] Of some prominence in the psychoanalytic community during the 1940s through the 1960s, conversion therapists worked under the assumption that homosexuality was a disease of the mind—a legacy of the medicalization of homosexuality in the scientific, medical, and psychiatric fields in the nineteenth and early twentieth centuries—that could be cured. The "treatments" developed for those "suffering homosexual affliction" ranged from psychoanalysis, counseling, and other forms of talk therapy to aversive conditioning (such as the application of electroshock therapy to the genitals or of nausea-inducing medicine during stimulation to curtail undesirable thoughts or behavior) to using even more brute and brutal techniques, such as general electroshock therapy, physical and chemical castration, clitoridectomy, and lobotomy.[20]

The strain of conversion therapy perhaps most influential in conservative Christianity is called reparative therapy, a term often used interchangeably with conversion therapy to refer to talking cures that aim to change an individual's sexual orientation from homosexual to heterosexual. Specifically reparative therapists trace the etiology of homosexuality to failed gender socialization, thus viewing homosexuality as a deficiency in gender that can be repaired through gender-affirmative therapy. This version of conversion therapy comes from the work of the psychoanalyst Irving Bieber in the 1960s but was popularized in the conservative evangelical community by the British psychologist and theologian Elizabeth Moberly in the 1980s and the clinical psychologist Joseph Nicolosi in the 1990s.[21]

Reparative therapists customarily attribute the failure in gender socialization to a dysfunction in the parent-child relationship, with same-sex desire being an individual's subconscious attempt to repair this dysfunction and feelings of inferiority, or what Moberly called the "reparative drive."[22] Therapy might involve trying to diagnose the root cause of the dysfunction—common explanations included an absent father, an overly affectionate mother, an emasculating experience in early childhood, sexual abuse, or the inability to perform normative masculinity or femininity—and prescribing participation in gender-affirmative activities, such as sports or other activities that are stereotypically gendered.[23] In many ways reparative therapy is born of anxieties over male fragility and the desire to police gender roles and is an expression more broadly of the historical project of compulsory heterosexuality.[24]

Beginning in the 1970s the predominant psychiatric and psychoanalytic organizations started to abandon the view that homosexuality was a mental condition requiring psychiatric treatment.[25] While increasingly marginalized in mainstream medical professions, the mantle of conversion therapy was taken up by conservative religious organizations like the now defunct Love Won Out, an ex-gay ministry launched by James Dobson's parachurch organization, Focus on the Family, and the ex-gay umbrella organization Exodus International, which eventually brought together hundreds of affiliated groups worldwide.[26] It was also taken up by ostensibly secular organizations such as the National Association for Research and Therapy of Homosexuality, commonly known as the NARTH Institute.[27]

In addition to the spiritual and emotional violence caused by perpetuating the myth that homosexuality is pathological, ex-gay ministries also have a parallel life of being leveraged as rhetorical weapons in Christian Right antigay activism. At the same time that gay and lesbian social movements were demanding fair and equal treatment on the basis that homosexuality is a normal variation in human sexuality, conservative Christian activists portrayed ex-gay ministries as the faithful Christian alternative and explicit refutation of such claims. The "success stories" of ex-gay ministries were a recurring theme in what Didi Herman calls the "antigay genre" of the Christian Right from its beginnings in the late 1970s.[28] A 1978 book called *The Unhappy Gays*, by Tim LaHaye, a widely influential evangelical pastor and author of the *Left Behind* series, is one early prominent example.[29] In addition to suggesting that the anti-Christ might be a homosexual, Mark Jordan points out, LaHaye cites successes of anonymous ex-gay men "to fortify his condemnation of those [homosexuals] who refuse to be healed."[30] The 1992 film *The Gay Agenda*, another example of the genre, included an interview with ex-gay activist John Paulk, along with footage of ACT UP and Queer Nation protests to portray gay people as social deviants bent on destroying America.[31]

The self-reported successes of the ex-gay movement continue to be a potent weapon in the Christian Right's antigay rhetoric. A prominent example is the work of Robert Gagnon, especially his book *The Bible and Homosexual Practice*, which is often cited by conservative evangelical writers as the definitive and authoritative statement on the "homosexual issue" in conservative Christianity. Gagnon parrots the work of reparative therapists such as Moberly and Nicolosi to dispute the claim that biology plays a role in homosexual orientation and cites organizations such as the NARTH Institute and Exodus International and anecdotal accounts of ex-gay men such as Frank Worthen and Joe Dallas—he refers to them as "ex-homosexuals"—as evidence of successes "in managing, and significantly decreasing or eliminating, homosexual impulses."[32]

The faith in the efficacy of reparative therapy expressed by Gagnon and other writers among the Christian Right diverges from the consensus of mental health professionals and even some leaders and participants in ex-gay ministries. The American Psychiatric Association, for example, in its 2000 position statement on conversion therapy, concluded that "Psychotherapeutic modalities to convert or 'repair' homosexuality are based on developmental theories whose scientific validity is questionable. Furthermore, anecdotal reports of 'cures' are counterbalanced by anecdotal claims of psychological harm. In the last four decades, 'reparative' therapists have not produced any rigorous scientific research to substantiate their claims of cure." Moreover, during her fieldwork with a residential ex-gay program, Tanya Erzen found that the ex-gay men and women with whom she spoke often "disassociated themselves from the politics of the Christian Right" and "resent[ed] that the wider ex-gay movement showcases and distorts their stories to promote an anti-gay political agenda."[33] In contradiction to exaggerated claims of permanent sexual orientation change, "many ex-gays admit that although some changes in behavior and identity take place, it is more probable that they will continue as 'strugglers' their entire lives."[34]

More recently a series of public controversies and failings have lessened the credibility of the broader ex-gay movement, and some leading evangelicals have begun to distance themselves from ex-gay therapy altogether. For example, Exodus International closed operations in June 2013 after a series of scandals, and some prominent leaders began to express publicly their loss of faith that sexual orientation change is possible. After announcing the closure of the organization, the former president of Exodus International, Alan Chambers, issued a public repudiation of the organization's mission and an apology for the harm caused to the lesbian and gay community.[35] Nevertheless, even as some conservative Christians are now distancing themselves from reparative therapy, others are recasting conversion therapy as a constitutionally protected religious belief, and many of the organizations formerly affiliated with Exodus International continue their work under other names and affiliations.[36]

The shadow of the ex-gay movement colored much of the gay Christian activism I encountered during my fieldwork. In many ways evangelical gay Christian organizations like TRP, GCN, and The Marin Foundation, although they do not necessarily say so in their stated missions, are working to mend some of the spiritual, emotional, and psychological violence caused by the ex-gay movement and its exploitation by the Christian Right. A significant number of the stories I heard or people with whom I spoke attested to direct or indirect experience with ex-gay ministries or their messaging of sexual orientation change. This is not to say that all, or even most, lesbian or gay Christians have experience with conversion therapy or ever consider it as a valid option; nevertheless, the legacy of ex-gay ministries was omnipresent at TRP conferences.

Some recalled, for example, that considering conversion therapy was their first reaction to realizing they might be gay. Others recounted that a parent compelled them to pursue conversion therapy after discovering a browsing history of gay pornography or Google searches for "Is being gay and Christian okay?" I heard stories about secretive "homosexuals anonymous" groups, often affiliated with organizations like Exodus International, at churches they attended as children for members "struggling with same-sex attractions." Still others told stories about how they were urged to meticulously excavate childhood memories to find the parental dysfunction that must lie beneath their disordered sexuality. There are now ex-ex-gay support groups for people who experience lingering trauma from their experience with ex-gay therapy.[37]

Even with the diminishing faith in ex-gay models, a common message that lesbian and gay Christians often still hear in conservative Christian spaces is "It's okay to be gay as long as you don't act on it," an updated spin on "Love the sinner, hate the sin," a talking point that, Janet Jakobsen and Ann Pellegrini argue, "allows people to take positions that are punitive toward their fellow citizens, while at the same time experiencing themselves as being not simply ethical, but compassionate and even tolerant of difference."[38] There is, moreover, some disagreement even among participants in lesbian- and gay-affirming organizations like TRP and GCN about the value of ex-gay ministries. For example, some would argue that ex-gay therapy should remain an option for consenting adults who desire help in managing their same-sex desires, whether for personal convictions or social reasons.[39]

Side A/Side B

As the previous discussion indicates, gay Christian identity work in evangelical communities often requires a fair amount of grit and creativity. One way in which some gay Christians in such spaces navigate the relationship between their sexuality and Christian faith is by using the language of Side A/Side B.[40] Side A/Side B is a taxonomy used as shorthand to describe internal disagreements over the inherent morality or sinfulness of same-sex desire and sex. Very roughly, Side A gay Christians believe gay sex is morally acceptable; Side B gay Christians do not.

The language gained some prominence in this community primarily through GCN. As mentioned in the introduction, GCN is a nonprofit organization that provides a platform and communal space for LGBTQ and LGBTQ-supportive Christians through an online community and annual conferences. When Justin Lee built the GCN website in the early 2000s, he imagined a sort of virtual safe space, an online community where other gay Christians like him could meet and talk, without fear or judgment, about the spiritual and social needs unique to being both gay and Christian.[41] While GCN began as an online community, Lee started organizing annual conferences in 2005, and these have become the largest yearly gatherings of LGBTQ and ally Christians in the world.[42] And while the conferences and online community are somewhat ecumenical, the organization has roots in and still draws a large number of participants from conservative and evangelical Christian traditions. As such, over its decade and a half of existence, GCN has functioned as an important subaltern counterpublic in evangelicalism for the creation and circulation of oppositional interpretations of what it means to be Christian and gay.[43]

Lee borrowed and modified the Side A/Side B language from a 1990s website called Bridges across the Divide.[44] Bridges across the Divide began in the late 1990s as an email exchange between two Christians who disagreed about the morality of homosexuality. Maggie Heineman, a PFLAG member in Philadelphia who was moderating an email listserv advocating for marriage equality, received an email from Steve Calverley, a self-identified ex-gay man who was writing in response to a post that questioned the efficacy of attempts to change one's sexual orientation.[45] What began as an exercise in mutual understanding and open dialogue between Heineman and Calverley turned into an effort to provide a platform for others to have similar conversations. The mission of Bridges across the Divide was to be "a cyberspace initiative providing models and resources for building respectful relationships among those who disagree about moral issues surrounding homosexuality, bisexuality and gender variance."[46]

In the context of GCN, Side A and Side B gay Christians share the acceptance of the reality of homosexuality as a natural variation in human sexuality. What separates Side A from Side B Christians is a disagreement over the morality of gay sex. As Lee explains, "SideA holds that gay sex (like straight sex) is morally acceptable in the right circumstances. SideB holds that gay sex is inherently morally wrong."[47] As such, Side A/Side B explicitly parts ways with the ex-gay framework that has characterized much of evangelical discourse on the nature and morality of same-sex sexual desire and acts—or "Side X," as it's sometimes called, although individuals who identify as ex-gay rarely, if ever, use this term themselves.

Lee decided early on that GCN would include both Side A and Side B gay Christians in its online community.[48] The website provides forums for both Side A and Side B Christians to congregate either together or separately and to discuss a range of matters relating to the relationship between their sexuality and faith. At the same time, participants are required to follow certain community rules. Reflecting on the early days of the website, Lee notes that "both 'Side A' and 'Side B' people would be welcome at GCN, and within this space, both sides would agree not to try to convert or talk down to one another. GCN was to be a neutral zone, a place for people to put the culture war aside and know they were among friends."[49]

The Side A/Side B taxonomy, as Lee himself acknowledges, oversimplifies the range of beliefs, identities, desires, and practices reflected at TRP or GCN conferences or on GCN's online forums. Side A gay Christians, for example, might agree that gay sex is morally acceptable but disagree about when and what constitutes morally acceptable sex. Side B gay Christians also differ: some might choose a life of celibacy or "singleness," others might enter sexless "mixed-orientation" marriages, and still others use the space to cultivate spiritual friendships.[50] Moreover, the inclusion of Side B gay Christians by GCN is not without its critics. Some participants in the community argue, for example, that their fellow gay Christians who maintain that celibacy is a higher calling for gay people perpetuate the idea that the only good gay person is a celibate gay person. Some also worry about how the Christian Right exploits the stories of celibate gay Christians—like its exploitation of the stories of ex-gay men and women for political gain—to shame sexually active gay Christians.[51]

During my fieldwork it was not uncommon to hear individuals describe themselves as Side A or Side B Christians, similar to how a Christian might identify as an Arminian or a Calvinist. I also heard Side A/Side B used to describe a person's acceptance of or opposition to LGBTQ people (no matter the person's sexual orientation or gender identity), doing roughly the same work as the language of affirming and nonaffirming. The difference might be that Side A/Side B originated in, and is still principally used within, the context of questions concerning the morality of gay sex, whereas affirming/nonaffirming reflects more recent conversations in evangelicalism on not only sexuality but also gender identity and the inclusion and support of LGBTQ people in all aspects of church life.

Still Side A/Side B reflects more than a theological debate about the inherent morality or sinfulness of gay sex. While not all gay Christians use or even accept this framework, I came to recognize it as an important space for doing the complicated work of negotiating gay and Christian identity in conservative Christian contexts. On the one hand, Side A/Side B functions to organize shared identities and form the basis of community. But as I will illustrate, it also functions as a space for individuals to modify how they understand the relationship between their sexual body and their spiritual health.

Prayer was a big part of all three of the conferences I attended. Each day began with half an hour of worship and prayer; Bible-breakout facilitators opened and closed sessions with prayer; panel discussants and keynote presenters often led conference attendees in prayer; it was common to see small groups of three or four huddled together, heads bowed, in the aisles and hallways in between panel discussions or Bible breakouts. There were also prayer or serenity rooms—hotel conference rooms or church basements repurposed as spaces for prayer and reflection—at all three conferences. Speakers at the conferences regularly encouraged attendees to use the prayer rooms. When a panel discussion at the Atlanta conference turned to the topic of sexual violence, for example, a panel discussant prefaced her comments by reminding the audience that the prayer room was available if participants found the content triggering.

The prayer rooms were typically divided into different stations. In Atlanta, for example, the room was organized into two rough halves: as people entered, a sign in the middle of the room directed them to an "activity prayer area" on the left and a "quiet prayer area" on the right. The activity prayer area included two round tables with instructions and materials for engaging in different tasks while praying—clay play, coloring, making prayer bracelets and origami. A coloring station provided sheets of paper with line art and colored pencils and pens for coloring, with instructions to "lift others in prayer and lift your concerns/thanksgivings/joys as you color a page."

The quiet prayer area contained a circle of ten chairs facing inward, interrupted in two places by round wood end tables upon which were tissue boxes, small vases with flowers, dimly lighted lamps, and running tabletop water fountains. A wall adjacent to the quiet area was converted into a prayer wall. It included instructions to write prayers on sticky notes and add them to six brightly colored posterboards taped to the wall. Several signs requested that people refrain from conversations out of respect to others in the room.

Although prayer played a less visible role at the steering committee meetings I attended, the committee did have a designated prayer team

4. Instructions and materials for the Coloring Station in the Activity Prayer Area of the prayer room at TRP's regional training conference in Atlanta, June 2015. Photo by the author.

responsible for planning and setting up the prayer room for the three-day Kansas City conference. A few months after I started attending meetings, the prayer team leader announced that she had created a private Facebook group for the steering committee members and other conference volunteers for prayer requests and to "infuse the whole process with prayer." Aside from a few inspirational Bible verses posted in the beginning, the Facebook group was never really used. In the days leading up to the conference, a prayer team volunteer sent a group email to the steering committee asking for our favorite Bible passages so that they could be displayed in the prayer room. A few responded with favorites—Micah 6:8; 1 John 4:7–12; Psalm 27:1; Joshua 1:9. I suggested the first clause of 1 Corinthians 13:12.

Reconciliation Narratives

As noted previously, one of the more recurring themes I encountered throughout my fieldwork—in interviews, at TRP conferences, and through reading gay Christian blogs and autobiographies—was "reconciliation narratives," stories people would tell about their "faith and sexuality journey" in the context of conservative evangelical conversations on what it means to be gay and Christian.[52] In their most basic form, reconciliation narratives recount the process through which people came to "reconcile" their sexuality with their faith or came to understand their sexuality as no longer an existential threat to their salvation and perhaps even crucial for living their faith authentically. The more I became familiar with these stories, the more I realized that this genre of storytelling was not only regulated by shared narrative patterns but also served personal, social, and political purposes for the storytellers and the community the stories helped constitute and legitimize.

As a genre of storytelling, the structure and function of reconciliation narratives share a family resemblance with both coming out and conversion narratives, both of which tend to describe a linear progression from oppression to liberation, confusion to enlightenment, or darkness to light that results in dramatic personal transformation.[53] Like coming-out stories, reconciliation narratives reconstruct how the speakers "came out" as gay to themselves, their family and friends, or—important in the case of reconciliation narratives—to God. The coming-out aspect of reconciliation narratives also often includes an element of "reclaiming a hidden, authentic self," to use Steven Seidman's language about coming-out stories.[54] Kenneth Plummer argues that narrating the process of one's coming out is a personal act that is also social and political. While such stories are of a highly personal experience, they often follow shared narrative formats that reflect a joint storytelling of a community. Coming-out narratives, therefore, play an important role in constituting communities in that they foster collective identity and motivate social change. "For narratives to flourish," Plummer argues, "there must be a community to hear; [and] for communities to hear, there must be stories which weave together their history, their identity, their politics."[55]

Reconciliation narratives also resemble conversion stories, a genre of storytelling common among evangelicals wherein an individual narrates a conversion experience or the moment of being saved or "born again."[56] Conversion stories often contain personal experiences interwoven with biblical stories and rhetorical flourishes to draw the listener into a communal transformational experience.[57] Christians sometimes refer to the telling of conversion stories as "witnessing" or "sharing a personal testimony." Susan Harding argues that witness accounts are rhetorically structured both to provide evidence of a change in world-view and to be "a method of bringing about that change in those who listen to it."[58] Reconciliation narratives likewise are a form of witnessing, not in the sense of attempting to convert or save the listener but to change the way fellow Christians view gay people and their intimate relationships. Conversion stories also recast, reorganize, and reinterpret experiences before and after the conversion experience in light of the pivotal life-changing moment. The conversion event marks the boundary, a moment of radical change, between what came before and what came after.[59] Similarly reconciliation narratives describe a moment of profound personal transformation.

Some of the reconciliation narratives I heard built up to a mystical experience—although the people with whom I spoke might reject this language—that marked and confirmed a change in the way individuals understood the relationship between their sexuality and their faith. Courtney Bender, in her study of the narratives of divine encounters told by mystics and other spiritual practitioners, argues that such stories are "highly regulated and shaped by theological norms that they also reproduce" and that they are structured in such a way as to "make claims for their authenticity and authority as religious experiences."[60] Similarly in the reconciliation narratives, the divine encounter is presented as evidence that God affirms—language the storytellers would use—their gay and Christian identity. That is, the reconciliation narratives make regulated and shared claims for the authenticity and authority of the mystical experience, or series of experiences, that culminates in accepting one's identity as a gay Christian. At the same time, the reconciliation narratives contribute to a world-building process that makes it possible for gay Christian stories to be heard. In this way these reconciliation narratives and the mystical experiences that sometimes accompany them are themselves a mode of counter-conduct.[61]

Although variations exist and not all lesbian and gay Christians would see themselves in the stories discussed here, many of the reconciliation narratives I heard followed familiar rhetorical paths.[62] Reconciliation narratives often begin by an individual's describing a period of intense questioning and doubt followed by a religious experience—an embodied experience where an individual receives a message of love or affirmation—that results in peace, clarity, and a new faith in being a gay Christian. The new faith arises not from the acquisition of new knowledge alone; it's born of the felt reality of the embodied religious experience. Following the religious experience, there might be a period of faith-testing wherein an individual "acts on faith" to tell others about the newfound knowledge, and after doing so, the individual's faith might be confirmed by a sign. Sometimes at the end of the reconciliation narrative, an individual might turn the experience into a general lesson about the nature of faith and knowledge.

I begin with Paul Creekmore's story from the interview I discussed briefly at the end of chapter 2.[63] Paul's reconciliation narrative provides a clean outline of the primary features of these narratives: the intense questioning and doubt, a mystical experience, faith-testing and a sign, and a transformation in identity grounded in embodied knowledge. Paul also described his experience using the language of Side A/Side B. At the center of Paul's story of how he transitioned from a Side B to Side A Christian—a change that Paul claims was more challenging for him than accepting his sexual orientation—is a life-altering mystical experience.

To remind the reader, when Paul first accepted that he "might be this thing that people called 'gay,'" his gut reaction was to commit to a life of celibacy in keeping with his belief that gay sex was inherently sinful: "I was initially Side B. That was my initial reaction [to accepting that I was gay]. That's how my mind works: something has changed; I took the smallest step possible." Later Paul went through a valley of doubt and loneliness before turning to the internet in search of other people like him. Then on the same evening of intense questioning and searching, Paul had an experience that ultimately led to, as Paul describes it, "a change of heart":

In the course of that evening, [I had] what remains the most vivid and powerful experience of God I have ever felt. . . . Christians talk about "hearing from God," and sometimes I'm skeptical of that. (I'm not a very hyper-supernaturalist person; I'm really not.) But if there is one time in my life where God has ever spoken to me—and it's not words you hear in the air, it's that thought in your head—that was it.

And it was so outside of myself. In the absolute franticness and panic in my mind, the—call it "the presence"—the presence that joined me, I suppose, was so inexplicably powerful and impossibly calm and peaceful at the same time and very, very quiet. And in my own experience with God up until that time, that is what God was in my mind. That was my intellectual encounter of God; it was those things. And this was the most powerful combination of all those all at once with this very simple message: "It's okay. You need to allow yourself to love and to be loved."

And that was—I want to say "sentence," at least "idea"—so powerful that I could not, absolutely could not, ignore it. . . . That's all I had . . . this spiritual experience. . . . I'm quite a rational, intellectual person. So, in a sense, that was the only way I was ever going to change my mind. Because I was never going to make rational sense out of [what I experienced], there was never gonna be a logical conclusion. Well, I've learned now that, yes, there is a logical conclusion that I could come to in support of same-sex relationships, but at the time I didn't know about it.

Part of what Paul was describing is not unique to gay Christians like him who wrestle with the relationship between their faith and sexuality; it's a common practice among some contemporary Christians, according the anthropologist Tanya Luhrmann, of learning how to interpret audiovisual and bodily sensations as evidence of God's presence, direction, and blessing.[64] Paul also pauses throughout to address possible counterarguments to his narrative, a rhetorical technique discussed by Courtney Bender in her ethnography of contemporary American spirituality. Like Paul, Bender's interviewees often organized their narratives in such a way as to "respond to a variety of imagined interlocutors who might pose counterarguments about the narratives' validity and authenticity."[65] Paul, for example, pauses his narrative of his embodied experience of God's presence to assert his rationality and general suspicion of such experiences. This technique functions, Bender argues, to "[protect] experiential knowledge from external critique" by "articulat[ing] the authority of the experience through its untranslatability, where the moment of experience itself stands outside of normal cognition."[66] In Paul's case, though, it does even more work. It demonstrates that his change of heart was not personal whimsy, as some of his critics might claim, but propelled by an overwhelming and patterned experience of presence.

The next morning Paul questioned his new embodied knowledge. The questioning, however, did not undermine the legitimacy of the experience but rather provided further verification. In Paul's telling of the story, the next step was to act on the new embodied knowledge as an exercise in faith-testing, which again was based on his previous relationship with and experience of God. The entire experience was later affirmed by a sign:

> So I had this spiritual experience—this wild, wild night, all night long. I couldn't sleep. And the next day, I had to deal with the reality of my experience: "Am I actually going to go on that? This crazy story? How am I going to tell people why I changed my mind? They're going to laugh at me!"
>
> And I had to tell people about this. I had to tell my best friend about this, to whom I was already out, but out as Side B. And I had to tell him, "Well, uh, God told me this was okay." I mean, what's he going to do with that?! And I did. And he reacted just like I expected him to. He tried to explain it away as some kind of frantic state of mind I was in and [that I had] told myself what I wanted to hear, and all this stuff.
>
> But I had a choice to make at that point, and that was: do I go with this or not? And in my experience, when God tells me something, he says it once, and then it's my job after that. And I didn't expect to have a divine lightning bolt again. What it came down to, for me, was sort of a question of the reality of my faith. If that was not God, then nothing in my life ever has been, and the entirety of my faith is on the line. So I had to have had [the experience]. I had to try and see what happened. So I did. I stuck with . . . what I had chosen that night, really, and didn't go back on it and saw how it played out in my life.
>
> And, I mean, the short [version] of the story is that, without question, a fundamental degree of joy that I never knew I was missing flooded back into my life. My mom visited me [a little later when I

was living in Los Angeles], and after tons of objections to this decision, . . . out of the blue, she just said, "You're happy." And it was [an] absolute visible change in my life. The reality of that was so clear that I couldn't really question the choice I had made. . . .

And Jesus teaches in Matthew that we can identify right from wrong, good from evil, through our personal experience. In Matthew, it says "a good tree does not bear bad fruit and a bad tree does not bear good fruit," and this is how you can discern for yourself what is right and wrong when there's a question about it.

As I learned during my fieldwork, "fruit" is often used in evangelical discourse as a test to determine whether a decision or action is sanctioned by God, especially in situations where there is no clear guidance in Scripture. The language comes from the parable of the Tree and Its Fruits in the gospels of Matthew and Luke, which Jesus uses to instruct his disciples in how they could determine whether a prophet had been sent from God.[67] In its contemporary use, in the same way that good fruit comes from a healthy tree, an individual can determine whether God approves of a decision or action based on the fruit it bears.[68] "Fruit," in other words, is a technology through which one can make an ethical decision and determine a truth about the self.[69]

A little later in our conversation, when we came back to the subject of how he had changed from Side B to Side A, Paul described the change using the language of "conversion." Although Paul had reservations about using such language in that it called to his mind someone converting from one religion to another (which Paul stressed was not how he viewed his change from Side B to Side A), he admitted that the experience led to "profound life changes." While not a conversion from one religion to another, the experience did lead to a reorientation in how he understands the relationship between his sexuality and spiritual health:

PAUL: So, the Side B/Side A [searching for words], my conversion to Side A, happened spilling out of undergrad.

JON: Do you hear other people talking about this experience using the language of conversion, by the way? Or is that just how you like to think of it?

PAUL: Mmmm?

JON: Because it does sound like a conversion experience.

PAUL: Yeah, oh yeah. . . .

JON: Maybe not in that exact language?

PAUL: I don't know. . . . I was trying to find a different word just then before I used it. . . . I don't have specific objections to it. It sounds like a conversion from one religion to another—maybe that's why I want to avoid that term, 'cause . . . that's not how I look at it.

JON: Yeah, yeah.

PAUL: It's not that severe. It's just altering one aspect of my belief system, just one tiny aspect. It's really just removing. . . .

JON: But it changed your whole life!

PAUL: [Laughing.] Yes, yes it did. Just simply removing gender from sexual morality—just doing that—means profound life changes. Profound life changes.

Paul's reconciliation narrative hinges on a mystical experience that transpired over the course of a single evening. For others reconciliation narratives might include several distinct moments where they felt or heard messages from God about their gay Christian identity. Shae Washington (introduced in the previous chapter) described her experience of reconciling her faith and sexuality as a guest speaker during a Bible-training session at the Kansas City conference (November 6, 2015). Washington introduced herself as a queer Black woman who is still active in the conservative evangelical church she attended while coming out, hoping to be an example and to create change from within. In her reconciliation narrative she mentions several "reconciling messages" that led up to her coming out as queer and Christian:

I came out maybe three or four years ago. I had friends who knew I struggled with same-sex attractions, but they thought I was over it and that it was in the past. I went on this journey where I experienced several distinct moments in a process of reconciling my sexuality with my faith. I received several reconciling messages from God during this time. It was a time where I was really wrestling and struggling with God. I knew that coming out might mean I would lose my friends and my family and my church. My friends had also been taught that being gay is a sin.

So I was very concerned about losing these relationships, and I didn't want people to think of me any differently. But most important to me: I didn't want them to think I didn't love Jesus. It was during this time that I was praying one day, and I felt like God told me that he had already set me free on the cross and that I should come into the light and be who he created me to be. And I felt this profound peace.

It was after she received this sign of peace (as mentioned in the previous chapter) that Washington acted on faith to test her new embodied knowledge, despite not yet having the biblical knowledge to support her decision.

Another reconciliation narrative shared with me during an interview illustrates how past life events can later be reinterpreted in light of the mystical experience. The interview was with a person I will call Jonah, a volunteer for a time on the steering committee for the Kansas City regional training conference.[70] Jonah is a white gay man in his late thirties who grew up in central and western Missouri before settling in the Kansas City area after college. I felt an immediate connection with Jonah. We were both raised by single mothers with absent fathers, we spent a period of our childhoods living with our grandparents, both of our first jobs were at restaurants as teenagers, and I knew from firsthand experience what Jonah meant when he said he began rebelling in his late teens to escape childhood worries. Religion was also a big part of both our lives growing up, although Jonah grew up Methodist and I, Pentecostal. Long after our conversation, two of Jonah's remarks stayed with me in particular: "I really believed that there was a God and that he hated me"; and, "Life [should be] about a lot more than this."

Jonah got involved with TRP because he wanted to bring together two communities and two aspects of his identity that often seemed to be at odds with one another. Despite being active and feeling, for the most part, welcome in his current church home, he at times felt isolated and excluded. On a few occasions some of his fellow church members raised concerns with senior pastors about Jonah's leading small groups because he was gay. At the same time Jonah felt disconnected from other gay people he knew. "The other struggle," Jonah told me, "was that, outside of the church [there were] people in the gay community who seemed so ostracized by the church [and] who really didn't understand why I cared . . . or why having a relationship with a church and with God was important to me. And I understand that." This dynamic, one that I encountered on a few occasions, provides important insight into how individuals negotiate and co-construct different aspects of their identities. Although not true for all, I got the impression that many of those who came to TRP conferences came because they didn't always feel fully at home either in their faith communities or with other LGBTQ people. Some, for example, sought to distance themselves from certain stereotypes of LGBTQ people, whether as represented in popular culture or perpetuated by the Christian Right.

Jonah, like Paul, describes the moment when he accepted being gay as a Christian in language reminiscent of a conversion experience. In fact Jonah connected his first conversion experience of being born again with the second conversion using the language of "claiming," the only two times he used such language during our conversation. Jonah told me that he "always knew [he] was different," but long before he came to accept his sexuality, a few early childhood experiences had shaped what he thought it meant to be gay. Because he had grown up in Methodist churches in the 1980s and 1990s, some of his earliest memories on the topic were of his family members—including his mother, an aunt and uncle who were "still very, very conservative," and another uncle who was a Methodist pastor—all "[seeming] to agree . . . that being gay is wrong." This would sometimes include "matter-of-fact" conversations about gay people: "Well, that's what they choose, and they'll go to hell." Jonah also remembers being intimately aware of the AIDS crisis at a time when it was still being reported as "the gay disease" and a "plague on gay men": "I remember it being on the news—people were scared. I remember asking my mom, 'How do I not get it?' and being really worried about getting it at like seven or eight. [My mom] was like, 'Of course you have nothing to worry about [because you're not gay].' That was one of her big concerns when she [later] found out that I was gay."

Jonah had his first religious experience while attending a small Christian summer camp in Missouri when he was around ten years old. Although he remembers his grandparents teaching him a "love for God," Jonah told me he didn't really remember claiming his faith until the religious experience at the camp: "I remember I had to be maybe in the fifth or sixth grade when I went to this camp and sort of had that conversion experience, and it really was what I would call being born again. I had and felt this experience, and I was on a high from that for a while. And that's when, [after] we came back, I got involved in a youth group."

By middle school and early high school Jonah began to feel that he no longer fit in with his friends. Then, while waiting tables during high school, Jonah met an openly gay person for the first time, and it was this "experience with someone who seemed comfortable and seemed fine with who they were" that Jonah first began to accept his sexual orientation: "Okay, this is probably what I am." Jonah came out to his mother and, as he described it, began rebelling from his family and his childhood faith. Jonah describes this period in his life as one of acute cognitive dissonance, agony, and doubt:

JONAH: I was heading into middle school, and I had friends, but I was never athletic. And it really was becoming apparent at that point in time that I was not like the other guys. . . . Even in youth group, I felt like, "Even here I can't really be who I am." And then when I started coming to terms with being gay, . . . there was this huge cognitive dissonance . . . : "How do I deal with the person I think I am versus what the church is telling me and, what I think by virtue of that, God has told me?" I mean, that's hard because you grow up and you're told all your life there's nothing you can do for which God will not forgive you or love you, and suddenly you are now the worst possible thing, or at least you imagine it that way. . . .

But . . . when I finally accepted being gay, I just shut everything out. . . . I really don't know why, other than I think it was a coping mechanism for feeling so hated. I mean, I really believed that. I thought, "Okay, God hates me. I'm not at all what he wants." And so the only way to really deal with that was to void my life of that completely.

JON: What changed about you during that time? Did you think about life any differently? Did you do anything differently? Did you ever stop believing in God? . . . Did you continue to pray?

JONAH: No, I don't think so. Well, that's not completely true.

JON: You just sort of felt exiled maybe?

JONAH: Very. [When I did pray during this time,] the prayers were often, "Okay, change this." Or, "I don't want to be this. . . . This can't be; I can't be this because. . . ." And then [the prayers became,] "If you really wanted me to be straight, make me. You can do anything." I mean, that verse: *I can do all things through Christ who strengthens me.*[71] All of those verses: *Nothing's impossible with God.*[72] That makes you feel really guilty because suddenly [it's my fault that] I don't have enough faith or whatever it is that isn't working out and fitting into this, you know, picture-perfect image. But . . . I did get to that point where it was like, "Okay, I want nothing to do with God."

Jonah spent several years in this liminal state. Looking back, however, he retrospectively interprets a series of events as signs that God never left him:

JONAH: Over time that changed. I mean, this was years of [feeling like God hated me]. Looking back, I can say, "I am a Christian, and I own that." . . . He was always chasing me. . . . I mean it's almost chilling because there was never a moment for me that I was out of His grasp.

JON: Tell me how you know that.

JONAH: [Laughing.] I don't know. That's a weird thing to say. I mean, it's almost internal. I don't know!

Jonah went on to describe a series of events that led him to feel that he needed to try something different, to try to find a way to manage his sexuality and reconcile himself with God. He had tried attending a few different churches during this time—a congregation affiliated with the

Metropolitan Community Church, a Unity church, and a Buddhist temple—but they "never took." He had fallen in love, only later to find out after an eight-month relationship that his boyfriend had also been dating someone else the entire time. Another pivotal moment came when his cousin died in a car accident a month before her twenty-second birthday. Jonah was only a year older, and they had been very close growing up but had grown apart since he had come out.

All of this culminated with Jonah's feeling that he needed to try something else, and he believed that to renew a relationship with God he could no longer be gay. Although he had resisted the advice for years, Jonah finally relented to his mother and agreed to consider ex-gay counseling. He even went on a few dates with women. Around the same time Focus on the Family happened to be sponsoring a Love Won Out conference in the Kansas City area, and Jonah attended with some optimism, hoping that his lack of faith would not get in the way this time. Despite being skeptical about the testimonies he heard from various speakers at the conference on how they had left homosexuality behind, Jonah decided to follow up with a counselor who had been recommended by the organization:

> I met with him probably four or five times in total. But when I met with him, . . . he was very much like, "What are your objectives?" And I said, "Well, I don't want to be gay anymore." And he was very like, "Do you think that's possible?" [Laughing.] And I was like, "Well, you tell me! You're the one sitting in the counselor's chair. You tell me!"
>
> And he never said yes or no, but he had very much indicated that he didn't think it was possible. So I was then really confused because I prayed about getting a counselor, I know my mother had prayed about it, and here I was with this counselor that was recommended by Focus on the Family [who was telling me orientation change wasn't possible].

The sessions ended with the counselor's recommending that Jonah seek out a gay-affirming church. Jonah remarked that he thought Love Won Out probably wouldn't have recommended this counselor if it had known he would give such advice. He interpreted this happy coincidence as evidence of God's continued direction. When Jonah followed the advice, he found that the "gay issue" was not as settled among Christians or in Scripture as he had been raised to believe. Jonah's next reaction was to resign himself to a life of celibacy, but then he was set up on a blind date with the person who is still his partner. At the time, though, Jonah felt he was at a crossroads: "What do I do with Christianity and God? And does God really hate me through all of this?"

During a night of intense prayer Jonah had an experience that led him—like when he had "claimed" his Christian faith after the born-again experience when he was ten years old—to finally say of his sexuality, "Okay, I'm going to claim this." Jonah describes the experience of God's presence and voice as something he felt as much as he heard, and it was this moment that resulted in a "certainty" and "knowledge" about his reconciled identity:

> JONAH: I basically prayed all night on the floor in my apartment one night going, "God, what do you want me to do? I've been through now a ten-year journey of having been out and trying to run away from you." And, I think, part of the way I knew was—in that prayer—feeling an answer to prayer: "I've never let you go." So hearing God say that . . . [after] all those years that I had been saying no to him, or pushing him away, [I was] really feeling this affirmation that "I've never let you go. You've always been mine." And . . . (it was nothing audible; I've never heard an audible response from God) there was a moment just in that night where it was so repeated and clear and just, "There's nothing you can do." . . .
>
> JON: Was this an embodied experience for you?
>
> JONAH: Well, I could hear a voice in my head. . . . Then you start thinking, "Okay, was it my own voice?" But no, . . . there were several things that were said because I was asking, you know, really praying, and saying, "If you don't want me to do this, I need an answer." I remember being very adamant: "I need, *I want*, an answer." And I had never prayed that way with God where I was just, "Tell me. I want this settled." And then, what the answer was, it was over and over and over: "I'm okay with this." Over and over and over.

And it sort of settled it in my mind. I came away from that night with clarity, with certainty in my mind at least, that God doesn't think this is sinful. I don't think God views it as sinful; I know it's not. . . . I wanted a legitimate answer. I really wanted to know: "I've heard what the church has said loud and clear. I know what I've dealt with. I want to know what you think, God." And that was what I felt and kept hearing. I mean, it was this repeated: "You are mine; this is not an issue for me." And that night changed my life.

Reconciliation narratives do not always end with reconciliation. Sometimes they end with an identity still in process and in tension. In other words, they don't always tell a story with a teleological progression from darkness to light but one of a constant negotiation between one's sexuality and spirituality. A reconciliation narrative a gay man I will call Brian told at the Kansas City conference illustrates this tension. Brian had been invited to share his reflections on a play called *Blueprints to Freedom*, which many in the audience had seen the night before.[73] *Blueprints to Freedom* is about the life of Bayard Rustin, a key leader of the civil rights movement. The play dramatizes how Rustin, a man of deep conviction and personal faith, was marginalized in the movement for being openly gay and his struggles with a God who sometimes seemed to be at odds with not only racial justice but also Rustin's sexuality.

The play happened to be on a three-week run at the Kansas City Repertory Theatre's Copaken Stage, just four blocks away from the hotel where TRP was holding its conference in downtown Kansas City. Recognizing that the themes of the play—the intersections of sexuality, gender, race, faith, and social justice work—would dovetail with the conference's content, Matthew Vines scrapped the Friday evening schedule a week before the conference and secured one hundred discounted tickets for the Friday evening performance.

Early the next morning, following the worship session that began each day of the conference, Brian shared his reflections with the audience. Brian is a white man in his late forties or early fifties who at one point identified as evangelical but at the time of the conference was attending a large United Methodist Church in a southern Kansas City suburb. Brian had been married to and raised children with a woman, and he had only recently come out after spending years trying "to pray the gay away." An intense embodied experience was a turning point for him; Brian described it, through tears, for the audience: "I spent years trying, as they say, to pray the gay away, but nothing worked. And I became so angry with God and almost left. I just kept asking him, 'How can I be gay and be your follower?' But then I had this very intense experience. I felt Jesus come up behind me and kiss me on the back of my neck. He smiled and said to me, 'You are my gay son.'"

Despite this experience, Brian told the audience that he was still "asking [himself] if it's okay to be gay and Christian." This is why the play's portrayal of Bayard Rustin wrestling with God resonated so strongly with him. Toward the end of the play there is a scene where Rustin is alone on stage in a moment of crisis and self-doubt. Rustin found himself increasingly marginalized in the civil rights movement, his sexuality seen as too great of a liability by some of its leaders, and on the eve of the 1963 March on Washington, which he was hard at work organizing, Senator Strom Thurmond in an effort to discredit the march accused Rustin of being a Communist and homosexual on the Senate floor.[74] In a scene reminiscent of the biblical book of Job, Rustin accuses God of being silent in the face of injustice.[75] It was this scene in particular that resonated with Brian:

> After the play last night, when we were asked what part stood out to us, I thought it was the part where Bayard screamed at God. This is the way I felt and continue to feel. But in the end, after Bayard yelled at God, he submitted himself to God. And this was comforting to me. It's as if God was saying to me at that moment, "I know how you're suffering and what the church has done to you." But I'm terrified that if I ever confronted God in the same way, he would reject me. And even though I can still hear Jesus saying, "You are my gay son," I'm still not sure if it's okay, and I'm wondering if other people here feel the same way.

Purity and Pollution

As the previous reconciliation narratives illustrate, sexuality and spirituality are often tightly interwoven in this community, where what it means to be a gay Christian is a matter of concern. People would often articulate and interpret their sexuality using language and frameworks drawn from their faith experience and, at the same time, describe how their identity as a Christian was shaped by their sexual identity.

Sexuality was often characterized as a natural and powerful force that is social, spiritual, and consequential. It was common for participants at TRP conferences to spiritualize and accept as natural and given "the dividing up of all sexual acts—indeed all persons—under the 'opposite' categories of 'homo' and 'hetero,'" as Eve Kosofsky Sedgwick describes the construction of sexuality in our present historical moment.[76] This is not to say that this binary understanding of human sexuality was never called into question by some of the people I met. As with debates in the broader lesbian and gay community, participants at TRP conferences sometimes disagreed over what has been characterized as "essentialist" versus social constructionist views of human sexuality.

Those I met emphasized the shared experience of humans as sexual beings. Activists and participants at TRP conferences would often emphasize the naturalness and "goodness" of human sexuality. As my interlocutors might say, they view not only their sexuality but also human sexuality more generally "as a gift"; I came to understand that this expression meant that sexuality is a built-in feature of human nature that enables an individual to reflect the divine. When God declares in Genesis that "it is not good that the man should be alone," the passage attests to, some in this community might argue, humanity's innate need for intimacy and sexual relationships.[77] As such, much of the discourse in these spaces functions as a naturalizing discourse for not only the hetero-homo binary but also for the type of sex essentialism described by Gayle Rubin or "the idea that sex is a natural force that exists prior to social life and shapes institutions."[78]

If sexuality is a gift, it is also sacred. Sexual desire was characterized as something that transcends the personal, and it can have varied positive or negative social and spiritual consequences. "Don't say with your body what you're not willing to say with your life" was one such cautionary tale about the potency of sex that I heard expressed. At the same time, sexual desire is not necessarily something to be repressed but rather managed and disciplined toward particular ends. Individuals often spoke of sexuality as something that requires diligent protection and care, as if it were a substance that could be spoiled and depleted if not carefully attended to, and human will as the valve that could direct the flow in different directions.[79]

In this way sexuality in this community resembles how sexuality is constructed more generally in evangelicalism. Amy DeRogatis writes, for example, that "evangelicals contend that sexual desire was created by God, affirmed in Scripture, and is an integral part of heterosexual marriage. Sexual pleasure serves to unite married couples, it produces offspring, and it can strengthen the mystical relationship with the divine."[80] Therefore, activists and participants at TRP conferences would often affirm this existing framework while attempting to fold in same-sex sexual desire and pleasure.

The sacredness of sex became particularly clear in conversations on the nature and purpose of marriage, or the "covenantal relationship" as it was often called, such as with Vines's arguments for marriage equality. In *God and the Gay Christian*, for example, Vines similarly characterizes sexuality as a natural, good, and essential feature of human nature: "Creation is good. The body is good. Sexuality, as a core part of the body, is also good."[81] In a chapter titled "What the Image of God Teaches Us about Gay Christians," Vines further pushes the significance of humans being sexual beings. While he makes larger claims about the "essence of marriage" being about "mutual self-giving" and a reflection of the "relational" nature of a Trinitarian God, he also frames marriage as a site for managing desire and the unruly sexual body.[82]

If sexual desire as a natural force can be both productive and destructive, individuals can harness that force to create authentic "covenantal bonds" that reflect the divine. In these covenantal bonds, Vines argues, humans can "discipline and sanctify [their] sexual desires."[83] Vines goes on to suggest that the "animalistic drive for self-gratification can instead be transformed into a powerful bonding agent in the context of marriage. Through the covenantal potential of our sexuality, we can reflect the image of our relational, covenant-keeping God."[84]

Thus Vines makes a theological and Christian anthropological rather than an identity- or rights-based argument for same-sex marriage. To deny gay people access to marriage, Vines argues, denies them the ability to "sanctify" their own sexual desires and ultimately the ability to bear the image of God: "If we reject the desires of gay Christians to express their sexuality within a lifelong covenant, we separate them from our covenantal God, and we tarnish their ability to bear his image."[85] Or as he summarized it at one point during a Bible-training session at the Atlanta regional training conference, "For every other desire there is some path to sanctification, but for same-sex desire there is nothing."

One of the goals of TRP, therefore, is to facilitate change so that the same sexual ethics that apply to heterosexual Christians can be extended to lesbian and gay Christians. To be more precise, the goal is to move specifically coupled and monogamous same-sex relationships to the inner part of the evangelical charmed circle of sex, to use another one of Rubin's concepts.[86] As Moon and Tobin argue in a series of articles based on an interdisciplinary, ethnographic-based study of LGBTQ conservative Christians (including those at TRP conferences), the LGBTQ conservative Christian movement has a complicated relationship with homonormativity. On the one hand, this movement "was made possible by decades of *homonormativity*," which queer theorists have identified as a strategy among some lesbian and gay organizations of demonstrating the compatibility of homosexuality with mainstream society through conformity with the binary gendered and sexual norms and values of heterosexuality.[87] On the other hand, Moon and Tobin go on to argue, this movement also goes beyond homonormativity by working to challenge the narrative that men and women are complementary halves, a relationship that defines proper gender roles and normal sexual desire.[88]

Similarly I encountered some tension in this community over the attempt to challenge an evangelical sexual hierarchy that positions gay sex as beyond the pale while at the same time emphasizing the sanctity and sacredness of sex. To do so, some point out, misses the opportunity to rethink the sex essentialism and sex negativity that animates evangelical sexual ethics and perpetuates a culture of stigmatization, exclusion, and shame. In particular it leaves unchallenged the relationship among so-called traditional marriage, conservative sexual ethics, the regulation of women's bodies, and the production and protection of patriarchy.[89]

One of the places this tension came up at TRP conferences was in discussions of evangelical purity culture. The evangelical purity culture movement promotes the ideal of adolescent sexual purity through valorizing virginity and requiring abstinence before marriage. Purity culture is perpetuated by influential Christian abstinence organizations like True Love Waits and Silver Ring Thing; by chastity clubs, purity balls, and other rituals for pledging one's abstinence or becoming a "born-again virgin"; by a vast purity literature illustrated by books such as the 1990s best seller *I Kissed Dating Goodbye*; and by ostensibly secular efforts to promote sexual purity at the state and federal level.[90] Providing federal funding for abstinence-only education programs and restricting access to contraception are but two examples of the latter. However, given that purity culture disproportionately places the onus on young women to be sexually pure, it "reinforces," critics argue, "women's oppressed sociosexual status as the property of men."[91]

The problem of evangelical purity culture was something with which Vines and other speakers grappled during a few poignant moments at TRP conferences. Although not addressed in *God and the Gay Christian* or to any great extent at the first TRP regional training conference in Washington DC, Vines raised the issue several times during Bible-training sessions at both the Atlanta and Kansas City conferences. One such exchange took place between Vines and the evangelical ethicist David Gushee at the Atlanta conference after the talking point on same-sex marriage had been introduced. Gushee had just finished making the point that same-sex relationships meet the biblical standard of marriage as a "union of sanctifying grace." Before moving on, Vines interjected his concern with how Gushee seemed to portray sexuality as something that can be "lost," and what followed was a lengthy digression that illustrates the tension over the linkages between how sexuality is constructed in evangelicalism and the violence of purity culture. Vines also took the opportunity to critique the deficiency and dogmatism that characterizes much of evangelical discourse on sexuality:

GUSHEE: Because we are embodied creatures, when we do something with our body sexually with another person, we are saying something. We are connecting with a person in a way that matters. [The New Testament scholar James Brownson] likes to say, "Don't say with your body what you're not willing to say with your life." So it's a teaching against promiscuity or casual sex. In a sense, when we have multiple sexual partners, we leave a little part of ourselves in every relationship, and something's lost. That does not mean there's not second chances and forgiveness as we move toward covenant. We have had enough shame culture in Christianity. . . .

VINES: Can we talk about that more before moving on? . . . A lot of us probably grew up in conservative churches that basically said, "Don't have sex until you're married because God said so." And if that's the extent of what you learned, . . . then when you realized there's something the church taught you about a core aspect of your sexuality is wrong, it's very easy to say, "Well, maybe everything else they taught me about my sexuality is wrong, too." Especially when what they taught you was based in their hypercertainty biblical interpretation, and you've come to believe that their certainty was misplaced. . . . I am not interested in telling people in a directive way, "You need to do this, or else." . . . We've already had that done so often; we don't need that. . . .

With The Reformation Project, we're specifically asking churches to affirm same-sex relationships—and specifically same-sex sex—in the context that they already affirm sex for everybody else, which is the context of a marriage that is monogamous. However, there are very understandable reasons why a lot of people do not find that compelling. A lot of that has to do with . . . the way churches have talked not just about LGBT sexuality but sexuality across the board.

And so if you're in a place where you're like, "I really don't agree with that"—that's okay. You're very much welcome here and welcome to share these thoughts. . . . We don't need to be having church cultures where this is the one answer, and if you don't agree with it, you can leave. Right? . . . Can we still have gracious space in the midst of that?

One question I want to ask: I know there are a lot of concerns that people have with the way that churches talk about sexuality in general, which is that people can talk about it in ways that . . . contribute to shame. And the people who have received the brunt of that shame have been women, LGBT people, and especially women of color. So often women's bodies are talked about as though they are rightfully men's, and therefore if a woman has sex before she is married—which a vast majority of women and men will do—then she should feel shame. . . . The idea is that she should feel shame for having taken something away from her husband—a.k.a. her virginity—and to me this is very troubling. . . .

[Speaking to Gushee] Like this idea that people lose something when they have sex. I feel like I get what you're saying, but I also wonder, what does this mean for the people who have had sex against their will? Have they lost something? Because I don't think so. . . . I think that's part of the concerns people have about this sexual ethic: does this contribute to the marginalization of women? . . . When you look at it this way, it's easy to see how this is a function of patriarchy, right? And, therefore, [it] should be rejected along with patriarchy.[92]

Vines's comments reflect how some wrestle with not only the exclusionary politics of evangelical sexual ethics but also disagreements over the strategies and goals of LGBTQ Christian activism in conservative Christian spaces. Similar conversations in the contested spaces between sexual diversity and sexual regulation unfolded during my fieldwork in Bible breakouts and passing conversations. TRP too increasingly featured panel discussions and keynote presentations pushing the boundaries of how many evangelicals think about sexual identity and diversity. For example, Eliel Cruz, a bisexual Christian writer and activist, provided a primer on bisexuality at the Kansas City conference. At the Los Angeles conference in late 2016, TRP invited Lianne Simon, who is intersex and Christian, and Megan DeFranza, a theologian and author of *Sex Difference in Christian Theology*, to give a shared keynote presentation on the implications of intersexuality for conservative evangelical sexuality and theology. As such, the conferences are productive and rich spaces for challenging conversations on how to rethink evangelical identity and community through thinking about sexual variance and the experience of people with non-normative sexual identities, including the potential consequences of not interrogating evangelicalism's long-standing investment in the regulation of gender and bodies through the regulation of sexuality.

The conversations at TRP conferences and related spaces using sexuality as a site for the negotiation and production of Christian values are valuable and necessary. At the same time, they reflect a fundamental tension astutely summarized by the theologian Laurel Schneider (along with many other queer theorists and theologians). Despite the frequently necessary political work of asserting the naturalness of homosexuality—what has been called "strategic essentialism" in gay and lesbian movement demands for social justice—doing so reproduces heterosexuality itself as natural and stable. Without "disrupt[ing] the stability and natural givenness of heterosexuality as well," Schneider argues, "I am convinced that lesbian and gay liberation attempts in theology will not be able to avoid the mimesis that conditions homosexual inclusion in a heteronormative communion. They will not be able to avoid, in other words, advocating 'good' homosexuals who incidentally look and act a great deal like good heterosexuals at the expense, perhaps, of many of the rest of us."[93]

Moreover, to return to Jakobsen and Pellegrini, there are limits to debates about sexual diversity that are grounded in sex essentialism, or "born that way" arguments, in that they "do not give us strong grounds for protecting *conduct*, whether that conduct be associated with gender, race, and/or sexuality."[94] While Jakobsen and Pellegrini are seeking a foundation consistent with American ideals of pluralism and freedom that will protect sexual conduct beyond any single religious directive, or even the frameworks of love and intimacy, their critique resonates with what I found at times to be a concern with advocating for the morality of same-sex sexual desire using the same political tools that have been used to exclude those very same people in the first place. In the end what is also distinctly "conservative" about conservative gay Christian activism, in addition to a particular orientation toward Scripture, is a conservative sexual ethic that reifies sexuality as sacred, and thus far it has left a critical evaluation of sex itself still a bridge too far.

4   Transgender Figures and Trans Inclusion

On a brisk Saturday afternoon on the last day of TRP's regional training conference in Washington DC, I joined about twenty-five of the other conference attendees in an untidy and well-used music room in the sprawling undercroft of the National City Christian Church to attend a panel discussion titled "Advocating for Transgender Inclusion." The four panel discussants, all of whom were Christian and either transgender or genderqueer, were there to talk about their experiences working on transgender inclusion in Christian spaces as clergy, activists, and everyday Christians.[1] Much of the discussion centered on their faith and gender journeys, their struggles identifying as trans Christians in often inhospitable spaces, how to create more inclusive churches, and what a Christian ministry to transgender people should actually look like.

When the floor opened to questions, an audience member began, candidly, with the question, "So what's the church's problem?" Although the somewhat pointed question made the panel discussants and audience laugh, it wasn't immediately obvious what the person meant. "It just doesn't make sense," he clarified. "How does the church justify its opposition to transgender people? Like, are there passages in Scripture it can actually point to?"

It must be a jarring experience to have to parrot back words others have used to justify one's oppression or even deny one's very existence, something I thought about often during my fieldwork. Somewhat surprisingly, though, the panelists struggled to come up with examples of biblically based arguments that they'd heard from other Christians. One individual remarked that sometimes other Christians will ask them, "If you're transitioning away from what God made you, are you transitioning away from God?" Otherwise they agreed they didn't hear too many "trans clobber verses" in the same way some Christians use Bible passages—turned into acrimonious platitudes like "God made Adam and Eve, not Adam and Steve"—to justify discrimination against gay people. "The reactionary position of the church today," one of the panelists suggested, "simply isn't rational. It's about privilege. It's about a majority group leveraging its privilege over a minority group." Another of the panelists added, "It's also because of how trans people get lumped together with gay people. I honestly don't think they know these are different things." "It's also about power," another said. "When you name yourself, you take away another's ability to name you. You are attacking their power over you."

The panelists' collective witness on their struggles and experiences as transgender Christians is the inspiration for this chapter.[2] For one thing, their discussion provides insight into the contemptuous, confused, and contradictory nature of much of the Christian Right's recent rhetoric about transgender people. The announcement on June 26, 2015, of the U.S. Supreme Court's decision in *Obergefell v. Hodges*, extending the right to marry to same-sex couples, rocked the conservative evangelical world.[3] After decades of campaigning against same-sex marriage in particular and against equal rights and protections for gay Americans in general, it appeared to some commentators that the Christian Right's influence was in retreat and the culture wars were finally coming to an end. Instead transgender rights quickly emerged as the newest frontier in a seemingly rejuvenated culture war.

Conservative evangelical leaders and parachurch organizations rallied their congregations and organized resources and public influence campaigns in response to a series of contemporaneous events in the United States involving transgender people and movements for transgender protections and rights. In early 2015, for example, the Obama administration expressed support for a campaign to introduce a bill that would ban conversion therapy in the United States. Known as Leelah's Law, the proposed legislation was named after Leelah Alcorn, a seventeen-year-old transgender girl whose tragic suicide gained national attention in late 2014.[4] Around the same time in another event that attracted much national attention and conservative evangelical scorn, Caitlyn Jenner came out as a transgender woman in April 2015. In May 2016 the Obama administration issued Title IX federal protections for transgender students.[5]

Then there are the so-called bathroom bills, legislation requiring individuals to use restrooms and changing facilities corresponding with the sex identified on their birth certificates.[6] In March 2016 the North Carolina legislature passed the controversial Public Facilities Privacy and Security Act, better known as House Bill 2 or HB2, becoming the first state to pass such legislation. The original language of the bill reveals that a moral panic over transgender rights was used as cover to rescind local LGBTQ protections and to advance conservative economic interests. For example, HB2 included language that reversed a Charlotte ordinance that extended nondiscrimination protections to LGBTQ people and restricted local governments from setting minimum wage requirements in addition to implementing other workplace protections.[7]

With these and other recent events and controversies, the word "transgender" began entering the lexicon of many evangelicals for the first time. Transgender people and rights quickly became a topic of heightened discussion from pulpits, in posts on evangelical blogs and articles in online magazines, in books from evangelical publishing houses, and at evangelical conferences. Given the self-assuredness with which some conservative evangelical commentators speak on the subject and the majority opposition to transgender people and rights among conservative evangelicals, it is easy to assume that Christian tradition and Scripture obviously justify and sanction Christian opposition.[8]

However, there's no Christian tradition regarding transgender and gender-nonconforming people. Even if the Bible-based arguments used to justify the exclusion of and discrimination against gay people don't hold up under scrutiny, they at least have the appearance of being "rational" and "obvious" and "settled" for many conservative Christians, if only through, Mark Jordan has noted, their repetition.[9] By contrast, there are no ready-to-hand verses like Leviticus 18:22 or traditions like the sodomitical tradition to declare transgender people as sinful in the way conservative Christians have done with lesbians and gay men. Nevertheless, as another transgender Christian sitting in the audience at the panel pointed out, an effort is now under way by some conservative evangelicals to solidify a biblical argument.

In what follows I map some of the broad contours of this emergence and consolidation of "transgender" as an object of discourse and rhetorical figure in recent conservative evangelical discourse. Similar to David Valentine's interests in *Imagining Transgender*, my goal is not to evaluate the theological or intellectual worth of specific claims or arguments but to call attention to some of the rhetorical strategies at play and the effects they produce.[10] Much like John Boswell, Dale Martin, Mark Jordan, and others have argued concerning Christian discourse on homosexuality, I suggest that this recent discourse on transgender figures represents the active construction of Christian Scripture and tradition as incompatible with trans people as some conservative evangelical thinkers and leaders return to the text and tradition to justify and rationalize their opposition to transgender rights. Thus I show in the first half of the chapter how some conservative evangelical thinkers and leaders draw on, while folding transgender people into, the established rhetorical toolkit of the Christian Right's antigay activism of the 1970s through today for their emerging antitransgender activism. I document how this transgender rhetorical figure is put to work not only in the construction and maintenance of the gender binary but also in struggles over democratic citizenship, the nation-state, and cultural hegemony.

At the same time, the Washington DC panel provides a window into how some transgender and ally Christians are attempting to disrupt the exclusionary politics of conservative evangelicalism, a politics that provides cover for many evangelicals to openly question whether trans people even exist; even more, the panel exposes some of the politics and potential shortcomings of this corner of LGBTQ Christian activism itself. I turn to these twin issues in the last half of the chapter using a few episodes from my fieldwork, beginning with people's internal struggles and conversations on how to make LGBTQ Christian activism in conservative Christian spaces genuinely inclusive and representative. I close the chapter with a discussion of the rhetorical strategies used by some in this community to create space and compassion for transgender and gender-nonconforming people in conservative Christian spaces.

The Cisgender Bible

Conservative evangelical discourse on trans figures goes back at least to the early 1980s with two books, to which I will return, by the conservative Christian ethicist Oliver O'Donovan.[11] Throughout the 1990s and early 2000s talk about transgender and transsexual people made periodic appearances in conservative Christian magazines and newspapers like *Christianity Today* and the *Christian Post*. O'Donovan and a few other writers excepted, when the categories "transvestism," "transsexual," or "transgender" appeared in conservative evangelical writings during this time, they usually came in the context of anxieties about homosexuality and the so-called gay agenda, with transgender identity not discussed on its own in any substantive or sustained way. Only later would transgender people, often referred to as "transgenders" or "the transgendered" in this discourse, begin to be isolated as a distinct matter of concern as evangelical writers and thinkers began, in response to broader changes in society, to talk more explicitly about "transgenderism" or "the transgender problem" or "the transgender movement." Nevertheless, as I will discuss, there continues to be much conflation of categories in this discourse. There is now a growing body of monographs authored by conservative Christian thinkers that focuses on transgender identity either in whole or in part.[12] However, online magazines, blogs, news aggregate websites, and other online media platforms popular among conservative evangelicals are still the most vibrant forums for this recent talk about transgender people.

Some of these commentators don't attempt to ground their objections to transgender people or protections in Christian Scripture or tradition; instead they often use extreme examples to portray all trans people as monsters and threats to the social order. For example, in an article written for *The Federalist*, a conservative- and libertarian-leaning online political magazine, an evangelical pastor named Mark Narankevicius Jr. used the story of Rodrigo Alves, a British man who has undergone more than fifty plastic surgeries (perhaps as the result of body dysmorphic disorder), to argue that transgender people who choose to undergo sex reassignment surgery suffer a similar "mental disorder."[13] Another writer, Heather Clark, in an article published on the online conservative Christian news aggregate website the *Christian News Network*, latched onto a story about Vinny Ohh, a California man using plastic surgery in order to become a "genderless alien," suggesting that Ohh's story represents what happens when individuals transition from what God made them.[14] Michael Brown, a prolific opponent of LGBTQ Christians and self-described Messianic Jew, in an article published on the conservative Christian website *Charisma News*, linked together stories about Caitlyn Jenner, the debates surrounding Rachel Dolezal and the possibility of a transracial identity, a woman who used drain cleaner to blind herself, a man who identifies as a furry, and a trans woman who lives her life as a six-year-old girl. The common thread, Brown suggests, is that these individuals "have some deep psychological issues, and rather than celebrating them we should pray for them."[15]

Among conservative evangelical writers who do attempt to ground their arguments in Christian Scripture or tradition, a few other patterns emerge. Even in cases where writers do try to parse what's explicitly sinful about transgender identity, they often conflate gender identity with homosexuality or gay sex. As such, some writers will use the categories "transgender," "homosexual," "gay," and even "LGBT" almost interchangeably. One of the immediate reasons for this conflation is that writers on the Christian Right have seized the coalitional acronym LGBT in their efforts to delegitimize any politics they find threatening.[16] As such, transgender people and issues specific to gender identity are often swept up as emblematic of the broader "LGBT activist agenda."

Another reason for this conflation, as other scholars of the Christian Right's antigay rhetoric have pointed out, is that Christians who view homosexuality as sinful often see the sin as a failure in gender.[17] This is why—to return to a point I made in the previous chapter—it's still common for ex-gay ministries to prescribe stereotypical gender performances for participants to learn how to perform proper heterosexuality. In this line of reasoning if homosexuality is a pathological sexuality that can be traced to gender trouble, then transgender people must also be sexually deviant. Some conservative evangelical commentators will, therefore, use the very same Bible verses in their condemnation of transgender people as have been used for gay people with little or no qualification, not going much further than indiscriminately adding transgender people to the established antigay tradition of the Christian Right.

An opinion editorial by Bethany Blankley on the *Charisma News* website illustrates these conflations and strategies.[18] Blankley is a self-identified conservative evangelical writer and political pundit who has contributed to the *Washington Times*, Breitbart News, and Fox News

Radio. Blankley published the editorial two weeks after President Barack Obama's comments at a town hall in Indiana on June 1, 2016, where he invoked Scripture and Christian morality while answering an audience member's question about his administration's decision to issue guidelines protecting transgender students from discrimination. "The question is," Obama explained, "how do we just make sure that . . . children are treated with kindness? That's all. And you know, my reading of Scripture tells me that [the] golden rule is pretty high up there in terms of my Christian belief."[19] Blankley attempts to dismiss and delegitimize this position by claiming that proper Christian faith and the "transgender agenda" are incompatible, accusing Obama of "misusing the Bible" in his support of transgender protections.

However, rather than explicitly addressing what Christian Scripture may or may not say about transgender identity and rights, Blankley inserts the word "transgender" into what could otherwise be a conservative evangelical editorial on homosexuality. To set up her evidence, Blankley begins by saying, "One need only look to the numerous verses and texts within the context of the entire Bible, both the Old and New Testaments, to discover that there are no transgendered people in the Bible and this type of sexual confusion/perversion is specifically identified, defined and prohibited."[20] Not only does this confuse transgender identity with a "type of sexual confusion/perversion," the first verse Blankley quotes in support conflates transgender identity with laws regulating clothing in the Deuteronomic code: "A woman must not wear man's clothing, nor is a man to put on a woman's clothing. For all that do so are abominations to the Lord your God."[21]

To put aside for a moment the other issues with using this verse in the context of transgender identity, this prohibition has a highly specific cultural and social context. Part of the pastiche of written and oral traditions that were collected in the Book of Deuteronomy, the prohibition most likely emerged during a period of national and religious reform following an Assyrian conquest and the Babylonian Exile during the seventh and sixth centuries BCE. Bible scholars mostly agree the prohibition's intent was either to regulate women as property or to distinguish Jewish temple practices from pagan cults, or it was in keeping with other rules in the Torah preventing the mixing of categories.[22]

Moreover, in their use of this verse, Blankley and other commentators conflate transgender and genderqueer identities with clothing norms and tastes. Clothing norms for men and women are of course highly variable across cultures and time. Men in Bible times, for example, wore clothes we might now call skirts (*kethoneth*), shawls (*simlah*), and decorative tassels (*zizit*).

Conservative Bible commentaries published in the last half of the twentieth century variously have acknowledged one of these possibilities or have described the verse as a prohibition against "transvestism" and, as at least one included, "homosexuality."[23] Before being repurposed for transgender people, the same verse has a different history of being used to police women's bodies, such as prohibiting women from wearing pants, in some conservative Christian traditions. Nevertheless, the verse is now increasingly read through an antitransgender lens. And if the word "transgender" ever enters an English translation of the Christian Bible, much like the word "homosexual" did in 1946, it will most likely be in this verse.

The rest of Blankley's editorial indiscriminately folds transgender people into the Christian Right's established antigay narrative using the same well-worn passages, including Leviticus 18:22 and Romans 1:24–27, used to justify discrimination against lesbians and gay men. Immediately following Deuteronomy 22:5, which she presents without further comment or explanation, Blankley asserts: "Not to mention the numerous verses that address homosexuality and what is described as sexually immoral and deviant behavior." After citing Leviticus 18:22, Blankley sets up the passage from Romans 1 by saying, "Here's a list of what the Bible says about homosexuals, lesbians, transgenders and those who identify as one of the LGBTQ categories." She also suggests "there are serious consequences to sexually deviant behavior, which affect an entire community." In the last lines of the editorial, therefore, Blankley turns to biblical stories of divine wrath that have come to be read as the consequences of cities and nations tolerating homosexuality—such as the story of Sodom and Gomorrah—to drive home the stakes of the Obama administration's "advancing the transgender agenda": similar "abominations . . . were so wicked that God brought a flood to destroy the entire Earth in Genesis and later turned an entire city of people into a pile of salt."[24]

In this way Blankley suggests that tolerance of "transgender behavior" as a sexually deviant behavior has implications for the existential health of the nation-state. Crudely put, for Blankley the transgender figure emerges as a cross-dressing sexual predator, a characterization exploited by conservative evangelical commentators in recent controversies over so-called bathroom bills. In fact, in the opening paragraphs of the editorial, Blankley repeats an unsupported claim that legislation allowing transgender people to use bathrooms corresponding with their gender identity subjects children to "predators" and has already led to "numerous acts of violence."[25]

Recent books by conservative evangelical authors dedicated in whole or in part to "transgender issues" have some of the same characteristics described previously, but they also tend to rely on and perpetuate the notion of gender complementarianism.[26] In the evangelical context the theory of gender complementarianism suggests that there are essential—biological, psychological, spiritual—but complementary differences between women and men that provide the basis not only for proper gender roles but also normal sexual desire. The doctrine, based on a selective reading of Scripture, maintains that women and men have distinct roles in public and private life, that women are to submit to men, and that men are to be the spiritual and civic leaders. Contemporary theories of gender complementarianism took shape as a response to feminist critiques of patriarchy in evangelicalism, in particular by evangelical feminists, in an effort to clothe male dominance and female subordination in more egalitarian language.[27] It was further refined in, and continues to provide much of the intellectual grist for, the Christian Right's antigay rhetoric.

This belief in the essential and complementary differences between men and women inform, for example, Oliver O'Donovan's *Transsexualism and Christian Marriage* and *Begotten or Made?* In both books, which are perhaps the first examples of a Christian author's discussion of the trans body at some length, O'Donovan considers the ethical and theological implications of advances in modern medicine, such as artificial insemination and sex reassignment surgery, for traditional Christian marriage. In *Begotten or Made?* for example, O'Donovan relies on gender complementarianism throughout, including in a passage that uses language resembling the Aristotelian concept of formal cause: "When God made mankind male and female, to exist alongside each other and for each other, he gave a form that human sexuality should take and a good to which it should aspire."[28]

As part of this God-given form, O'Donovan insists that the body, including gender, has a metaphysical integrity that makes altering the body through procedures like sex reassignment surgery beyond the bounds of God's intended use for the body. "It is not humane," O'Donovan concludes, "for us to attempt to alienate ourselves from ourselves and become other than ourselves."[29] For O'Donovan sex reassignment surgery is inhumane and perhaps inhuman in that it involves an "othering" of the essential self. Despite O'Donovan's arguments being limited to what he calls "transsexual surgery" and his never seriously considering gender expression, gender identity, or gender-variant people more generally, they nevertheless continue to be influential in shaping current conservative evangelical discourse on the transgender rhetorical figure.[30]

Published in 2015, R. Albert Mohler Jr.'s *We Cannot Be Silent* is an example of the recent emergence of conservative evangelical discourse on transgender figures using gender complementarianism as a framework. Mohler is a member of the Council on Biblical Manhood and Womanhood, the current president of the Southern Baptist Theological Seminary, a former member of the board of directors for Focus on the Family, and an influential and prolific conservative evangelical writer. Like many of his other books, *We Cannot Be Silent* is a lament over what Mohler sees as America's moral decline away from traditional Christian values, especially regarding sexuality, gender, and marriage. Mohler attributes this moral decline to several things—the sexual revolution, radical academics, postmodernism—but especially secularism.

The specter of the secular looms large in the book. On several occasions Mohler references sociological scholarship on the secularization thesis and Charles Taylor's *A Secular Age* to express his concerns over religious pluralism and the declining influence of conservative evangelicalism in the public sphere. In his view marriage equality and the "transgender movement"—and the celebration of what he calls "erotic liberty" more generally—at the expense of religious liberty are striking symptoms of America's moral decline.[31] Mohler seems unconcerned with hedging his arguments in the ideals of religious tolerance and the disestablishment of religion in the United States. In other words, to borrow language from Janet Jakobsen and Ann Pellegrini, Mohler is unapologetic in his belief that to be traditionally American means to be Christian in a certain way.[32]

Chapter 5 of *We Cannot Be Silent* is a stand-alone chapter on what Mohler refers to as "The Transgender Revolution." According to Mohler, the stakes could not be much higher: "The transgender revolution, even more than the movement for gay liberation, undermines the most basic structures of society."[33] He frets that "we observe an entire civilization collapsing."[34] For the most part Mohler returns to the toolkit of the Christian Right's antigay rhetoric to make his case. Earlier in the book Mohler rehearses the narrative, encapsulated in works like the 1992 film *The Gay Agenda*, that traditional Christian America is under siege by a shadowy and powerful "cadre of homosexual activists" who came "together to hatch a revolution that would one day transform every dimension of American public life."[35] In Mohler's reconstruction of the various lesbian and gay rights movements, the homosexual movement was highly organized and strategic, receiving its "marching orders" from books like Kirk and Madsen's *After the Ball*.[36]

When Mohler gets to his chapter on "The Transgender Revolution," he adds trans people to the narrative while also drawing on other familiar rhetorical strategies. He emphasizes the threat posed to impressionable youth, suggesting that children are being indoctrinated in public schools into a transgender worldview through sex education programs that include sensitivity training and information on sexual orientation and gender identity.[37] In another move drawn from the antigay playbook, Mohler associates transgender people with the demonic.[38] With the transgender revolution, Mohler writes, "We are confronting principalities and powers no previous Christian generation has encountered. . . . The fact that we fight not against flesh and blood, but against principalities and powers, is perhaps never more poignant and important than in the midst of a struggle."[39]

The language of "principalities and powers" would resonate with an audience familiar with the evangelical worldview, calling to mind a grand spiritual battle against powerful demons trying to trap a Christian nation in spiritual bondage.[40] As Mohler suggests in the next sentence, with a rhetorical wink, "The transgender movement reminds us whom we are really fighting."[41] The transgender revolution, according to Mohler, is yet another symptom of the spiritual pathology unleashed by secularism and the perceived decline of conservative Christian cultural hegemony; the sexual revolution, divorce rates, feminism, gay and transgender rights—all are teleological manifestations of dark forces waging war on Bible-believing Christians.

Mohler roots his specific arguments against transgender people in theories of gender complementarianism and sex essentialism as revealed through, in his view, natural law, Scripture, and common sense. He asserts that the creation myths found in Genesis demonstrate "our embodiment as male or female as essential to our self-identity."[42] Like O'Donovan, Mohler talks about the fundamental integrity and sanctity of the body. He repurposes Psalm 139:13, a verse popular among pro-life advocates, to suggest that the integrity and deterministic nature of body morphology are integral to God's creation.[43] Similarly he uses the birth narratives of Luke 1 as evidence of sex essentialism, suggesting that because the sex of both Jesus and John the Baptist were prophesied before their births, it proves "their biological sex was important before they were even born."[44]

Even though Mohler acknowledges that ideas about gender can be shaped by culture—though, in his view, ultimately insignificantly—he rejects the distinction between sex as a biological category and gender as a social construct as a "postmodern," and therefore illegitimate, "development."[45] He also rejects the social construction of sex, cruelly dismissing people born with sex characteristics that do not fit into the gender binary, often grouped as intersex, as a "[reminder] that the consequences of Adam's sin even impact our genetic chromosomal structure."[46] Instead Mohler maintains that one's gender identity, and by extension normal sexual desire, are inextricably linked to body morphology, the brute facts of genitalia, brain structure, and chromosomes. In this way, according to Mohler, gender-affirmation medical procedures are not only a form of body "mutilation" but also an "act of defiance against the Creator's purpose" for the body.[47] Finally, Mohler asserts a causal and deterministic relationship between this body morphology and consciousness.

In an apparent inversion of long-standing Christian theories about the primacy of the will over a corrupt and unruly body, Mohler suggests that in situations where there is a "disconnect between self-consciousness and embodiment," individuals must make their self-perception conform to the body.[48]

Throughout the chapter Mohler collapses a range of gender identities and expressions into the single transgender rhetorical figure. It represents a case wherein, similar to what Valentine argues, the transgender rhetorical figure is used to "not only *explain* non-normative genders but also *produce the effect* of those differences by effacing others."[49] For example, Mohler often conflates transgender, genderqueer, and transsexual people, such as when he claims that the primary threat posed by the "transgender movement" is the "[discarding of] the 'binary system of gender' as part of the goodness of God's created order."[50] Although the category of transgender does potentially trouble the sex/gender binary, Mohler fails to acknowledge that while not all self-identified transgender people situate themselves within the gender binary, in many cases transgender identity often works within the gender binary rather than discarding it.[51] In other places Mohler conflates transsexual and transgender categories and seems to assume most of the people he groups together as transgender desire and seek gender-affirmation medical procedures.

These conflations function to stabilize the gender binary by eliding variation and difference and constructing gender-variant people as outside the gender binary. They also allow Mohler to oppose transgender people as a threat to the gender binary without ever having to define what he means by "maleness" and "femaleness." It allows him to never seriously interrogate the complicated and enigmatic relationship among biology, gender identity, gender expression, and culturally bound notions of what it means to be a woman or a man. Instead Mohler uses the transgender rhetorical figure to achieve his broader aim. It is only in the context of so-called traditional Christian marriage—and by implication, traditional gender roles and hierarchy in public and private life—that gender can achieve its fullest definition, expression, and potential.

In the end Mohler's reading of Christian Scripture and tradition regarding gender and marriage is highly selective. For example, he suggests that the paragon of marriage in Scripture is lifelong monogamy when the assumption of the Old Testament is polygamy and the advice of the New Testament is singleness or celibacy. He also ignores the variability of gender in Scripture, some of which I discuss in the following section.

Politics of Trans Inclusion

TRP's regional training conference in Kansas City was just four months away. It was a blistering-hot late afternoon in mid-July 2015. I had made the twenty-minute drive from my house near downtown Kansas City to the suburbs and rolling hills of western Shawnee, Kansas, to attend one of the several meetings of the programming subcommittee. The subcommittee's job was to brainstorm and organize the Bible training, panel topics and speakers, keynote presentations, worship, and other content for the conference.

I happened to pull into the long horseshoe drive winding down to Mary's home, one of the subcommittee members, just after Peter and Chelsea, who drove together. Mary greeted us at the door with a plate of freshly baked chocolate chip cookies, offered us glasses of milk, and invited us in. Peter quickly got to work setting up a Google Hangouts connection for a final member, John, who was joining us remotely. The four of us chatted about a range of topics to fill the time before the meeting began: Royals baseball; a local pastor who, Mary and Chelsea were excited to hear, had agreed to speak at the conference; how the global reach of the United Methodist Church shapes interdenominational politics regarding LGBTQ inclusion.

After Peter resolved a few technical issues, John joined our discussion from a television screen in Mary's living room by asking if we had heard the news about Julie Rodgers. Rodgers, who described herself at the time as an openly gay but celibate Christian, had recently resigned from a ministry position at Wheaton College after being pressured by the administration to not speak publicly about her changing views on the morality of same-sex sex and marriage.[52] "Did she go from Side B to Side A?" Peter asked excitedly. "Yeah, she went affirming," John replied. "She made an announcement about it earlier today." John continued, joking, "I'm actually a little sad she changed her mind. I have very few good friends who are Side B. But, in all honesty, it's a good thing that she's now affirming, especially because conservatives were using her to argue that celibacy is a valid option for all gay Christians."

The discussion soon turned to conference planning. Of the range of topics that came up during the meeting, which ended up running late into the evening, two stood out to me in particular. The first was how to make the Bible content more accessible and engaging. Based on feedback from previous conferences, some attendees suggested that there was too much information being presented during the multi-hour Bible-training sessions to be effective. The other primary focus was diversity and inclusion, a desire to ensure that the conference speakers and message were as diverse and representative as possible. These two issues came to a head late in the evening.

Our discussion had returned to the instruction of the talking points, and Chelsea, a transgender woman who had joined the steering committee two months earlier, told us about the first time she saw them. A month before, Chelsea, along with me and a couple of other members of the steering committee, had worked an informational table at Kansas City PrideFest to promote the upcoming conference. The table was flanked by two tall pull-up banners displaying a version of the ten talking points at the heart of TRP's Bible-training content, among them the following: "Condemning same-sex relationships is harmful to LGBT people"; "Sexual orientation is a new concept"; "Paul condemns same-sex lust, not love"; "Marriage is about commitment."[53] "The first time I saw the talking points at Pride," Chelsea told us, "I didn't see myself there. I love the talking points and think they're really important, but I didn't see how they speak to the issues transgender people face in the church."

Chelsea's comments that evening called attention to an important aspect and shortcoming of some LGBTQ activism in conservative Christian contexts. While TRP's stated mission is to transform conservative Christian teaching concerning *both* sexual orientation and gender identity, often using the inclusive language of "LGBTQ Christians" to describe the organization's focus and participation, the talking points reflect the interests of primarily cisgender gay people and committed, monogamous gay couples. At the same time that transgender and gender-nonconforming people encounter growing politicization and misrepresentation in conservative evangelicalism, there are also issues of visibility and representation even in spaces that are thought to be inclusive and welcoming, including at times LGBTQ Christian organizations like TRP.

A couple of the speakers on the "Advocating for Transgender Inclusion" panel in Washington DC, introduced at the beginning of this chapter, made similar observations about the lack of content specific to transgender people or gender identity at the conference. Chris Paige, the panel's moderator, talked about how they had raised this issue with Matthew Vines and had been working with him and other organizers on how to live up to TRP's mission of transforming evangelical teaching concerning gender identity in addition to sexual orientation.[54] Aside from the panel and the opening evening keynote presentation, which was delivered by a transgender Christian but not about trans identity or gender issues, there was no substantive discussion of gender identity or the issues that transgender people face.

While on the topic, Paige reflected further on being a trans person in affirming spaces. "LGBT is not a safe word for me," Paige told us. Paige, who is white and identifies as otherwise, nonbinary, or genderqueer, was referring not only to TRP's use of "LGBTQ Christian" but also the careless use of the acronym in society more generally. For some the acronym registers as progressive and inclusive; for others it's disingenuous and potentially dangerous. While it's a useful tool in coalitional politics, Paige worried that the acronym masked the distinctive experiences, politics, and needs of trans people in churches and society. Paige also called attention to the hypocrisy of churches that claim to be inclusive, welcoming, or affirming but are so in name only. "If you don't know anything about transgender identities or issues, if you don't have services dedicated to these issues, then don't say 'LGBT,'" Paige said. "The problem is that the acronym takes on a life of its own. Instead, we should be naming these issues. And people in the church have a responsibility to educate themselves."

In other words Paige and the other panelists were calling attention to how the language of "affirming" and "welcoming" can perform an institutional function similar to what Sara Ahmed argues regarding the language of "diversity." As commitments to diversity in institutional life are often "non-performative" in that they "do not do what they say," commitments to "affirming" and "welcoming" are sometimes little more than symbolic acts.[55] The language of affirming is sometimes used as cover for not addressing the institutional and theological habits that perpetuate exclusion in the first place. Likewise, while Paige and the other panelists were concerned with the careless and sometimes disingenuous use of LGBTQ as an umbrella term, the general critique was that if TRP and other advocates are sincere in their efforts to make evangelicalism truly inclusive, then they need to dig deeper than issues of sexuality and marriage equality.

These same concerns came up elsewhere during my fieldwork for related reasons. The day before at the Washington DC conference, for example, Bishop Vicky Gene Robinson also cautioned those working for LGBTQ social justice in Christian contexts not to have too narrow a focus. Robinson, who in 2003 became the first openly gay man in a relationship to be elected bishop in the Episcopal Church, was moderating a panel called "Advocating for Inclusion as a Pastor," with Amy Butler, Danny Cortez, Frank Schaefer, and Ken Wilson as guest speakers. When the floor opened to questions, in the audience a middle-aged white man of about forty asked the panel members what they thought would be the next controversy "after the church moves past the LGBT issue." Robinson responded resolutely, "We need to be careful about being too glib when talking about the LGBT issue almost being won."

Robinson perhaps had in mind the keynote presentation from the night before, when the speaker had triumphantly stated that wins in marriage equality and the growing acceptance of gay women and men, even in conservative Christian churches, were evidence that "the culture war is coming to an end."[56] While some churches and denominations, Robinson argued, have perhaps become more accepting of some gay people, they still fall short of challenging or reassessing their notions of gender and sexuality. "Transgender people," he argued, "pose a radical space to explore gender and sexuality in ways that many Christians have not yet begun to discover." Even more, Robinson continued, growing acceptance of gay people still leaves unaddressed the issues of violence and poverty that plague queer communities of color. "We need to be clear about who we're talking about here and who really needs help.

I'm not talking about affluent white gays whose biggest trauma is finding a brunch place. I'm talking about the queer woman of color with three kids who have no money and nothing to eat." Gay Christians in particular, Robinson went on, have an obligation to recognize that gay inclusion and gay marriage "isn't *it*."

The issues of marriage equality and the politics of representation came up for different but related reasons at the same programming subcommittee meeting described at the beginning of this section. The meeting took place just weeks after the *Obergefell v. Hodges* decision. Peter expressed concern that *Obergefell* would lead Christians who support LGBTQ social justice to think the work was done. "We have to find a way to address the gay marriage ruling at the conference," he said. "I see this happening all the time: people are already sick of hearing about this issue, and they shut down when you bring it up. And now I'm worried they'll be even more reluctant to talk about it because they think the fight is over. But there are still people sitting in churches all over the world being told that God hates who they are."

Mary pressed the issue further. In response to the *Obergefell* decision, Kansas governor Sam Brownback issued an executive order on July 7, 2015, that the administration presented as protecting the religious freedom of clergy and religious organizations who oppose same-sex marriage based on "sincerely and deeply held beliefs." The order prevents the state from withholding state aid or resources or otherwise penalizing religious organizations that discriminate against same-sex couples.[57] Beyond the fact that TRP conferences were too narrowly focused on issues of gay inclusion and marriage equality, Mary also thought they needed to be more overtly political. "We're in Kansas," Mary insisted. "We can't hold this conference in Kansas and not somehow deal with our governor."[58]

As a young and small organization, TRP was extremely receptive and responsive to internal criticism and pressure to create an organization and messages that were representative and inclusive. At the same time, activists and other participants working with TRP faced a dilemma like other, more mainstream, lesbian and gay organizations. As critics have often pointed out, national lesbian and gay organizations, in an effort to reach a bigger constituency, tend to focus most of their efforts on issues such as marriage equality that concern white, middle-class, cisgender gay men and women.[59] However, such a focus is often at the expense of the issues and interests of other gender, sexual, or racial minorities.

Similarly TRP activists and others at TRP conferences often wrestled with how to construct a message that could reach a mainstream evangelical audience without being rejected either as too "liberal" or too "queer." Even more, though, TRP activists wrestled with internal assumptions about what was at stake in the "LGBTQ Christian movement." Or, as Robinson had pointed out, they wrestled with how to build a movement for LGBTQ inclusion and equality in conservative Christian spaces that recognizes that gay inclusion and gay marriage aren't it.

The conversations on what is meant by an LGBTQ Christian movement and who gets to decide positively influenced TRP's approach to the Bible-training conferences over the year of my fieldwork. As the issues of race and privilege came more to the fore—a topic I discuss in the next chapter—conference organizers placed more emphasis on being trans-inclusive in the organization and content of the Atlanta and Kansas City conferences. This work primarily included incorporating more opportunities to address basic misconceptions, misrepresentations, and ignorance among evangelicals about transgender people and gender identity.

At a conference planning meeting in late September 2015, one of the members of the steering committee urged the other organizers to request that speakers and worship leaders use trans-inclusive language at the upcoming conference, such as using gender-neutral language during worship or presentations. Halfway through the Kansas City conference, Matthew Vines paused at the end of a Bible-training session to mention that several people had approached him that day, in person and on Twitter, to talk about using inclusive language at the conference. He said he was working with the worship team to make the song selection more inclusive going forward. TRP also invited transgender women of color as keynote speakers to talk specifically about their lives and experiences in Christian communities and society more generally. Thus Nicole Garcia opened the Kansas City conference by urging those present to center the lives and experiences of transgender women of color in their conversations on what it means to be Christian, including their responsibilities as citizens and members of Christian communities.

At the same time, to challenge conservative evangelical teaching regarding sexual orientation and sexually active gay couples remained the primary focus of the Bible-training sessions and talking points at the conferences. The fifth talking point is the one exception; it argues that the moral trajectory of Scripture tends toward greater inclusivity of women and people with non-normative sexual and gender identities. The talking point was used at all three conferences I attended to introduce a short discussion with a transgender guest speaker on how the talking point might apply to trans issues. Even so, in that the conferences were organized around the talking points—from the training sessions in the mornings to the breakouts to rehearse the talking points in the afternoons—an examination of gender itself and the issues specific to transgender and gender-nonconforming people continued to play a lesser role.

Ministry, Evangelism, Witness

I had the opportunity to talk in person with only four transgender Christians during my fieldwork, and only one of these interactions was more than a brief introduction and conversation. My other in-person engagement with transgender Christians, whether as panel discussants or keynote speakers, was at TRP conferences. Despite these limited interactions, I still think it's worthwhile to summarize a few of the themes that emerged regarding how transgender and genderqueer Christians negotiate identity and politics and seek to create space and compassion in Christian communities for trans people.

Like the other activism I encountered during my fieldwork, recourse to Scripture played a central role in transgender Christian efforts to disrupt the emerging antitrans rhetoric of the Christian Right.[60] For instance, a speaker on the Washington DC panel called attention to passages in Scripture that seem to suggest that the Judeo-Christian God is genderqueer, such as in the first of the two versions of the creation myth found in the first chapters of Genesis, which implies that God contains both female and male.[61]

Other speakers at TRP conferences highlighted examples of gender-variant characters and the multiple, often contradictory, representations of masculinity and femininity throughout the Bible. As Alex McNeill, one of the speakers on the Washington DC panel, pointed out, "Despite those who try to use passages as trans clobber verses, Scripture is actually full of gender variance." Both Vivian Taylor, a white transgender woman and executive director of Integrity, USA, speaking on the same panel, and Austen Hartke, a white transgender man and creator of the YouTube series *Transgender and Christian* speaking on a panel at the Atlanta conference, pointed to the eunuch, both as a character and rhetorical device, as but one example of Scripture's complicated message on gender variance.

The history of the eunuch in Christian discourse is exceedingly complex. It should be noted, at minimum, that the eunuch of the ancient world is not the equivalent of either today's "gay" or "transgender." In general, "eunuch" seems to refer to young men who had been forcibly castrated in preparation for certain types of work, such as handling money, entering slavery, or working near women, although the term was also sometimes used to refer to slaves, people who were celibate, and others who were not castrated. Nevertheless, it could be said that the eunuch represented a class of subjugated people who were violently relegated to a liminal space of neither male nor female. As such, there is a tradition in Christianity of using Bible passages about eunuchs as counter-discourse for the celebration of sexual and gender minorities. For example, as evidence of the radical inclusivity of the Gospel, some Bible scholars point to the fact that the Ethiopian eunuch of Acts 8—a gender/sexual minority of a different ethnicity and nationality—was perhaps the first Gentile convert to Christianity. The theologian John McNeill once referred to the Ethiopian eunuch as the first gay Christian.[62]

In addition to gender variance in Scripture, trans Christian speakers at TRP conferences argued that Scripture itself undermines the importance of the gender binary and points toward greater inclusion of people with non-normative gender and sexual identities.[63] Speakers also emphasized passages in Scripture that stress the importance of social justice or are critical of privilege and power, thus reclaiming the text as a document for the marginalized and the outsider. As one example, during the Washington DC panel, Vivian Taylor brought up the story of

Esther from the Old Testament. The Book of Esther tells the story of Esther, an orphan of Hebrew descent who became queen of the Persian Empire and who risked her status and life to save the Jewish people from genocide. The lesson, Taylor argued, is that "God calls us to check our privilege in our relationships."

Another important theme that emerged was the effort to challenge evangelical assumptions about what "ministry" and "evangelism" mean in the context of conversations around transgender identity, even for churches who already consider themselves to be welcoming and inclusive. In addition to Chris Paige's admonition not to refer to a welcoming church as LGBT-inclusive if it had not taken active steps to do things such as provide support services or include transgender members in leadership or decision-making positions, Paige went further to criticize Christian ministries that seek only to evangelize the transgender community. "It's not about bringing trans people into the church," Paige said. "It's about going to trans communities and meeting their needs where they're at." Vivian Taylor agreed, adding, "There's a pressing need to evangelize, to speak up in your own community, to address misrepresentations, to advocate on behalf of trans people, whether one identifies as a trans Christian or as an ally." It's not the transgender community that needs salvation, they argued, but Christian churches—even those that claim to be affirming—that need to be evangelized, to be educated and shaken out of their apathy and indifference to the everyday violence many transgender people face.

The transgender Christians that I heard from also drew on concepts common among evangelicals to give voice to their experience of gender and to establish a common ground for trans inclusion. Living one's life as a witness, as I also heard elsewhere during my fieldwork, was one such script. Some Christians use the word "witness" in the sense of evangelizing or sharing the Gospel with unbelievers.[64] But there is also another sense, drawn from Bible verses such as 1 Peter 2:12, of living one's life as a witness.[65] Essentially it means the totality of one's character and conduct toward others is an argument, stands as proof, for the grace and goodness of God. This in itself is a form of evangelism, the difference perhaps being that with witnessing change takes place through example as opposed to coercion. But being a living witness is also about the presence and testimony of bodies themselves that don't conform to ideological expectations. The secular counterpart to living as a witness might be the gay liberation mantra, "Coming out is a political act."[66]

Alex McNeill used witness in a similar sense at the Washington DC conference. McNeill told the small audience that he began his gender journey during college. He first identified as a lesbian and found that doing so opened gendered spaces previously unavailable to him, like the "butch dyke," to begin renegotiating his gender identity. McNeill eventually earned a Master of Divinity from Harvard Divinity School and began the process of legally and medically transitioning and presenting as male before undergoing the ordination process in the Presbyterian Church (USA) and accepting a position as the executive director of More Light Presbyterians. Despite his desire to be seen only as male, McNeill has chosen to remain visibly transgender by keeping his transition public and identifying specifically as a "transgender man." He told the audience that he has chosen to "always be transitioning in order to be a witness" to others in the church.

In a guest post on GLAAD's website, McNeill described his decision to always be transitioning as a calling: "I am called to remain open about my transition because I want to offer my journey to those who are struggling to make leaps of faith of their own, and to use my story to help the church welcome transgender people into their communities."[67] In this way McNeill presents his identity as a transgender man as a witness to others, keeping in tension and in view a form of unintelligibility as witness for its potential to disrupt hegemonic notions of gender and what it means to be Christian.[68]

McNeill's comments also point toward another strategy some transgender Christians use to translate their experience of gender into language that cisgender Christians can understand—that is, by calling attention to how cisgender Christians often describe the Christian self as unsettled and a journey and subject to continual transformation. I heard this often throughout my fieldwork—cautionary tales about becoming too comfortable in one's identity and admonitions to embrace a disrupted identity as an opportunity for spiritual and emotional growth. For some, comfort devolves into complacency, whereas the Christian life should be marked by humility, restlessness, and unpredictability. I heard this sentiment expressed many ways: "We are continually becoming who God created us to be"; "Jesus didn't call us to be comfortable"; "If you're comfortable in yourself, you're doing it wrong."

The common threads between gender transition and the Christian self came to the fore toward the end of a panel discussion at TRP's regional training conference in Atlanta on "Gender Identity and Transgender Issues." The discussion was moderated by Allyson Robinson (whom I introduced in chapter 1) and included three other transgender Christians.[69] Robinson introduced the panel's topic by reading a recent tweet from the theologian Broderick Greer to set the tone for the discussion: "Not all Christians do theology from perches of power. Some of us do theology as a form of survival."[70] The fifty minutes allotted went by quickly as the panelists talked about their individual "faith and gender journeys," their reflections on whether the growing acceptance of lesbians and gay men in some Christian churches also translates to greater inclusion for trans people, and passages in Scripture that have been useful for them on their journeys. Afterward, during a brief question and answer session, an audience member asked the panelists about their self-perceptions of their gender identity and how they will know their "transitions are complete." He added, addressing the panel, "All I see are people who are perfectly wonderful and normal looking."

Neo Sandja, a Black transgender man and immigrant from the Democratic Republic of Congo, responded first by calling attention to the politics of declaring things "normal." "When I hear people say, 'You look normal,' it makes me feel like you're saying this other person doesn't," he said. "Like you're saying, 'That person doesn't pass, but you pass.' But some people might not be able, no matter what they do, to pass. And some people don't *want* to pass in this binary world."

Another panelist, Carmarion Anderson, seconded Sandja's point while adding language, like McNeill's, about always-transitioning-as-witness. Anderson is a Black transgender woman who transitioned in her late teens, a move that led to her being excommunicated from her childhood Pentecostal church. She later found a home and became a staff pastor in an inclusive Black Baptist church in Dallas. "I transition daily," Anderson responded, "so I don't have an end mark. For me, when I move beyond transitioning, I move beyond my community and move myself into privilege." Anderson continued, "My personal testimony is that my transition is my purpose. It was not a choice. It is my duty. It is my 'yes' to ministry." Although Anderson didn't mention the verse, when she said, "I transition daily," a passage in I Corinthians where the Apostle Paul wrote "I die daily" rang in my ears.[71] Some have interpreted Paul's words to mean he saw suffering and affliction as vital to his calling. Whether or not Anderson had this verse in mind, she made a similar claim by suggesting that her daily transition, and the experiences of suffering and affliction that have accompanied it, enable her to minister more effectively to others who suffer and are afflicted.

Earlier in their conversation Carmarion invoked another passage from Scripture, this time explicitly, to translate her gender identity for the audience. She quoted Romans 12:2, as it's found in the KJV, from memory: "And be not conformed to this world: but be ye transformed by the renewing of your mind." Anderson said this verse inspired her in her transition. Just as Christians are called to transform themselves into something other than society's expectations, Anderson extrapolated, so too is she called to transform herself into the image she has of herself in her mind, despite society's expectations of what it means to be female-bodied. "I am not conformed to this society," Anderson said. "I have been transformed, if you don't mind, by the Holy Ghost."

At the end of their discussion, still responding to the original question, Allyson Robinson returned to the same passage in Romans used by Anderson to translate her experience of gender:

> For me, I *was* normal. I started this journey as normal. I was a normal, kind of privileged, white guy. And, thank God almighty, I don't want to be normal again. . . . The word normal just means "conform to the norms," and if I understood what Senior Minister Carmarion was saying a moment ago from the word of God, I'm not supposed to be conformed to the norms of the world, but I'm supposed to be remade in the pattern of my God. So I have no desire to arrive in a place where I decide this thing has run its course.

In the end, the language of "witness" and "calling" and the inherent instability of the Christian self provided a rich language for Robinson,

Anderson, and McNeill, along with some of the other transgender Christians I learned from during my fieldwork, to negotiate gender and faith and do the complicated identity work that is often necessary for transgender and genderqueer people in Christian spaces. It also provided purpose and motivation, not unlike constructions of LGBTQ Christian bodies as witnesses I heard elsewhere during my fieldwork, to stay resilient in hostile spaces and through challenging situations. And as the transgender and ally Christians I heard from might argue, just as individuals can learn to hold their Christian selves in tension and suspense, they can also learn how to hold their assumptions about another person's—and even their own—politics, gender, sexuality, doubts, and relationships in suspense.

5 Academies of Racial Justice

As noted in the introduction, Nicole Garcia is a Latina transgender woman and self-described "complete church nerd" and "total Jesus freak." A certified gender therapist and former law enforcement officer, Garcia entered seminary in 2013 to pursue ordination in the Evangelical Lutheran Church in America, putting her on a path to becoming the first openly transgender woman of color to be ordained by the denomination, one of the largest in the United States.[1] Garcia described her experience as a Christian and a transgender woman of color as the opening night keynote speaker for TRP's Kansas City regional training conference in November 2015. She opened her presentation with a challenge to mainstream evangelicalism's indifference to—and often complicity with—the discrimination and violence transgender Americans, especially transgender women of color, face in their everyday lives.

"To be perfectly honest," Garcia confessed to the audience, "I need your help. I need each and every one of you to help save my life." Garcia told the audience she had some trepidation about coming to the conference. In the months leading up to the event, a transgender woman of color had been brutally murdered in the streets of Kansas City. Tamara Dominguez's attacker ran her over with a truck, stopped, and ran over her several more times. The police officers, in their reports of the incident, misgendered Dominguez and used her pretransition name.[2] Dominguez immigrated to the United States in hopes of escaping discrimination against transgender people in her hometown of Veracruz, Mexico.[3] "Would I make it back to the hotel?" Garcia wondered aloud. "Would I be next?" As Christians, Garcia insisted, the audience members must ask themselves: "Who is being singled out by society for oppression and marginalization? Who is being seen as so different and being so dangerous to society that they have to be watched, monitored, closely followed, and, when appropriate or necessary, executed?"

Throughout the slides of her presentation, which were projected on the ballroom wall behind her, Garcia interspersed images of the twenty-three transgender women who had been murdered in the United States in 2015, most of whom were explicitly targeted for being transgender. However, when the photographs appeared on the large screen behind her, Garcia didn't acknowledge them or say the women's names, leaving the images on the screen for only a few moments at a time. Garcia's inspiration for the presentation came from #SayHerName, a hashtag campaign pioneered by the African American Policy Forum to mobilize a social movement and raise awareness about Black women who are the victims of police violence.[4] #SayHerName emerged as a criticism of media accounts and narratives of police violence, including at times by Black Lives Matter activists, wherein the stories of young Black men gain more public attention than Black women. Similarly Garcia flashed images of the transgender women throughout her presentation without saying their names or acknowledging their presence as a witness to how some lives are more disposable and forgettable than others.[5]

In this final chapter I examine TRP's approach to reforming evangelical racial politics. I focus on the practices through which activists and participants have sought to counter mainstream evangelicalism's production and protection of whiteness and the practice of minimizing, by personalizing it, the existence and violence of racism. Given the rhetoric and actions of some evangelicals in this regard, TRP activists and participants wrestled with a troubling question that any observer of contemporary evangelical racial politics might wonder: does the Christian God condone racial violence?

I explore the theme of racial justice in TRP's activism by discussing how activists put the body and affect to work. In addition to the other modes of counter-conduct described throughout this book—for example, a recourse to Scripture, the formation of new communities with new leaders to guide them, and the inventiveness and malleability of reverse discourse—TRP activists made implicit and explicit use of the body and viscerality in their racial justice activism.

I examine this theme primarily through a discussion of a workshop developed by TRP called the Academy for Racial Justice (hereafter "the Academy"). "The Academy will combine," the promotional materials for the Academy advertised, "biblical teaching, simulations, ethnic-specific break-outs, and significant cross-cultural dialogue around the intersection of racial identity and LGBT issues."[6] As a supplement to TRP's training on LGBTQ matters in Christianity, the Academy for Racial Justice represents an evolving interest among organizers in making explicit the connections between racial and LGBTQ violence and the incorporation of a broader critique of evangelical racial politics. As I learned from my participation in two of these workshops, the goal of the Academy—and of the conferences more generally—was to get participants to *feel* something. These were intensely emotional experiences and intentionally so. I left the workshops with the impression that organizers were as interested in my body as they were in my mind.

The Academy activists and participants seemed to take for granted that the body and embodied experience could be tools of resistance. They understood that bodies, similar to what Mark Jordan argues, are not only "shaped by religious powers" but also "use religious discourses or practices to resist powers."[7] They also understood that embodied experience is instrumental in creating shared meaning and purpose, in addition to being generative of spiritual and sacred knowledge.[8] Moreover, they recognized that (to borrow language from Sara Ahmed) "emotions *do things*" and could be put to work to register dissent and build attachments.[9]

In an effort to draw a connection between racial and LGBTQ social justice, the workshops put to work various technologies of the self or practices whereby people, according to Foucault, "effect by their own means, or with the help of others, a certain number of operations on their own bodies and souls, thoughts, conduct, and way of being, so as to transform themselves in order to attain a certain state of happiness, purity, wisdom, perfection, or immortality."[10] Such practices have the potential to function as counter-conduct. As Foucault writes elsewhere, these "exercise[s] of self on self [are] a sort of close combat of the individual with himself in which the authority, presence, and gaze of someone else is, if not impossible, at least unnecessary."[11] Central to the practices of tuning the body and fashioning the self that I encountered were experiences of violence, suffering, and marginalization. As I argue, participants in the Academy workshops were taught to cultivate, through embodied practices, a sensibility of shared vulnerability and precarity rooted in experiences of violence and suffering.

Violence against LGBTQ Americans continues to be common, especially LGBTQ Americans of color. According to a recent report by the National Coalition of Anti-Violence Programs, a national organization that tracks and combats violence within and against the LGBTQ community, about 20–25 percent of gay people experience a hate crime at some point in their lifetimes, and transgender and gender-nonconforming people—especially when also people of color—experience a disproportionate risk of homicide.[12] Even today, despite American attitudes on average trending over the last several decades toward greater acceptance of LGBTQ people, less than 35 percent of white evangelical Protestants believe homosexuality should be accepted by society, compared to 63 percent of all Americans.[13]

Such beliefs have consequences. Despite the attempts of many conservative evangelicals to distance themselves from more overt instances of anti-LGBTQ rhetoric and violence, the Christian Right's anti-LGBTQ campaign, and conservative evangelicalism's exclusionary teaching concerning sexuality and gender more generally, directly contribute to a culture of physical, emotional, psychological, and spiritual violence toward LGBTQ Americans. This tension was dramatically illustrated by the tortured responses from evangelicals to a shooting at the Pulse nightclub in Orlando, Florida, in June 2016. Evangelical commentators denounced and sought to disassociate their rhetoric from the violence while at the same time reaffirming their opposition to LGBTQ rights and protections.[14] At the same time, they sought to dismiss the violence as a distinctively American problem by constructing the shooter as an outsider because of his race. There's a long tradition of this type of rhetorical and moral maneuvering by the Christian Right. For example, Rebecca Barrett-Fox argues that the Christian Right uses the more extreme rhetoric and tactics of groups like Westboro Baptist Church as cover to "construct itself as compassionate to gay people."[15]

In what follows I show how participants were trained to read and embody an affective response to violence against sexualized and racialized bodies and to funnel feelings toward individual and collective action. I start with a brief discussion of evangelical racial politics and how and why TRP began to incorporate an analysis of race and racism into its training conferences. The main body of the chapter describes the work of the Academy, which is based on my participation in two Academy workshops. The first was at the Atlanta regional training conference in June 2015, when TRP introduced the Academy; the second was at the Kansas City regional training conference in November 2015. I use the Kansas City Academy as the primary backbone of the following discussion, with moments from the Atlanta Academy interspersed throughout.[16]

Evangelical Racial Politics and a Turn to Racial Justice

Evangelicalism's relationship to racism and whiteness in American culture cannot be stated in simple terms. On the one hand, the roots of today's evangelical movements can be traced to the racial anxieties of white conservative Protestant segregationists in the first half of the twentieth century, and the conservative Christian project since has continued to be deeply invested in the production and protection of whiteness.[17] On the other hand, it is also a mistake to conflate evangelicalism with white Christian conservatism. As I have discussed in the introduction, evangelicalism is a contested discursive and embodied tradition. Not only does conflating evangelicalism with white conservative Christianity elide the fact that roughly 25 percent of evangelical and conservative Christian Americans are people of color, but it also papers over the countless racial justice activists and organizations that arose within and situate themselves in the tradition of evangelicalism.[18] As Brantley Gasaway and others have argued, it was in fact "a sense of Christian responsibility to oppose racism and to reverse its unjust social effects [that] helped to propel the rise of contemporary evangelical progressivism" in the last half of the twentieth century.[19]

While difficult to summarize, a common distinction among evangelicals on theories and theologies of racism is between those who personalize racism and consider it something of the past and those who view racism as an ongoing systemic issue.[20] Most white conservative evangelicals to this day understand racism, insofar as they believe it to exist, in terms of individual actions, which are interpreted through narratives of personal sin and redemption.[21] Racism cannot be legislated away; it must be reconciled through self-transformation, which can only come from a personal relationship with God. In other words, as some evangelicals might say, when it comes to racial issues, America doesn't have a racism problem; America has a sin problem. Racism, moreover, is viewed as a personal issue because insofar as structural racism existed in America, it is a relic of the past. Although a great evil, racism ended with abolition and the civil rights movement.

By contrast, progressive evangelicals, including many of those with whom I spoke during my fieldwork, argue that racism is ongoing and is inflected in the structures and culture of mainstream evangelicalism and American society more generally. Addressing racism goes above and beyond personal transformation to the systems of power that reproduce it. But for many conservative evangelicals who interpret racism through the lens of individual discriminatory actions, continuing to raise the issue of racism as an ongoing systemic problem is in itself racist. In other words, because systemic racism has ended, it's racist to suggest that America continues to have a racism problem.

In what began as an effort to change conservative Christian teaching concerning sexual orientation and gender identity, over the year of my fieldwork there was a growing recognition at TRP conferences and related spaces that a reckoning with racial inequality must be part of the conversations on LGBTQ inclusion in conservative Christian communities. This is not to say that race wasn't a topic at TRP's first regional training conference. The Washington DC conference included several Friday afternoon panels devoted to the intersections of LGBTQ inclusion and race, including a panel on "Exploring Intersectional Justice" and three other panels on advocating for LGBTQ inclusion in Asian American, African American, and Latino and Hispanic church communities. However, race as an issue of power and privilege was definitely more of an emphasis at the Atlanta and Kansas City conferences. In addition to more keynote and panel speakers of color at these two conferences, issues of race and privilege became more of a framing mechanism for the conversations on LGBTQ inclusion and equality, in particular through the addition of the Academy for Racial Justice workshops that opened the conferences that followed.

TRP's turn toward a broader critique of evangelical racial politics was in part a response to the way many of its fellow evangelicals were reacting to a series of events that had taken place in American society over the previous year. These events were the backdrop to many of the conversations on race that took place during my fieldwork and provide important context to the Academy workshops described later in this chapter. Among these are the broad evangelical indifference to the high-profile police officer shootings of unarmed Black people; evangelical opposition to the protests and unrest in Ferguson, Missouri, and the emergence of the Black Lives Matter movement; and growing evangelical support of Donald Trump's presidential campaign and his open embrace of white nationalism and racism.[22]

In response to the Black Lives Matter movement, for example, the phrase "All Lives Matter" became a popular refrain among some evangelicals to counter what they saw as the divisive politics of Black Lives Matter activists and to deny the existence of structural and institutionalized racism in so-called postracial America. Just months before the Kansas City conference, Glenn Beck, a conservative radio and television pundit, organized an All Lives Matter rally in Alabama, drawing an enthusiastic crowd of twenty thousand and broad conservative Christian support.[23] At the same time, prominent evangelical leaders and thinkers like Jim Wallis have been increasingly vocal about evangelicalism's historical relationship to whiteness and white supremacy.[24] Taken together, such reactions illustrate the ongoing and complicated relationship among evangelicalism, the protection of whiteness, and colorblind racism in the United States.

In some ways TRP's activists, in their attempt to make explicit the connections between racial and LGBTQ social justice, were mirroring trends in other contemporary movements for social justice. As scholars of social movements such as David Roediger and Lisa Duggan have documented, U.S. history has seen the periodic emergence of cross-fertilization and coalitional politics among progressive movements for social justice.[25] This includes the solidarities that developed between (among others) antislavery activists and feminists during the Civil War era; between Black feminists and labor activists during the 1960s; and more recently between activists in the Black Lives Matter movement and national LGBTQ organizations. TRP is not alone among other mostly evangelical LGBTQ Christian organizations that are seeking to incorporate into their ministry and activism a critique of evangelical racial politics. GCN, whose predominately white and evangelical or conservative Christian participation resembles TRP's, also sought to address the issue of race at its annual conference in Houston in January 2016. An organizer for the conference, in providing a rationale for why the group wanted to include a discussion of race at the conference, explained, "We have to recognize that there are other minorities and we need to speak up for each other."[26]

For conference attendees at both TRP's Kansas City and GCN's Houston conferences, the discussion of race seemed to be met with a mix of confusion and surprise. At TRP, for example, conference organizers remarked that some had asked why they were having a conversation about race at all at a conference that was supposed to be about a biblical basis for LGBTQ inclusion in faith communities. This confusion was somewhat understandable given the advertised focus of the conference and the fact that a majority of TRP's volunteers and conference attendees are white and may not think of their whiteness in the context of race. The conference organizers tried to argue, however, that the problem with this narrow view is that roughly a third of LGBTQ Americans are also nonwhite, so to disassociate issues of systemic racism from issues of sexuality and gender would be to ignore the unique issues and problems that queer people of color face in the United States.[27]

TRP's turn toward race also stems from internal critiques that LGBTQ Christian activism and discourse is essentially a white discourse. Often such critiques took place in hallways and over lunch breaks or virtually on Twitter, even if they were not always reflected on the stage at TRP conferences. During the Atlanta conference, for example, participants used the official conference hashtag #TRPinATL to call attention to the racial disparity on panels and keynote presentations. One participant tweeted, "Majority white LGBT 101 panel and 2 white straight male keynoters tonight certainly indicate the intended audience @ #TRPinATL. work to do."[28] Such parallel virtual conversations taking place on Twitter and other social media platforms during the conferences provided tools for saying what was often being left unsaid during "polite" in-person conversations and played a role in shaping the general discourse of the conferences.

The conversations at the steering committee meetings for the Kansas City conference often revealed the deep concern of some TRP activists and volunteers about making sure the conferences were racially diverse and representative of all LGBTQ people. While this issue came up at most all the meetings, one was especially memorable. "I'm concerned," one participant said, "with people feeling excluded if the only thing they see on stage are more straight white men." This led to a discussion about whom to invite to lead worship and give presentations at the Kansas City conference. Some at the meeting had issues with the worship at the Atlanta conference, not because of the song selection or musician-ship but because it "was a bunch of straight white people leading the worship." The same was true with the invited speakers. At one point one of the steering committee members joked that he had considered implementing a "quota for straight white men" for speakers. He contin-ued, "It wasn't really intentional, but opening the Atlanta conference with a straight white worship team and two straight white speakers didn't really set the right tone for the conference."

I stopped by the prayer room on my way to the opening evening of TRP's regional training conference in Atlanta in search of a quiet place to clear my head and reflect after a long day participating in the Academy for Racial Justice. The prayer room was tucked away in a smaller confer-ence room just outside of the main meeting space in between the reg-istration area and the book table. I sat for a few minutes in the quiet area, gazed tiredly at the prayer wall, and entertained a thought about what my prayer would be if I had one. Because it was the first day of the conference, there were only five handwritten prayers on the wall—most of which appeared to be starter notes to prime the wall, written by who-ever had set up the room—for things like "safe travels for all who are traveling to Atlanta"; "for all speakers and facilitators of TRP"; and "for those feeling invisible and marginalized."

5. Quiet Area and Prayer Wall at TRP's regional training conference in Atlanta, June 2015. Photo by the author.

Two days later I made my way back to the prayer room on the last night of the conference just before the final keynote presentation and sat again in the prayer area. Although I was alone in the room and it was quite serene, I could hear the busy clinking of dishes and a periodic muffled roar of an industrial dishwashing machine from beyond the false wall behind me. The notes on the prayer wall had grown over the three days; they ranged from the exuberant to reflections on limited options and constrained lives, people trying and hoping for the best in impossible situations. Someone left a sticky note requesting prayers for someone named John, who had cancer. A few others called attention to the need for "reconciliation" or that family or friends would "finally affirm my sexuality." It was yet another reminder that people continue to suffer because of conservative Christian teaching on sexuality and gender.

My mind drifted back to when I first arrived in Atlanta three evenings before. I had just walked into the airport MARTA station to catch a train to downtown Atlanta when I passed by a young Black woman, in despair, pleading with an older white man, "What more do you white people want from me?!" I don't know what led up to the interaction, but the young woman's anguish seemed laden with painful memories of previous interactions with white people.

It was almost ten p.m. by the time I made it to the conference hotel in downtown Atlanta. I was tired and hungry after a day of travel, so I dropped off my things in my room and walked a few blocks north in search of a bar for a late dinner and a quick beer. Just before leaving to walk back to the hotel, I watched as a tall and slender young Black man, looking unkempt and a bit run down, made his way to the bar and pulled from his pocket a fistful of quarters to pay for a beer. "Sorry, we don't take quarters," the white bartender said, pointing the man toward the exit.

The clamor of dishes in the kitchen behind me brought me back to the prayer room and reminded me that I was in a corporate space masquerading as a sacred place. A young woman came into the room, walked directly to the prayer wall, and after some thought scribbled down a prayer, posted it, and left. I settled on a prayer myself. I gathered my fieldnote journal and conference program, walked over to the wall, and dutifully offered my prayer among the growing sticky notes: "For the forgotten in Atlanta." A few minutes later I added another: "For those who have lost faith and need more than a return." It was a familiar act. I had dutifully cultivated this type of sensorium for five or six years in my late teens and early twenties. It was strange to be on the other side of it now, but at the same time it was somehow still therapeutic. Although I no longer place any faith in the prayers, being in the space and going through the motions—reminding my body what it was like to engage in similar practices—still somehow worked its magic.

Tuning the Body

I walked into a second-floor conference room in a downtown Kansas City hotel and found a seat near the back of the room. It was a chilly November morning in 2015, and I was there with roughly forty others attending the eight-hour Academy for Racial Justice that kicked off TRP's three-day regional training conference. People were filing in and out of the room, making small talk and sipping coffee from paper cups while waiting for the day's activities to begin.

The small conference room contained seven or eight rows of long folding tables covered with black tablecloths. Along the left side of the room was a long window overlooking the fountains in the plaza below the Kansas City Marriott, a hotel known to locals for lighting up the Kansas City skyline with a vibrant wall of seasonal greetings. At the front of the room were large notepads propped up on easels for keeping track of "Community Garden" topics, issues that came up during the day's activities to be tabled for further discussion later, and the "Ground Rules," the rules of engagement for participating in the workshop. The beige wall behind the notepads contained definitions, each printed on sheets of white printer paper, of key terms in "the language of racial justice"—among others, colonialism, cultural appropriation, intersectionality, microaggression, tokenism, reverse racism, trigger warnings, white supremacy. Beginning on the wall to the right and wrapping around the room behind us was a timeline of racial justice and LGBT equality. Just before eight a.m., I watched as the workshop facilitators gathered discreetly in the back corner of the room and bowed their heads in prayer.

TRP's conference organizers were inspired to develop the Academy for Racial Justice after attending a similar program called the Racial Justice Institute at the National LGBTQ Task Force's annual conference in Denver in early 2015.[29] Amelia Markham, one of TRP's full-time organizers, wrote in a blog post in the months leading up to the Atlanta conference that TRP wanted to provide a similar workshop for its conference attendees but "from a specifically Christian standpoint."[30] The workshop's activities include primers on key terms and issues in racial and LGBTQ social justice, a Bible lesson on diversity and race, small group discussions, and other participatory activities designed to foster dialogue or raise awareness.

The Academy workshops were available to a limited number of participants for a separate registration fee and took place during the day on Thursdays before the conferences officially began on Thursday evenings. The participants in the workshops I attended reflected the demographics of the conference attendees more generally. The facilitators and participants in the Kansas City workshop, for example, came from a diverse range of church backgrounds and current church homes: Southern Baptist, Methodist, Church of the Brethren, Episcopalian, Catholic, Evangelical, and at least two agnostics. Most of the room was also white and straight, with seven or eight people of color—four of whom were the workshop's facilitators—and less than half identifying as either transgender, genderqueer, queer, lesbian, or gay.

The Kansas City workshop began with one of the facilitators I will call Lucine. She introduced herself as a Latina, activist, feminist, and straight ally, telling the participants, "I want you to feel safe to express yourself. Think of this day and space as a safe space, a place where you can feel free to have open and frank conversations about race and to express any emotions or feelings you experience throughout the day."[31]

The active construction of the conference room as a safe space is a practice, as theorists of safe spaces have argued, of cultivating a space "as a site for negotiating difference and challenging oppression."[32] Throughout my fieldwork I found that the language of "safe spaces" was often mapped onto more familiar spaces in Christian discourse and coupled with vulnerability. Speaking at a 2014 GCN conference, Jeff Chu, a gay evangelical and author of *Does Jesus Really Love Me?*, described his hopes for the church this way: "The table I long for—the church I hope for—is a place where we love especially when it isn't easy, allowing us to be vulnerable, inviting every voice to join the conversation, pushing us meal by meal toward community, toward communion."[33] A blogger writing about GCN's 2015 conference wrote similarly: "In its conference, GCN has created a safe and vulnerable community, a model of what God calls His Church to strive for, and I believe Evangelicals are starting to recognize this type of space as undeniably essential."[34] In this way the church and table and community and communion are also conceptualized as safe spaces. On this day the conference room was similarly constructed as a space for learning how to make oneself vulnerable to other people, to celebrate diversity, and to make authentic connections.

Joline, another of the facilitators, introduced herself as a queer Black woman who had grown up in an evangelical church. "Christ is central to everything I am," she added. Joline invited us to "stand up and get loose" and led us in what she called a "shakeout exercise." One, two, three, four: we shook our white, brown, and black limbs, each in turn, in increasing intervals to her count, preparing our bodies to be receptive to the affective labor to which we would be made subject over the next eight hours.

I use "affect" here to call attention to how we were instructed to read our bodies, to link individual emotions to a social body, and to use those attachments as a foundation for both collective identity and social and political action. Sara Ahmed uses the language of "affective economies" to describe the sociality and politics of emotions. "In such affective economies," Ahmed argues, "[emotions] align individuals with communities—or bodily space with social space—through the very intensity of their attachments."[35] Similarly in the conference room on that day we were being taught how to align our emotions, recognize attachments, and direct them toward political ends. This is what I understood Lucine to mean when, reflecting later that afternoon about her hopes for the Academy, she asked, "What would success for today's Academy for Racial Justice look like? My hope," she answered, "is that we can make a heart connection with each other and between these two groups and areas of social justice work. You're not truly doing social justice work if you're doing this at the expense of others."

While the facilitators labored to "name" emotions and experiences—a term they often used to pull difficult and ineffable things into the light to be appropriately examined and exorcised—we were also encouraged to take up the work ourselves. We were repeatedly instructed to be mindful of any emotions and feelings that came to the surface throughout the day's activities and to connect those body sensations to individual and collective action.

After the shakeout exercise and ten minutes to "meet and greet those close by," the first activity was a discussion of the workshop's ground rules, which were printed, along with information about the other activities, in a simple program that each of the participants received. "Conversations about race and injustice," the program stated, "can be powerful but also may involve some deeply personal revelations and trigger some intense emotions. As such, we'll need to establish some basic guidelines as a group to ensure that we all are able to come to the table with mutual respect and understanding." The rules included "Be Present"; "Practice Gracious Listening"; "Speak from Your Own Experience"; "Be Authentic." Another rule, "Take Care," included the following instructions: "Take care of yourself during this time (and all the time!). Drink your water, take a bathroom break, and be aware of your emotional and physical state. Don't run at the first sign of an uncomfortable conversation, but if something has really upset you it may be a good idea to spend a few moments cooling down."

Another facilitator, whom I will call Kali, said the purpose of the ground rules was to "make this a safe space for everybody." In the introductions before the workshop began, Kali—whose pronouns are both "he" and "she"—introduced herself as queer and genderqueer and a first-generation Chinese American who was raised Catholic before joining an evangelical church and eventually a Methodist church. Joline expanded on Kali's point by telling us that the ground rules were "an agreement to accountability." By agreeing to the ground rules, we pledged to hold one another accountable. Kali and Joline also encouraged the participants to contribute their own ground rules to the list, and Kali wrote these down on a self-stick easel pad with a thick black Sharpie so that they could be added to the other content already lining the walls. "Clarify instead of object," a man in his early twenties proposed. "Speak up so people can hear," a woman in her early fifties added. At the Atlanta Academy a thirty-something man suggested, "I'm white and will probably say something wrong today, but I ask that you give grace."

A little later in the morning Joline led us through an exercise called "Power Analysis," which she described as a "mapping power exercise" designed to help participants understand the "differences between individual and group power." Joline reminded us to "be aware of any feelings beginning to percolate and arise. Sometimes when we unmask power, which is designed to be invisible, it can be uncomfortable." Joline began by asking us to brainstorm groups who hold more power and those who hold less power in society, busily writing down the names on one of the large self-stick easel pads—again to be added later to the content already lining the walls—as people around the room joined in with suggestions.

As the list evolved, Joline placed the groups who typically hold more power on the left and those who typically hold less on the right: white people were paired with people of color (Kali interrupted to say, "I would say 'minorities,' but in reality such people are the global majority"); men with women and people who are genderqueer, gender nonconformist, nonbinary, trans; the rich with the poor, the economically disadvantaged, the 99 percent; citizens with the undocumented and immigrants; the able-bodied with those who are differently abled; those who are native English speakers with those who are not; and so on. Almost as an afterthought, someone suggested we should add "Christian" to the list, paired with people who do not identify with this dominant religion or any religion at all.

Joline then directed us to focus on how particular groups experience power differently. "How have straight people," she asked, "been afforded more power solely on the basis of their sexual orientation?" Joline continued acting as a scribe as participants—some nodding in agreement or voicing support, others sitting in thoughtful silence—offered intermittent examples:

Straight people are well-represented in the media

We're able to marry the person we love and choose

Not facing housing and unemployment discrimination

Along with the right to marry, LGBT people have been denied other sacraments like ordination, which is *deeply* un-Christian

As a straight person, I am labeled as, quote, "normal"

Not worrying about having to come out or being rejected by your family because you're straight

After the examples slowed to a stop, Joline then asked the LGBTQ people in the room to talk about how the responses made them feel:

Less than

Unworthy

Fearful

Second class

Ashamed

Unclean

Angry

Invisible

No connection to the divine

Isolated

Unbiblical

After a similar exercise exploring what white people are afforded based solely on the color of their skin, Joline asked the people of color in the room to respond to the same question:

Less than

Dangerous

Ugly

Unwanted

Ashamed

Objectified

Outside

Exoticized

Ineligible

When done writing, Joline stepped back and looked at the emotions captured on the sticky pad and remarked that "[this type of] internalized oppression can be dangerous and if gone unchecked can even present itself in the form of disease." Joline then instructed us to take a deep breath together: "Breath in what you've just heard." And we collectively pulled in air.

Another of the Academy activities, which organizers included at both the Atlanta and Kansas City conferences in which I participated, was a self-guided tour of a "Racial Justice and LGBT Equality Timeline." The timeline included pivotal moments—setbacks, turning points, victories—in the history of movements for racial and LGBTQ social justice in the United States. Each moment, perhaps fifty to sixty in total in this curated history—printed on individual sheets of white printer paper—included an image related to the event and a brief description.

The workshop facilitators adapted the timeline from a resource called "Immigrant Rights, Racial Justice and LGBT Equality Timeline in Pictures," which is a shared curriculum of Basic Rights Education Fund, an Oregon-based LGBT organization, and Western States Center, a nonprofit also based in Oregon that works to create a broader progressive social movement by connecting activists and organizers from across different organizations.[36] The curriculum suggests beginning with a short introduction by a trainer, followed by a tour of the timeline in discussion pairs, and finishing with a full group discussion or "debrief." Participants are encouraged to focus on the connections between racial and LGBTQ oppression and the policies, laws, strategies, structures, and biases that contribute to and perpetuate shared oppression. According to TRP's Academy program, the goals of the exercise, also adapted from the previous iteration of the timeline, were to "understand the systematic and institutionalized oppression of targeted communities and its impact"; to "identify the common strategies used to exclude and marginalize targeted communities"; and to "build awareness and common ground between communities."

I came to understand the tour of the Racial Justice and LGBT Equality Timeline as an exercise in putting on prosthetic memories. According to Alison Landsberg, this modern mode of cultivating collective memories, enabled by mass culture, "emerges at the interface between a person and a historical narrative about the past . . . [wherein] an experience occurs through which the person sutures himself or herself into a larger history . . . [thereby taking] on a more personal, deeply felt memory of a past event through which he or she did not live."[37] Such memories are then experienced as an extension of the body in that they are experienced on and through the body. As Landsberg underscores, there is nothing intrinsically progressive or conservative about the process or outcomes of acquiring prosthetic memories. Nevertheless, "The resulting prosthetic memory has the ability to shape that person's subjectivity and politics."[38]

After a brief introduction, the facilitators instructed us to take twenty minutes in silence interacting with the timeline while asking ourselves,

6. Academy for Racial Justice participants tour the Racial Justice and LGBT Equality Timeline at TRP's regional training conference in Kansas City, November 5, 2015. Photo by the author.

"What's missing from the timeline? What am I inspired by? What am I feeling?" They told us to be mindful of those feelings and feel free to step out of the room to pray or reflect if they became overwhelming. They also encouraged us to insert ourselves into the timeline, adding or modifying as we saw fit.

African American spirituals and contemporary praise and worship songs played softly in the background from an iPhone. Participants moved from moment to moment, some in quiet contemplation, some periodically taking pictures with cell phone cameras, others busily scribbling notes, embodying the memories. We quietly and deliberately let each moment—like a presence—inhabit us: 1619 and the beginnings of the American slave trade; the U.S. invasion of Mexico in 1848; electric shock therapy; lynching; Operation Wetback and the deportation of Mexican Americans in 1954; antisodomy laws; Stonewall; the 2015 murder of a trans woman named London Kiki Chanel (among others).

HERO
Beyond!!!!
Words!!!

1963

Bayard Rustin (left) and Cleveland Robinson in front of March on Washington headquarters.

Gay man, African-American civil rights and nonviolent movement leader Bayard Rustin is the chief organizer of the March on Washington.

Rustin is required to play a behind the scenes role because he was gay and was eventually pushed out of visible leadership in the civil rights movement.

7. While viewing a timeline of LGBT equality at TRP's regional training conference in Kansas City (November 5, 2015), a participant added their own experience to a moment in the history by penciling in praise of Bayard Rustin.

One of the moments read: "Gay man, African-American civil rights and nonviolent movement leader Bayard Rustin . . . is required to play a behind the scenes role because he was gay and was eventually pushed out of visible leadership in the civil rights movement." A participant used a pen to circle Rustin's name and write in the corner, "HERO Beyond Words!!!!" On another, someone crossed out "internment" to write in "concentration" so that a moment in the timeline would read that the United States had placed more than one hundred thousand Japanese Americans in concentration camps during World War II.

After the twenty minutes were over, Madlin, the fourth facilitator at the Kansas City Academy, who earlier had introduced himself as Episcopalian, a queer spawn, and Nikkei, began the debrief by asking for our reactions to the timeline and in particular any emotions we felt.[39] "None of this was covered in our history books," one of the participants began. Another participant, a middle-aged white man, said, "I just feel so sad and ashamed of the way people can vilify another group of people just for being different. And the fact that this happened because of white people, by people who look like me . . . I don't know how else to say it. I feel shame." Lucine jumped in to press the issue further. "What do you do with that feeling?" she asked. "With such a powerful feeling, how do you respond to that?"

Another participant, a middle-aged Black man, talked about how he struggled with how he should be feeling during the exercise. "I tried to read the timeline cerebrally, but my heart and emotion kicked in. This isn't in the past; it's still present with me. And I was reminded of that verse: *God is a very present help in a time of trouble.*"[40] He continued, referring to a recent successful campaign in Houston to vote down an LGBTQ nondiscrimination ordinance (a campaign that was supported by some African American churches), "How do oppressed people oppress people? And then the shame kicked in." Earlier in the morning the same participant had brought up, to an enthusiastic response from several of the other participants, that he had been reading Brené Brown's *Daring Greatly*. He said the book resonated with him in that it discusses the value of making oneself vulnerable and how people are conditioned not to show certain emotions. Similarly, during the timeline, he felt shame because of his emotional response and then questioned why he had been taught not to feel certain emotions. "And I wondered why I was having an emotional response and why I felt shame. It's a powerful exercise, and I'm grateful to be here," he concluded.

The conversations that followed the timeline exercise during the Academy that began the Atlanta conference were much the same. But a few of the comments also illustrate how some participants used religious language, concepts, and rituals to articulate emotions and to make sense of violence and suffering while aligning their experience with the experience of others. "I grew up Catholic," a white participant in that Academy said, "and the tour of the timeline reminded me of the Eucharist. Just like how during the Eucharist, when partaking of the body and blood of Christ I am participating in his death and suffering, I felt like I was going around receiving the body and blood of people of color and participating in their suffering and deaths." His sentiment seemed to resonate with others in the room. Another white participant agreed, saying that the experience "felt like performing the Stations of the Cross and meditating on the suffering and death of Christ." Another participant, a white woman who spoke through halting tears, tried to tether these abstract concepts to real-world action: "How do we actually make changes in homes and schools and churches to make sure this doesn't happen again?"

At the Kansas City Academy several of the participants also attempted to connect their experience of the timeline with a moral responsibility to act and to be politically engaged. One of the participants, for instance, brought up why he had changed "internment" to "concentration" on the timeline: "I was struck by how we have the ability to make history into what it wasn't or somehow soften the edges. We need to be honest about what happened instead of acting like nothing happened." Madlin followed up by connecting the writing of history to what it means to be a Christian. "Softening history," he said, "is not a Christian thing to do. We should be naming history." Another participant connected the Ferguson protests over the previous year with Stonewall: "I couldn't help but think of Ferguson after seeing Stonewall in the timeline. I think it's ironic and hypocritical how white queers today are criticizing the destruction of property in Ferguson when the Stonewall riots included much of the same." A middle-aged white woman said, "It just reminded me how much more I could be doing." "Either you're just bystanders," Madlin responded, "standing by and watching events like those on the timeline happen, which means you're complicit, or you do something about it." Later that day conference volunteers moved the timeline from the smaller conference room of the Academy to the ballroom walls of the main conference space so that other conference content could be stitched into the historical narrative represented on the timeline.

The last exercise of the day was called "Allyship and Speak-Out." As Joline described it to us, the exercise was designed to teach us about allyship, which she defined as "working on behalf of marginalized groups." "For me," she added, "true allyship means standing in the gap and working to interrupt violence. So it's not just about calling yourself an ally but actually being active." "Standing in the gap" is a phrase some Christians use to talk about acting on behalf of someone who is in need, usually with the connotation of coming to someone's defense. Sometimes "standing in the gap" is used in the context of what is called intercessory prayer or praying in the place of someone else.[41] Joline connected the role of an ally to "standing in the gap" but emphasized that "allyship shouldn't mean just helping in a paternalistic way but acknowledging our shared oppression."

We were organized into two rows—a "target group" and a "nontarget group"—sitting and facing one another. We did the exercise twice: once we were split into people of color on one side facing allies on the other; the second time, into LGBTQ people and allies. The facilitators asked the target group participants a series of questions and conducted them to direct their responses to the nontarget group. The nontarget group participants then repeated back to the target group what they had heard. Kali asked those in the people of color group, for example, "What do you never want to see, hear, or have happen to you again?" The responses included, among others, the following:

Police violence toward Black bodies

Racial profiling

Don't ever "Donald Trump" again

When finished, the nontarget group repeated the responses back across the aisle. In the next round the LGBTQ group was asked, "What is something you want people to know about you, your identities, your communities?"

> We are not all promiscuous
>
> It's okay if we are
>
> We're not recruiting your children
>
> It's okay if we are
>
> Who I have sex with is the smallest part of who I am
>
> We have so much to say about who God is

After the final question was asked and the final responses were voiced, Madlin turned to the nontarget group and instructed, "Breath in what they said. Think of each breath as a prayer." We obeyed and took in a collective breath, internalizing and interning in our bodies the words and experiences of the people sitting across the aisle.

Lucine had the final word of the day. She used the opportunity to remind us to be mindful of our bodies: "If you wake up tomorrow with anxiety, remember to be mindful and take time for self-care. Maybe something was stirred up in your spirit today. Don't run from that sensation. Take time to discern what it means."

Vulnerability

Throughout my fieldwork and the writing of this book I have often thought of the project as an ethnography of theodicy. To a certain extent this is what I think the activists and participants in the Academy for Racial Justice workshops were wrestling with. The workshops can be thought of as exercises in theodicy in that they are attempts to rationalize and reconcile the reality of racialized, gendered, and sexualized violence with a just God.

The workshops also remind me of Judith Butler's meditations in *Precarious Life*. To counter the violence of contemporary biopolitics—whereby some are more exposed and made subject to violence than others—Butler argues that we need to cultivate politics and ethics based on shared vulnerability. It is through the "apprehension of common human vulnerability," she argues, that "we might critically evaluate and oppose the conditions under which certain human lives are more vulnerable than others, and thus certain human lives are more grievable than others."[42] Similarly the argument of the workshops was that one's politics and conduct should follow from a mutual recognition of shared vulnerability.

Moreover, in working to make embodied connections between racial and LGBTQ social justice—seeking to bridge racial, sexual, and gender identities and differences—the workshops also work to mend some of "the factioning, fractioning, and fractalizing of identity," as Jasbir Puar summarizes it, that "is a prime activity of societies of control, whereby subjects . . . orient themselves as subjects through their disassociation or disidentification from others disenfranchised in similar ways in favor of consolidation with axes of privilege."[43] In other words, the labor of activists and participants in the workshops can also be thought of as resistance to what Foucault calls the "government of individualization," which "breaks [the individual's] links with others, splits up community life, forces the individual back on himself, and ties him to his own identity in a constraining way."[44]

Finally, I submit that the identity and community work that took place at the Academy workshops was also a form of conversion, which Foucault calls "one of the most important technologies of the self the West has known."[45] The experience was designed to cultivate new knowledge and to be transformational. It was a struggle over and cultivation of a different Christian subjectivity, a changed understanding and practice of what it means to be a Christian subject in conservative Christian spaces, especially as it relates to politics and conduct regarding race, gender, and sexuality and what it means to be LGBTQ and Christian. The conversations that took place at the workshops, and more generally in LGBTQ Christian activism in conservative Christian spaces, emphasized the ethical responsibility of centering the experiences of the marginalized and oppressed in conversations about Christian community and identity. And the activities helped train participants how to harness emotions to modify the self, cultivate a sense of shared vulnerability, and direct these toward political ends, a critical part of the labor of converting bystanders to allies and building more inclusive and equitable communities.

Conclusion

I have told two main stories throughout this book about the lives, frustrations, and hopes of the LGBTQ and LGBTQ-supportive Christians I met during my fieldwork. On the one hand, I have argued that this community of activists, volunteers, and concerned Christians, organized around LGBTQ social justice in evangelicalism, can be understood as a community of counter-conduct. The conversations and practices at TRP conferences, and similar spaces where what it means to be LGBTQ and Christian is an object of concern, are more than disputes over theology and belief; they are struggles over how one is conducted and conducts oneself in conservative evangelical communities as LGBTQ and Christian. This includes, among other struggles, contests over the treatment and inclusion of LGBTQ people and the ongoing negotiation of gender and sexual norms, values, and identities. The LGBTQ Christian activism I studied, far from being marginal to evangelicalism, represents a rich site for the production of identity, politics, and values while working both within and against evangelicalism as a historical project.

In chapter 1 I argued that the formation of communities in evangelicalism organized around LGBTQ social justice makes possible an environment for the exploration and negotiation of new ways of being and what counts as appropriate, and even necessary, "political" or "public" speech. In chapter 2 I discussed the role of Scripture as a contested space for the formation of LGBTQ Christian communities and identities. As I showed, while the substance and meaning of particular passages are undoubtedly material to these conservations, even more so are the contests over the proper relationship between the text and the self and the everyday reproduction of the Bible as a moral and sacred document.

The second broad story was about the struggle over not only evangelicalism as a collective project but also what it means to be both LGBTQ and a Christian and who gets to decide. For example, in chapter 3 I documented the invention and circulation in conservative evangelicalism of languages and scripts for people living as gay Christians. At the same time, some in this community worry about how the acceptance of ready-made categories of gender and sexuality reinscribes norms and values that have contributed to shame and the marginalization of women, people with non-normative gender and sexual identities, and queer desire. Chapter 4 documented, in part, how some transgender and genderqueer Christians negotiate identity and politics, both in the context of recent conservative evangelical rhetoric about transgender people and in spaces that are assumed to be welcoming or affirming. In chapter 5 I showed how TRP activists put the body to work in their attempts to disrupt the racial politics of mainstream evangelicalism and to make a connection between racial and LGBTQ social justice.

For Foucault, as pointed out by Davidson, what makes counter-conducts potentially disruptive as forms of resistance is the cultivation of alternative politics, ethics, and modes of life.[1] The anthropologist of religion Talal Asad, in an essay on the politics of belief and religious freedom in secular-liberal democracies, distinguishes between two modes of democracy: democracy as a state system and democratic sensibility as an ethical principle for guiding an individual's conduct and responsibilities as a member of a pluralistic society. According to Asad, democracy as a state system "is jealous of its sovereignty, defines and protects the subjective rights of its citizens (including their right to 'religious freedom'), infuses them with nationalist fervor, and invokes bureaucratic rationality in governing them justly; it is fundamentally *exclusive*."[2] At odds with democracy as a state system, Asad continues, is democratic sensibility— whether "religious" or "secular"—as an ethos that "involves the desire for mutual care, distress at the infliction of pain and indignity, concern for the truth more than for immutable subjective rights, the ability to listen and not merely to tell, and the willingness to evaluate behavior without being judgmental toward others; it tends toward greater *inclusivity*."[3]

In the case of TRP and the related conversations among and about LGBTQ Christians I studied, it was a cultivation of a democratic sensibility similar to Asad's description that characterized their counter-conduct—an ethos of shared vulnerability and mutual care that formed the basis of moral decisions and the production of identity and community. It was the nurturing of a political and ethical sensibility defined more by the mutual recognition that (to borrow from Judith Butler) "we're undone by each other."[4] In this way TRP's conferences can be thought of as local struggles over democracy and democratic values. They represent, like so many other spaces in American life, the attempt to negotiate identity and community in institutions and traditions where democratic values are not always valued nor perhaps even compatible.

As such, thinking about the negotiation of gender, sexual, and religious identities as a relationship between conduct and counter-conduct cuts to the heart of an ever-present tension in evangelicalism. That is, it calls attention to the tension between conservative evangelicalism's authoritarian tendencies, which attempt to lay claim to the totality of one's public and private life, and its ideals of self-transformation and individual freedom and responsibility. As Asad and others have argued, religious and sexual freedom in the United States is often only a protected right for some, and that is why Jakobsen and Pellegrini have argued that secularism in the United States should properly be understood as "Christian secularism."[5] Rather than treating all religious and sexual practices equally, a Christian presumption lies behind the religio-sexual order that the U.S. government works to protect, as illustrated by recent efforts to protect and codify conservative Christian "values" and "beliefs" through the various so-called religious freedom bills.[6] What is incongruous about the broad evangelical support of such legislation, however, is that if conservative evangelicals genuinely valued religious freedom and conscientious objection, they would respect their fellow Christians who support marriage equality or the right of LGBTQ Christians to conduct their lives according to their own religious convictions.

As I was writing this conclusion, a declaration called the Nashville Statement has been in the news since its release on August 29, 2017. Drafted by the Council on Biblical Manhood and Womanhood at the national conference of the Southern Baptist Convention in Nashville, this "Christian manifesto" outlines fourteen articles opposing "homosexual immorality or transgenderism."[7] The manifesto, signed by an initial coalition of more than 150 evangelical leaders, is an attempt to reassert what are perceived to be traditional evangelical values regarding gender, sexuality, and marriage. For those who are familiar with the rhetoric of the Christian Right, the intellectual and theological dishonesty of the document is disappointing but not surprising. Even though critics quickly declared the Nashville Statement another sign of the final "death rattle" of the Christian Right and an affront to queer Christians and the evangelicals who support them, it's a reminder of how entrenched these views are and the broad institutional support that sustains them.[8] It's also a reminder of how vital organizations like TRP are and just how much more work remains to be done.

There were many other reminders, over the months of my fieldwork, of the stakes and challenges of reforming conservative evangelicalism's teachings and conduct concerning gender, sexuality, and race—for example, the tepid response among conservative evangelicals to the Orlando nightclub shooting on June 12, 2016, in particular how some conservative evangelicals used this tragedy to politicize Islam, to deny their own complicity in violence against LGBTQ people, and to remind the public that their opposition to marriage equality is somehow compassionate and holy; the embracing of the phrase "All Lives Matters" by some evangelicals to discredit the Black Lives Matter movement; and the unprecedented support among self-identified evangelicals for the Trump presidential campaign.

These and other recent events in the United States raise critical questions for scholars of American religion, not least of which is whether evangelicalism is incompatible with sexual, gender, and racial diversity and equality or perhaps even liberal democracy itself.[9] The answer, as I hope this book has underscored, is of course not. However, for those who are trying to change conservative evangelicalism from within, it will require a fundamental rethinking of conservative evangelicalism's courting of power and cultural hegemony; its investment in regulating normative gender and sexuality; and its illiberal, boundary-drawing, and authoritarian tendencies.

Research on the relationship between cultural identity and belief has shown that belief is often more about affiliation and "moral tribes" than about facts and objective truth.[10] In other words, affiliation with a moral community influences what an individual believes and accepts as truth—for example, when one *must* believe that homosexuality is sinful becomes tethered to legitimate Christian identity—and to interrogate another's beliefs is to question their very understanding of the self and status as a member of a particular moral community. As such, reasoned debate will have its limits.

It's true that some of those I met at TRP conferences sometimes placed too much faith in the force of an argument and the assumption that other actors were responding in good faith. Some seemed to assume that disagreements in belief were rooted in a misunderstanding of the facts, that if presented with the right information people would recognize the incontrovertible truth. At the same time, I think lessons can be learned from how they attempted to reason with their fellow travelers. As the same body of research has suggested, people are more likely to consider information as trustworthy or factual when it comes from a person who they believe share similar values.[11] As such, people tend to be more receptive to arguments made from members of their own community and when the arguments are based on a combination of reason and an appeal to shared morality.

Therefore, while activists and speakers at TRP conferences often stressed that it's important to correct mistruths, to educate and inform others on the issues that matter in a measured and factual way, they also emphasized that such conversations are less productive outside of the context of established relationships and shared values. A member of TRP's staff remarked at one point that perhaps 90 percent of the people who attended the Atlanta conference were there because of personal relationships, and volunteers were encouraged to accompany the people they invited throughout the conference and to continue cultivating those relationships long after the conference ended. The very purpose of the conferences in this way was to be catalysts for forming such relationships, to provide a foundation for later conversations.

While largely optimistic and hopeful, the TRP activists and conference participants I met knew that this work would take time. Rather than giving up when things become contentious or engaging only in the types of drive-by social activism common on social media, people in this community often encouraged one another to keep going, to be resilient, and to remember that cultivating relationships for change is a painstakingly long and singular process.

Notes

Introduction

Unless otherwise specified, all quotes throughout this book are based on my fieldnotes. I followed the anthropological practice of producing daily fieldnotes based on "jottings" made while in the field (Emerson, Fretz, and Shaw, *Writing Ethnographic Fieldnotes*). When possible, I supplemented the quotes drawn from my fieldnotes with TRP's recordings of its events.

1. Gwendolyn Ann Smith, "Transgender Day of Remembrance: Why We Remember," *Huffington Post*, November 20, 2012, https://www.huffingtonpost .com/gwendolyn-ann-smith/transgender-day-of-remembrance-why-we -remember_b_2166234.html.

2. Zach Stafford, "Woman Killed in Illinois Is 19th Transgender Homicide Reported This Year," *The Guardian*, August 26, 2015, https://www.the guardian.com/us-news/2015/aug/26/keyshia-blige-trangender-homicide -illinois.

3. From the About section of Blige's now-memorialized Facebook profile.

4. I define my use of "evangelicalism" and "the Christian Right" later in this chapter.

5. I use "LGBTQ Christian" to refer collectively to individuals in this community who identify as Christian and either lesbian, gay, bisexual, transgender, or queer. Here I follow the lead of those I met who use "LGBTQ Christian" as a coalitional and social category to describe a community and collective sense of identity. When talking about specific individuals, I try to use the language with which those individuals describe themselves. In some places, such as in chapter 3, I use "gay Christian" when referring specifically to lesbians and gay men or issues pertaining to sexuality rather than gender identity. Even so, such a distinction has rarely been made in the conservative LGBTQ Christian literature I have read or by those with whom I have spoken. Even when talking explicitly about issues of sexuality, individuals still often used the term "LGBTQ Christian." Moreover, I seek throughout to resist a unitary notion of identity, calling attention to the fact that what

it meant to identify as LGBTQ and Christian was varied and contested. My interest was in discovering what these terms and labels meant for the people I met. Finally, "LGBTQ Christian" and "gay Christian" are not only coalitional and social categories but also objects of discourse. That is, the categories serve as discursive spaces for talking about a range of other issues: the body and desire, difference and inclusion, shame and vulnerability, and the meaning and significance of being LGBTQ and Christian, among others.

6. I use "object of concern" in the Foucauldian sense of how a thing enters discourse and is "problematized, becoming an object of concern, an element for reflection." Foucault, *The Use of Pleasure*, 23–24.

7. Foucault, *Security, Territory, Population*, 201. Given the history of the Christian Right's rhetoric about "homosexual conduct," it's important to emphasize that I am not using "conduct" in this sense. As will become clear in the discussion of counter-conduct later in the introduction, I use "conduct," following Foucault, in the broader sense of the government of human beings, both the direction of an individual's conduct or behavior and the way in which individuals conduct themselves. Davidson, "In Praise of Counter-Conduct," 26–27.

8. Matthew Vines, "The Gay Debate: The Bible and Homosexuality," YouTube .com, https://www.youtube.com/watch?v=ezQjNJUSraY, accessed October 18, 2017.

9. Burrow-Branine, "Blogging While Gay and Christian."

10. Andrew Sullivan, "The Next Generation Speaks," *The Dish* (blog), April 8, 2012 (11:17 a.m.), http://dish.andrewsullivan.com/2012/04/08/a-spiritual -sabbatical/.

11. For a history of religious and political centrism and progressivism in Kansas and a healthy corrective to its conservative reputation, see Wuthnow, *Red State Religion*.

12. Garriott and O'Neill, "Who Is a Christian?," 378–88.

13. Vines, *God and the Gay Christian*. TRP is a 501(c)(3) nonprofit.

14. "Mission and Vision," ReformationProject.org, https://www.reformation project.org/mission-and-vision/, accessed November 3, 2017.

15. I discuss the focus and structure of the leadership-development cohorts and regional training conferences in chapter 2.

16. D'Emilio and Freedman, *Intimate Matters*, 395.

17. See, for example, Butler, *Bodies That Matter* and *Gender Trouble*; Foucault, *History of Sexuality*; Katz, *Invention of Heterosexuality*; and Rubin, "Thinking Sex."

18. The critical race theorist Kimberlé Crenshaw is usually credited with first articulating the need for an intersectional framework in the study of identity and systems of oppression. Crenshaw, "Demarginalizing" and "Mapping the Margins." For a recent discussion of methodological and theoretical issues in intersectionality studies, as well as an example of how religion is sometimes overlooked in this literature, see Cho, Crenshaw, and McCall, "Intersectionality Studies."

19. For a succinct statement on the relative lack of theorizing religion in LGBTQ studies and queer theory, see Pellegrini, "Testimonial Sexuality."

20. See, for example, Jordan, *Recruiting Young Love*, xiv; Schneider, "Homosexuality, Queer Theory, and Christian Theology," 6; and Wilcox, "Outlaws or In-Laws?"

21. D'Emilio and Freedman, *Intimate Matters*, 395.

22. Puar, *Terrorist Assemblages*, 13.

23. Puar, *Terrorist Assemblages*, 55; emphasis in original.

24. Jakobsen, "Sex + Freedom = Regulation," 287–88.

25. On the role of gender and sexuality in the negotiation and maintenance of religious identity and communities, see Bartkowski, *Remaking the Godly Marriage* and *Promise Keepers*; Davidman, *Tradition in a Rootless World*; Davie, *Women in the Presence*; DeRogatis, *Saving Sex*; Griffith, "Sexing Religion"; Moon, *God, Sex, and Politics*; Petro, *After the Wrath of God*; Rudy, *Sex and the Church*; and Stein, *Stranger Next Door*. On the role of gender, sexuality, and religion in the maintenance of secular power and consolidation of national identity, see Herdt, *Moral Panics, Sex Panics*; and Jakobsen and Pellegrini, *Love the Sin*. On the role of the Christian Right in influencing LGBTQ activism and shaping sexual politics, see Barrett-Fox, *God Hates*; Cobb, *God Hates Fags*; Fetner, *How the Religious Right Shaped Lesbian and Gay Activism*; and Herman, *Antigay Agenda*.

26. A recent succession of edited volumes brings together some of this scholarship: Boisvert and Johnson, *Queer Religion*; Comstock and Henking, *Que(e)rying Religion*; Talvacchia, Pettinger, and Larrimore, *Queer Christianities*; and Thumma and Gray, *Gay Religion*.

27. Erzen, *Straight to Jesus*; McQueeney, "'We Are God's Children, Y'all'"; Sumerau, "'That's What a Man Is Supposed to Do'"; Wilcox, "When Sheila's a Lesbian" and *Coming Out in Christianity*; and Wolkomir, *"Be Not Deceived."*

28. Fetner, "Ex-Gay Rhetoric" and *How the Religious Right Shaped Lesbian and Gay Activism*; Herman, *Antigay Agenda*; and Thumma, "Negotiating a Religious Identity." Recent interdisciplinary articles by Dawne Moon and Teresa W. Tobin are notable and important exceptions: "Sunsets and Solidarity";

"Humility"; "Politics of Shame"; see also Moon, Tobin, and Sumerau, "Alpha, Omega, and the Letters in Between."

29. H. R. White, "Proclaiming Liberation." See also Buzzell, "Gay and Lesbian Activism"; Comstock, *A Whosoever Church*; and Udis-Kessler, *Queer Inclusion*.

30. Puar makes a similar point in "Reading Religion Back into *Terrorist Assemblages*," 55.

31. Althusser, "Ideology and Ideological State Apparatuses"; Asad, "Religion and Politics"; Bernauer and Carrette, *Foucault and Theology*; and Jakobsen and Pellegrini, *Love the Sin*.

32. Csordas, "Embodiment as a Paradigm for Anthropology"; Griffith, *Born Again Bodies*; McGuire, "Religion and the Body"; and Turner, *Religion and Modern Society*.

33. Asad, *Genealogies of Religion*, 76–77; Davidman, *Becoming Un-Orthodox*; Luhrmann, *When God Talks Back*; and Orsi, *Between Heaven and Earth*.

34. Dean, *Governmentality*, 10.

35. Dean, *Governmentality*, 10.

36. Wuthnow, *Restructuring of American Religion*.

37. I discuss denominationalism in chapter 1 in the context of how evangelical polity influences LGBTQ-inclusion efforts.

38. Hunter, *Culture Wars*. For a summary of these debates and an argument for viewing these divides less in binary than in multidimensional terms, see Kniss, "Mapping the Moral Order."

39. Dochuck, *From Bible Belt to Sunbelt*; Dowland, *Family Values*; Williams, *God's Own Party*; and Young, *We Gather Together*.

40. Marsden, *Fundamentalism and American Culture*, 4, and *Understanding Fundamentalism and Evangelicalism*, 1.

41. Marsden, *Fundamentalism and American Culture*, 232.

42. Fetner, *How the Religious Right Shaped Lesbian and Gay Activism*, 1.

43. Fetner, *How the Religious Right Shaped Lesbian and Gay Activism*, 8. Parachurch organizations, including faith-based nonprofits like TRP, are independent religious organizations often working without the oversight of denominations or churches. Most parachurch organizations, the influence of which expanded dramatically beginning in the 1960s, are Protestant and evangelical.

44. For the connections between white Christian fundamentalism and the protection of whiteness, see Harding, "Representing Fundamentalism"; and Jones, *The End of White Christian America*.

45. Herman, *Antigay Agenda*, 60–91.

46. Jordan, *Recruiting Young Love*, 136.

47. Fetner, *How the Religious Right Shaped Lesbian and Gay Activism*, 9–10.

48. Fetner, *How the Religious Right Shaped Lesbian and Gay Activism*, 58–61.

49. See, for example, Fetner, *How the Religious Right Shaped Lesbian and Gay Activism*, 65–74.

50. Patrick J. Buchanan, "1992 Republican National Convention Speech," Buchanan.org, http://buchanan.org/blog/1992-republican-national-convention-speech-148, accessed October 17, 2017.

51. Cadge, "Vital Conflicts."

52. Wuthnow, *Restructuring of American Religion*, 10.

53. See, for example, Herman, *Antigay Agenda*, 32, 50.

54. Jordan, *Recruiting Young Love*, 148–49; emphasis in original.

55. For histories of the various lesbian and gay rights organizations, see Armstrong, *Forging Gay Identities*; D'Emilio, *Sexual Politics*; and Faderman, *Gay Revolution*.

56. Jordan, *Recruiting Young Love*, 106.

57. Fetner, *How the Religious Right Shaped Lesbian and Gay Activism*, 30.

58. Fetner, *How the Religious Right Shaped Lesbian and Gay Activism*, xiv.

59. On the history of LGBT organizing in Christian traditions, see H. R. White, "Proclaiming Liberation" and *Reforming Sodom*; and Jordan, *Recruiting Young Love*.

60. Formed by George Augustine Hyde and John Kazantks, the first known church in the United States to minister to openly gay people was the Eucharist Catholic Church in Atlanta during the late 1940s and early 1950s. For more on this history, see "Profile: Rev. George Augustine Hyde," LGBTran.org, https://www.lgbtran.org/Profile.aspx?ID=96, last modified September 2004. See also Jordan, *Recruiting Young Love*, 69–70; and H. R. White, "Proclaiming Liberation," 104.

61. Quoted in Jordan, *Recruiting Young Love*, 119. MCC membership then and now reflects a wide range of faith traditions, including both high and low traditions of Protestantism and Catholicism, Buddhism, Judaism, atheism, and more. H. R. White, "Proclaiming Liberation," 108–10.

62. D'Emilio, *Making Trouble*, 54. According to a report on MCC's website, the church as of 2012 had a presence in forty countries through nearly 250 affiliated churches and ministries. Darlene Garner, "Global Presence of Metropolitan Community Churches," MCC Office of Emerging Ministries, June 23, 2012, http://mccchurch.org/files/2009/08/MCC-GLOBAL-PRESENCE-as-of-June-23-2012.pdf.

63. Jordan, *Recruiting Young Love*, 197.

64. Jordan, *Recruiting Young Love*, 125; and H. R. White, *Reforming Sodom*, 149, 155.

65. Jordan, *Recruiting Young Love*, 67–68, 71, 73, 95; and H. R. White, *Reforming Sodom*, 61, 67, 86, 105. One notable moment in this history includes a four-day retreat in 1964 in San Francisco, called the "Consultation on Religion and the Homosexual," which brought together local Protestant clergy and representatives from several homophile organizations.

66. Dignity, a Catholic LGBT organization, was even earlier. It was formed by Patrick X. Nidorf in 1972 as a support group for gay Catholics and ex-Catholics. See Jordan, *Recruiting Young Love*, 121–27. The UCC Gay Caucus later became the Open and Affirming Coalition, United Church of Christ.

67. Ralph Blair founded Evangelicals Concerned in 1975, and the organization hosts conferences, Bible study groups, and other events to help lesbians and gay men integrate their sexuality with their Christian faith. Soulforce, founded in 1988 by Mel White and Gary Nixon, organizes public education events and nonviolent protests. Andrew Marin founded the Chicago-based Marin Foundation in 2005 with the aim of inspiring dialogue between the conservative evangelical and LGBTQ communities. The Marin Foundation is perhaps most well known for its "I'm Sorry" campaign, where participants attend gay pride parades with signs that apologize for the treatment of LGBTQ people by the conservative Christian church. GCN, now known as Q Christian Fellowship, is a Christian nonprofit founded in 2001 by Justin Lee; it hosts and moderates online forums for LGBTQ Christians and organizes annual conferences to foster community and raise awareness and understanding of LGBTQ issues in conservative churches. See chapter 3 for more on GCN.

68. Many of the people I met had previous or current experience with a wide range of other organizations working at the intersection of LGBTQ issues and Christianity, including the following: Association of Welcoming and Affirming Baptists; Reconciling Ministries Network; Integrity USA; More Light Presbyterians; Open and Affirming Coalition, United Church of Christ; Welcoming Congregations/Guardian Angels Network for the Southwest California Synod of the ELCA; the Fellowship of Affirming Ministries; GRACE (Gay Reconciling Asian Christian Empowerment); Network on Religion and Justice; Intercollegiate Adventist Gay-Straight Alliance Coalition; Center for Lesbian and Gay Studies in Religion and Ministry; KC Coalition of Welcoming Ministries; Equality House; Human Rights Campaign; Evangelicals for Marriage Equality; Evangelicals Concerned; Gay Christian Network; The Marin Foundation; Canyonwalker Connections; Tyler Clementi Foundation; Level Ground; Other Sheep; Rainbow Stoles; Believe Out Loud; Queer Faith Tumbler; Str8apology; #FaithfullyLGBT;

Transfaith; TransSaints Ministry of the Fellowship of Affirming Ministries; Transgender and Christian; and the Transgender Faith Tour.

69. Grenz, *Welcoming but Not Affirming*.

70. According to the Pew Research Center's 2014 "Religious Landscape Study," evangelical Christians—whether self-identifying as evangelical or affiliated with one of the many denominations or nondenominational churches historically lumped together as evangelical—constitute the largest religious group in the United States. More than a quarter of all Americans, and more than a third of the 70 percent of Americans who are Christian, are affiliated with evangelicalism. "Religious Landscape Study," Pew Research Center, http://www.pewforum.org/religious-landscape-study/, accessed October 17, 2017. A 2016 study by the Pew Research Center on the American public's support of same-sex marriage and homosexuality found that just 34 percent of white evangelical Protestants believe homosexuality should be accepted by society, compared to 63 percent of all Americans. Hannah Fingerhut, "Support Steady for Same-Sex Marriage and Acceptance of Homosexuality," Pew Research Center, May 12, 2016, http://www.pewresearch.org/fact-tank/2016/05/12/support-steady-for-same-sex-marriage-and-acceptance-of-homosexuality/.

71. Biblicism, crucicentrism, conversionism, and activism, otherwise known as the "Bebbington quadrilateral," is a fourfold definition of evangelicalism proposed by the sociologist of religion David Bebbington; see Bebbington, *Evangelicalism in Modern Britain*. Ethnographic studies of "America's folk religion" (as Randall Balmer calls it) include the following: Balmer, *Mine Eyes Have Seen the Glory*; Bartkowski, *Promise Keepers*; Elisha, *Moral Ambition*; Harding, *Jerry Falwell*; and Luhrmann, *When God Talks Back*. On the emergence and characteristics of modern American evangelicalism, see Gloege, *Guaranteed Pure*; Sutton, *American Apocalypse*; and Worthen, *Apostles of Reason*. On the origins of evangelicalism in the United States, see Brekus, *Sarah Osborn's World*; and Porterfield, *Conceived in Doubt*. On the place of evangelicalism in broader American religious history, see Marty, *Pilgrims in Their Own Land*.

72. I borrow this language predominately from Talal Asad and his conceptualization of Islam as a discursive and embodied tradition. Asad: *The Idea of an Anthropology of Islam*; *Genealogies of Religion*; "Thinking about Religion, Belief, and Politics"; and "Thinking about Tradition, Religion, and Politics in Egypt Today." For a discussion of extending Asad's arguments to the idea of an anthropology of Christianity, see Robbins, "What Is a Christian?"

73. Some scholars include conservative Catholicism in the Christian Right. Although I met a few gay Catholics during my fieldwork, TRP attracts participants who come from primarily mainline and evangelical Protestant traditions.

74. Fletcher, *Preaching to Convert*, 3.

75. Hulsether, *Religion, Culture, and Politics*, 155–56.

76. Bebbington, *Evangelicalism in Modern Britain*, 2–3.

77. Gasaway, *Progressive Evangelicals*, 7. Contemporary Christians who express their Christian identity in political activism and social justice work thus share in a long tradition of progressive social and political activism in American Christianity: the religiously motivated fervor of Christian abolitionists in the early nineteenth century; the marrying of personal salvation and good works in the Social Gospel movement of the early twentieth century; and the coevolution of the new Protestant Left with the progressive social movements of the 1950s and 1960s and the emergence of liberation theologies, to name a few. See also Kniss, "Mapping the Moral Order." On the role of religion in American radicalism and activism, see McKanan, *Prophetic Encounters*.

78. On progressive evangelicalism and the evangelical Left, see Gasaway, *Progressive Evangelicals*; and Swartz, *Moral Minority*. On socially engaged evangelicals, see Elisha, *Moral Ambition*. On new or neo-evangelicalism, see Streenland and Goff, *New Evangelical Social Engagement*. For the related history of the broader Protestant Left, see Hulsether, *Building a Protestant Left*.

79. Elisha, *Moral Ambition*, 24–25. Elisha, borrowing from Jasper's *The Art of Moral Protest*, argues that the socially engaged evangelicals he studied do not adhere to a single activist identity. As such, Elisha prefers the language of "activist orientation" to draw attention to how they center social justice work as part of their religious identity.

80. Coley, *Gay on God's Campus*, 3–7.

81. Foucault, *Security, Territory, Population*, 191–226. Counter-conduct is still a somewhat unexplored aspect of Foucault's rethinking of power and resistance, although there has been some growing interest in the concept among scholars since the 2007 publication in English of Foucault's 1978 Collège de France course, "Security, Territory, Population." This includes a recent special issue of *Foucault Studies* devoted to counter-conduct. Binkley and Cruikshank, "Counter-Conduct." Recent scholarship in social movements studies has put counter-conduct to work in the analysis of various protest movements. See, for example, Conlon, "Hungering for Freedom"; and Death, "Counter-Conducts." Mark Jordan, *Convulsing Bodies*, 25, draws on

Foucault's writings on religion and resistance to think about the religious energies of "counter-communities" as resistance movements against twentieth-century political regimes.

82. Foucault, *Security, Territory, Population*, 193. I have omitted the variations on the French *conduite*, used by Foucault in this passage and that the translator included in the English translation.

83. Foucault, *Security, Territory, Population*, 194. In the lectures on "Security, Territory, Population" Foucault explores how and when modern forms of governmentality emerged from the medieval Christian pastorate and the shared logic between these regimes of power. He argues that the common thread between the governmental logic and target of the secular nation-state and the Christian pastorate is conduct. The various modes of counter-conduct represented by the antipastoral movements of the Middle Ages eroded the power of the pastorate, enabling the rise of secular forms of pastoral power in the form of modern nation-states. While Foucault spends the most time in his lectures on the antipastoral movements of the Middle Ages, he also references other examples of counter-conduct movements throughout, such as Luther's reformation, which he calls "the greatest revolt of conduct the Christian West has known," and the Methodist movement of the nineteenth century (*Security, Territory, Population*, 196).

84. Foucault, *Security, Territory, Population*, 195. Foucault identifies five main forms of counter-conduct that emerged during the Middle Ages: asceticism, communities, mysticism, Scripture, and eschatological beliefs (*Security, Territory, Population*, 204–16). For further reading on counter-conduct as an analytical category and its place in Foucault's genealogy of the pastorate and governmentality, see Davidson, "In Praise of Counter-Conduct"; Chrulew, "Pastoral Counter-Conducts"; and Lorenzini, "From Counter-Conduct to Critical Attitude."

85. Foucault, *Security, Territory, Population*, 194–95. I have omitted the French *conducteurs* from the quote.

86. Compare Foucault, *Security, Territory, Population*, 149.

87. Death, "Counter-Conducts."

88. Foucault, *Security, Territory, Population*, 215.

89. Foucault, *History of Sexuality*, 101.

90. Binkley and Cruikshank, "Introduction," 3.

91. Davidson, "In Praise of Counter-Conduct," 27.

92. Compare Luhrmann, *When God Talks Back*, 190.

93. The Kansas City steering committee, chaired by Paul Creekmore, was subdivided into several subcommittees, or action teams, led by other volunteers. When I joined the steering committee in April 2015, the teams were

for volunteers, worship, hospitality, promotions, prayer, discover the city, and fundraising. These teams were reorganized and consolidated in the two months leading up to the Kansas City conference into four subcommittees: logistics, public relations and marketing, organizing and turnout, and programming. I am unable to speak to the composition of the steering committees of the other two conferences I attended.

94. At the time of my fieldwork, TRP's board of directors included two white cisgender straight women; two white cisgender gay men; and a cisgender straight man who identified as Nikkei.

95. Registration fees began at $99 and increased to $199 in the weeks before each conference. TRP does offer discounted tickets for groups and volunteers and offers a limited number of need-based scholarships. Conference attendees came from all over the United States with a few international attendees.

96. It is my understanding that at least some of the conference speakers and panelists were reimbursed for travel expenses or provided honorariums.

97. Foucault, *Use of Pleasure*, 12–13.

98. Thomas, *Doing Critical Ethnography*, 4.

99. Madison, *Doing Critical Ethnography*, 5; emphasis in original.

100. Abu-Lughod, "Writing against Culture." See also Behar and Gordon, *Women Writing Culture*; and Weston, "The Virtual Anthropologist."

101. Okely, *Anthropological Practice*, 21–23.

102. See, for example, Barrett-Fox, *God Hates*; and Erzen, *Straight to Jesus*.

103. Compare Harding, *Jerry Falwell*.

104. Tanya Erzen relates a similar story in *Straight to Jesus*, 6–7.

105. Mapping is a technique used by community organizers to get people invested in a cause by building and sustaining relationships with them. The process begins with an individual recruiting a target number of people in their sphere of influence who then, in turn, identify a target number of people to do the same.

106. Luhrmann, *When God Talks Back*.

107. Latour, "From Realpolitik to Dingpolitik"; Fraser, "Rethinking the Public Sphere," 123; and Rochon, *Culture Moves*, 8.

108. Isaac, Jacobs, Kucinskas, and McGrath, "Social Movement Schools."

109. Ahmed, *Cultural Politics of Emotion*; and Landsberg, *Prosthetic Memory*.

1. Grace-Filled Conversations

1. K. Ryan Jones and Shawn Willis, "Is This the Most Radical Preacher in America?" MSNBC Digital Documentaries, September 30, 2014, http://www.msnbc.com/msnbc/watch/is-this-the-most-radical-preacher-in-america-335687235881.

2. Allyson Dylan Robinson, "The Three Temptations of the Affirming Church: A Sermon Delivered at the Opening of the Reformation Project's 2014 Washington DC Regional Conference," *Allyson Dylan Robinson* (blog), November 8, 2014, https://medium.com/@allysonrobinson/the-three-temptations-of-the-affirming-church-b524086fc77b#.xut1cy9zg. Quotations in the next several paragraphs come from this source as a supplement to my fieldnotes.

3. The story of the temptation of Christ appears in all three Synoptic Gospels. Robinson draws mainly from the Gospel of Luke's version (4:1–13) of the story. Although often translated as "tempted," the Greek *peirazo* means "to try" or "to test" in the sense of putting someone or something to the test. During Jesus's time in the wilderness, the devil comes to him and presents him with three tests: to turn stones into bread to relieve his own hunger; to throw himself off a high point to demonstrate his faith that angels will break his fall; and to worship the devil in exchange for political power.

4. Mirroring practices I found elsewhere during fieldwork, Robinson positioned herself as speaking on behalf of both the LGBTQ Christian and broader LGBTQ communities while critiquing what she simply referred to as "the church," which she separated into affirming and nonaffirming. According to Robinson, broader support of marriage equality, nondiscrimination protections, and increasing acceptance of LGBTQ Americans in churches and society are evidence that the culture wars are coming to a close.

5. TRP's inaugural regional training conference took place during the Obama administration.

6. Moon and Tobin, "Sunsets and Solidarity" and "Politics of Shame."

7. "There is in fact another, to a certain extent opposite way of refusing submission to pastoral power, which is the formation of communities." Foucault, *Security, Territory, Population*, 208.

8. Moon, *God, Sex, Politics*, 2.

9. The trend, especially among younger white evangelicals, of identifying as "spiritual but not religious"—and similar expressions such as "follower of Christ"—also reflects this dynamic. In my experience those who identify as "spiritual but not religious" are sometimes seeking to distance themselves from evangelicalism's role in the culture wars, which they see as a "politicization" of religion. On "spiritual but not religious" as a social and political practice, see Bender, *New Metaphysicals*, 183.

10. Asad, *Formations of the Secular*, 200; emphasis in original. See also Asad, *Genealogies of Religion*, 27–29. Similarly Foucault suggests that the relationship between religion and politics in modern Western societies should be defined less in terms of the "interplay between Church and state" than

"between the pastorate and government." Foucault, *Security, Territory, Population*, 191.

11. As a corrective, Courtney Bender has argued that scholars of religion should study "practicing religion" rather than "religious practices" or the processes through which ideas, practices, and institutions become religious or political ("Practicing Religions," 274–75).

12. Latour, "From Realpolitik to Dingpolitik."

13. Latour, "From Realpolitik to Dingpolitik," 13. Thus Latour proposes the term "Dingpolitik" as a substitute for "Realpolitik."

14. Latour, "From Realpolitik to Dingpolitik," 5.

15. Latour, "From Realpolitik to Dingpolitik," 13; emphasis in original.

16. Latour, "From Realpolitik to Dingpolitik," 31. In this way Latour's focus on assemblies constituted through disagreement is a critique of the Habermasian vision of a public sphere constituted by some underlying agreement or commitment to consensus. The public sphere envisioned by Jürgen Habermas is a space where "private people come together as a public" to form public opinion by engaging in open dialogue and critical debate; Habermas, *Structural Transformation*, 27. Habermas considered the public sphere to be an inclusive space accessible to all. Critics, however, have called attention to how the public sphere is always constructed by exclusion. Cody, "Publics and Politics," 40. Often, marginalized groups are systematically excluded from the public sphere for not conforming to what is accepted as legitimate public discourse or practice. This is true also regarding LGBTQ people in many Christian traditions.

17. For discussions on what could be called "religious publics," how religions "go public" through mass media and other means, and more generally on the relationship between religion and the public sphere, see Asad, *Formations of the Secular*; Casanova, *Public Religions*; Engelke, *God's Agents*; and Hirschkind, *Ethical Soundscape*.

18. Other denominations have similar organizations but use different language to describe churches that have become reconciling. For example, Presbyterian churches might become More Light congregations; churches in the United Church of Christ use the language of Open and Affirming; and the Evangelical Lutheran Church in America uses the language of Reconciling in Christ.

19. Methodism refers to a broad movement in Protestantism rooted in the life and teachings of John Wesley, an eighteenth-century Church of England minister who established parishes in the Colony of Georgia in the late 1730s. Methodism has come to represent a theological position that embraces Arminianism in opposition to Calvinism, in particular rejecting

the Calvinist notions of total depravity and the elect in favor of Christian perfectionism and free will. For the history and culture of Methodism in the United States, see Vickers, *Cambridge Companion to American Methodism*.

20. Denominationalism as a theoretical concept was developed in the early twentieth century by sociologists of religion to categorize religious bodies— primarily Protestant—that share a common commitment to a particular faith tradition but nevertheless have somewhat distinct polities, cultures, and beliefs. Weber, "On Church, Sect, and Mysticism"; Niebuhr, *Social Sources of Denominationalism*; and Troeltsch, *Social Teachings of the Christian Churches*. Denominations have played a significant role throughout American religious history in mediating between the twin tendencies of either withdrawing from society and creating spiritual ghettos or attempting to abolish the lines between church and state, tending instead to assume a more accommodationist orientation to the demands of a pluralistic society. Berger, *Sacred Canopy*, 106. At the same time, denominationalism as an analytical category has suffered from the inability to account for variation, conflict, disagreement, and dissent within particular denominations and religious communities, giving the impression that denominations are more homogenous than they are in reality. In fact, some would argue that denominational instability has always been a defining characteristic of American religious life. Moore, *Religious Outsiders*.

21. Often called *The Discipline*, the book outlines the law and doctrine of the UMC. The full passage in the 1972 version reads, "Homosexuals no less than heterosexuals are persons of sacred worth, who need the ministry and guidance of the church in their struggles for human fulfillment, as well as the spiritual and emotional care of a fellowship which enables reconciling relationships with God, with others and with self. Further we insist that all persons are entitled to have their human and civil rights ensured, though we do not condone the practice of homosexuality and consider this practice incompatible with Christian teaching." Bucke, Hole, and Proctor, *Book of Discipline*, 256. For a history of the "homosexual issue" in the UMC denomination, see Udis-Kessler, *Queer Inclusion*.

22. Good News began as a magazine by the same name in 1967, and as an organization it has had a presence at General Conference since 1972, advocating for a range of conservative social issues. Transforming Congregations was formed in the late 1980s as a response to the successes of RMN. At one point affiliated with Exodus International, Transforming Congregations coordinates ex-gay ministries in the UMC, developing educational materials and workshops devoted to helping congregations respond to the "sex-

ually confused and broken." "About," TransformingCongregations.org, http://transformingcongregations.org/about/, accessed October 17, 2017.

23. Brief biographies of both men can be found on the LGBT Religious Archives Network's website. "Profile: Dr. Rick Huskey," LGBTran.org, https://lgbtran .org/Profile.aspx?ID=39, last modified October 2003; "Profile: Gene Leggett," LGBTran.org, https://lgbtran.org/profile.aspx?ID=236, last modified October 2009.

24. Quoted in Udis-Kessler, *Queer Inclusion*, 28–29.

25. The following history and summary of the reconciliation process are based on RMN promotional and educational materials, as well as conversations with individuals during my fieldwork. See "Become a Reconciling Congregation or Community," RMNetwork.org, https://rmnetwork.org/take -action/become-a-reconciling-congregation-or-community/, accessed June 22, 2016; "Our History," RMNetwork.org, https://rmnetwork.org/who-we -are/history/, accessed June 22, 2016.

26. In 1989 the program, now called Reconciling Congregations, was incorporated as an independent nonprofit and in 2000 was renamed again as the Reconciling Ministries Network. By the end of 1984 the organization had shepherded nine churches through the process of becoming reconciling congregations; by mid-2016 the number of reconciling communities totaled nearly eight hundred.

27. "Become a Reconciling Congregation or Community."

28. The "public and visible" includes publishing a statement of inclusion called a "Welcoming Statement," which should be on church letterhead and placed in one or more public places, such as the church marquee, promotional materials, or a Facebook page. Churches should think of the Welcoming Statement "as placing your 'Welcome Mat' on the outside of the building, not just the inside." RMN suggests language for and makes final approval of the Welcoming Statement, noting that "because *The Book of Discipline* specifically singles out lesbian and gay persons for harm, and because RMN is committed to ensuring that bisexual and transgender persons are equally valued and included, it is critical that each statement explicitly welcomes lesbian, gay, bisexual, and transgender persons (full spelling preferred)." "Become a Reconciling Congregation or Community."

29. Moon, "Difficult Dialogues," 184.

30. Moon, "Difficult Dialogues," 183–84.

31. Rebecca Voelkel, David Lohman, and Tim Feiertag, "Building an Inclusive Church, a Welcoming Toolkit 2.0: Helping Your Congregation Become a Community That Openly Welcomes People of All Sexual Orientations and Gender Identities," RMNetwork.org, http://www.rmnetwork.org/newrmn

/wp-content/uploads/2014/10/welcomingtoolkit.pdf, accessed June 22, 2016. The Institute for Welcoming Resources became a program of the National LGBTQ Task Force after a merger in 2006. The toolkit was written and compiled with the help of several "partner Welcoming Church Programs," including representatives from the Reconciling Ministries Network, More Light Presbyterians, Integrity USA, the Association of Welcoming and Affirming Baptists, Room for All in the Reformed Church in America, ReconcilingWorks, and GCN. Quotations in the next several paragraphs come from this source.

32. Likewise the toolkit draws on the work of Marshall Ganz, a scholar influential in various social movements, to encourage the practice of public storytelling as a strategy for inspiring action. With the communication of values through emotional storytelling as opposed to talking points, the goal is to build a foundation for empathy and shared experience that will ultimately translate into political action. The authors of the toolkit see a family resemblance between Ganz's storytelling strategy and the work of reconciliation. After all, they write, "Jesus was first and foremost a storyteller," and "the opportunity to listen deeply to one another through a Welcoming Process is one of the characteristics that mark it as sacred." Voelkel, Lohman, and Feiertag, "Building an Inclusive Church, a Welcoming Toolkit 2.0."

33. For a brief discussion of different types of ecclesiastical polity, see Balmer, *Encyclopedia of Evangelicalism*, 460.

34. Balmer, *Mine Eyes Have Seen the Glory*, xv.

35. The National Association of Evangelicals represents about thirty million evangelicals from forty-five thousand churches across forty denominations. As of 2015 the Southern Baptist Convention had a membership of more than fifteen million. "About NAE," NAE.net, https://www.nae.net/about-nae/, accessed June 15, 2017; Travis Loller, "Southern Baptists See 9th Year of Membership Decline," Associated Press, June 7, 2016, http://bigstory.ap.org/article/e1afa2371ff44136ae3683ff0eb8c6e7/southern-baptists-see-9th-year-membership-decline.

36. Fuist, Stoll, and Kniss, "Beyond the Liberal-Conservative Divide," 65–87.

37. Fuist, Stoll, and Kniss, "Beyond the Liberal-Conservative Divide," 78.

38. Fuist, Stoll, and Kniss, "Beyond the Liberal-Conservative Divide," 78. The authors cite Evangelicals Concerned as an example.

39. Compare Fuist, Stoll, and Kniss, "Beyond the Liberal-Conservative Divide," 81.

40. Fraser, "Rethinking the Public Sphere," 123.

41. "Past National Conferences," ReformationProject .org, https://www.reformationproject.org/past-national-conferences/, accessed October 18, 2017.

42. Rochon, *Culture Moves*, 8.

43. Rochon, *Culture Moves*, 69.

44. Max Kuecker interview with author, March 4, 2015.

45. Bartkowski, *Promise Keepers*, 37.

46. I have borrowed the language of deep hanging out from my dissertation advisor, Ben Chappell, who uses this language to describe the practice of ethnography.

47. I use "gay Christians" in this section because VanderWal-Gritter's focus and argument pertain, for the most part, to lesbians and gay men.

48. See, for example, a critique of VanderWal-Gritter's book written by Side B Christians: "A Review of Generous Spaciousness by Wendy VanderWal-Gritter," *A Queer Calling* (blog), May 22, 2014, http://aqueercalling.com /2014/05/22/a-review-of-generous-spaciousness-by-wendy-vanderwal -gritter/.

49. Foucault, *Use of Pleasure*, 12–13.

50. Luhrmann, *When God Talks Back*.

51. VanderWal-Gritter, *Generous Spaciousness*, 12, 19, 41.

52. See VanderWal-Gritter, *Generous Spaciousness*, chapter 3, for a discussion of ex-gay therapy and ministries.

53. VanderWal-Gritter, *Generous Spaciousness*, 14.

54. VanderWal-Gritter, *Generous Spaciousness*, 16.

55. "Our History," GenerousSpace.ca, https://www.generousspace.ca/our history/, accessed October 17, 2017.

56. VanderWal-Gritter, *Generous Spaciousness*, 14.

57. VanderWal-Gritter, *Generous Spaciousness*, 50.

58. VanderWal-Gritter, *Generous Spaciousness*, 13.

59. Frei, "Response," 24. See also Frei, *Theology and Narrative*.

60. Springs, *Generous Orthodoxy*, 17.

61. Springs, *Generous Orthodoxy*, 17.

62. Grenz, *Renewing the Center*; and McLaren, *Generous Orthodoxy*.

63. VanderWal-Gritter, *Generous Spaciousness*, 26.

64. VanderWal-Gritter, *Generous Spaciousness*, 106.

65. VanderWal-Gritter, *Generous Spaciousness*, 106.

66. VanderWal-Gritter, *Generous Spaciousness*, 107.

67. Wilson, *Letter to My Congregation*, 81–110.

68. See, for example, Rom. 14:1–23; Wilson, *Letter to My Congregation*, 81–110.

69. Danny Cortez, "Why I Changed My Mind on Homosexuality," YouTube .com, https://www.youtube.com/watch?v=WqYvkVqVLF0&feature= youtube, accessed October 18, 2017.

70. Bob Allen, "Southern Baptists Oust 'Third Way' Church," *Baptist News*, September 23, 2014, https://baptistnews.com/article/southern-baptists -oust-third-way-church/.

71. Matthew Vines, "Elevating the Dialogue on LGBT Inclusion," Facebook .com, https:// www .facebook .com /vinesmatthew / ?hc _ref = search, accessed November 14, 2016. As of mid-2018, TRP had organized at least three such events: on August 9, 2016, in Atlanta at the nondenominational Renovation Church; on October 21, 2016, at TRP's Los Angeles regional training conference; and on May 18, 2017, at Northland Church, an evangelical church in Longwood, Florida.

72. Butler, *Precarious Life*, xix.

73. Butler, *Precarious Life*, xix.

74. R. Albert Mohler Jr., "There Is No 'Third Way': Southern Baptists Face a Moment of Decision (and So Will You)," AlbertMohler.com, June 2, 2014, http:// www .albertmohler .com /2014 /06 /02 /there -is -no -third -way -southern-baptists-face-a-moment-of-decision-and-so-will-you/.

75. Ruth Graham, "Is It Too Late for Evangelical Christians to Honestly Discuss Same-Sex Marriage?: A Dispatch from This Year's Q Ideas Conference, or the Christian TED Talks," *Slate*, April 29, 2015, http://www.slate.com /articles/life/faithbased/2015/04/q_ideas_conference_2015_how_does _the_christian_ted_talks_deal_with_same.html.

76. Eric Teetsel and Owen Strachan, "Colson, Conversation, and Questions about Q Ideas," *The Manhattan Project* (blog), April 15, 2015, http://www .patheos.com/blogs/manhattanproject/2015/04/qideas/.

77. Matthew Lee Anderson, "The Limits of Dialogue: Q Ideas, Gay Marriage, and Chuck Colson," *Mere Orthodoxy*, April 17, 2015, https://mereorthodoxy .com/limits-dialogue-q-ideas-gay-marriage-chuck-colson/.

78. Carol Kuruvilla, "United Methodist Church Makes Small Step toward Accepting Same Sex Marriage," *Huffington Post*, February 14, 2015, http:// www.huffingtonpost.com/2015/02/14/united-methodist-church-gay -marriage_n_6680290.html.

79. Candace Chellew-Hodge, "God and the Gay Christian: An Interview with Matthew Vines," *Religion Dispatches*, May 7, 2014, http://religiondispatches .org/god-and-the-gay-christian-an-interview-with-matthew-vines/.

80. Agamben, *Time That Remains*, 116.

81. Agamben, *Time That Remains*, 119.

82. Agamben, *Time That Remains*, 123. Agamben is referencing Mauss's classic essay *The Gift*, where Mauss theorizes that gifts, contrary to popular belief, are never actually free but draw one into an obligation of reciprocity and exchange.

83. Lee, *Torn*, 232.

84. Lee, *Torn*, 210.

85. I discuss these workshops in greater detail in chapter 5. The quotes in the next several paragraphs are reconstructions based on my fieldnotes of discussions at TRP's Atlanta and Kansas City regional training conferences (June 2015 and November 2015 respectively).

86. Davis, *In Defense of Civility*, 159. Original quote in italics.

87. Moon, "Difficult Dialogues," 197.

88. Herbst, *Rude Democracy*, 4; emphasis in original. See also p. 148.

2. The Problem of Scripture

1. Kevin DeYoung, "40 Questions for Christians Now Waving Rainbow Flags," *Kevin DeYoung* (blog), July 1, 2015, http://blogs.thegospelcoalition.org /kevindeyoung/2015/07/01/40-questions-for-christians-now-waving -rainbow-flags/. According to the organization's website, the Gospel Coalition is a "fellowship of evangelical churches" founded in 2005 by Don Carson and Tim Keller. The organization's leadership includes a council of fifty-five theologians and pastors, among them Carson, Keller, DeYoung, R. Albert Mohler Jr., and John Piper. The Gospel Coalition's mission is to influence and educate church leadership through conferences, the production of educational resources and position pieces, and other initiatives. See "Foundation Documents," theGospelCoalition .org, https://www .thegospelcoalition.org/about/foundation-documents, accessed October 18, 2017. Unless otherwise noted, quotes in the next several paragraphs are from DeYoung, "40 Questions."

2. Several Christian bloggers decided to take DeYoung's questions seriously. See, for example, Ben Irwin, "40 Answers for Kevin DeYoung," *Ben Irwin* (blog), July 2, 2015, http://benirwin.me/2015/07/02/40-answers-kevin -deyoung-gay-marriage/; Susan Cottrell, "40 Real Answers to Your 40 Questions: To Kevin DeYoung and the Gospel Coalition," *FreedHearts* (blog), July 3, 2015, http://www.patheos.com/blogs/freedhearts/2015/07/03 /40-real-answers-to-your-40-questions-to-kevin-deyoung-the-gospel -coalition/; Buzz Dixon, "40 Questions for Christians Now Waving Rainbow Flags," *Above All, Love* (blog), July 2, 2015, http://www.patheos.com /blogs/unfundamentalistchristians/2015/07/40-questions-for-christians -now-waving-rainbow-flags/. Matthew Vines countered with his own list of forty questions, "40 Questions for Christians Who Oppose Marriage Equality," *Corner of Church and State* (blog), July 3, 2015, http://tobingrant .religionnews.com/2015/07/03/40-questions-for-christians-who-oppose -marriage-equality-guest-commentary/. Another blogger responded with

just one question: "When are you going to listen to the answers to your questions?" Alise Wright, "1 Question for People Who Won't Wave the Rainbow Flag," *Knitting Soul* (blog), July 3, 2015, http://knittingsoul.com /2015/07/03/1-question-for-people-who-wont-wave-the-rainbow-flag/. The responses illustrate how the issue is not as settled as DeYoung assumes it to be, even among evangelicals.

3. The scholarship on this topic is vast. The main works I drew upon include Boswell, *Christianity*; Jordan, *Invention of Sodomy*; and Martin, *Sex and the Single Savior*.

4. Bielo, "Introduction: Encountering Biblicism," 2. Bielo borrows this language from the anthropologist John Bowen, "Elaborating Scriptures."

5. Foucault, *Security, Territory, Population*, 213.

6. Ammerman, *Bible Believers*; and Harding, *Jerry Falwell*.

7. Bebbington, *Evangelicalism in Modern Britain*, 2–3.

8. Smith, *Bible Made Impossible*.

9. Bielo, *Words upon the Word*, and Luhrmann, *When God Talks Back*.

10. Harding, *Jerry Falwell*, 27.

11. Compare Orsi, *History and Presence*. See also Bialecki, "Bones Restored to Life."

12. Bielo, "Introduction: Encountering Biblicism," 2.

13. Many evangelical churches are just now beginning to grapple with transgender and gender-nonconforming identities. I return to this topic in chapter 4.

14. Thumma, "Negotiating a Religious Identity"; and Wolkomir, *"Be Not Deceived."*

15. H. R. White, *Reforming Sodom*, 1. "Do you not know that the unrighteous will not inherit the kingdom of God? Do not be deceived; neither the immoral, nor idolaters, nor adulterers, nor homosexuals, nor thieves, nor the greedy, nor drunkards, nor revilers, nor robbers will inherit the kingdom of God" (1 Cor. 6:9–10 RSV). While the complete RSV wasn't published until 1952, the New Testament was released in 1946.

16. H. R. White, *Reforming Sodom*, 35. In addition to 1 Cor. 6:9–10, the other most cited passages include Gen. 19, Lev. 18:22 and 20:13, Rom. 1:24–27, and 1 Tim. 1:10. White points to the twelve-volume *The Interpreter's Bible*, a series of biblical criticism and commentary published in the 1950s, as an example of the emerging homosexual tradition.

17. Hornsby, "Heteronormativity/Heterosexism," 326.

18. H. R. White, *Reforming Sodom*, 3.

19. H. R. White, *Reforming Sodom*, 35.

20. Jordan, *Invention of Sodomy*.

21. Boswell, *Christianity*; Jordan, *Invention of Sodomy*; and Martin, *Sex and the Single Savior*.
22. Katz, *Invention of Heterosexuality*, 14. See also P. Brown, *Body and Society*.
23. Foucault, *History of Sexuality*, 43.
24. Jordan, *Recruiting Young Love*, 8.
25. Quoted in Jordan, *Recruiting Young Love*, 8.
26. Jordan, *Recruiting Young Love*, 8.
27. Jordan, *Recruiting Young Love*, 8.
28. Jordan, *Recruiting Young Love*, 9–10.
29. Foucault, *History of Sexuality*, 43.
30. Katz, *Invention of Heterosexuality*, 20.
31. Carter, *Heart of Whiteness*.
32. H. R. White, *Reforming Sodom*, 17. Mark Jordan identifies the Anglican clergyman Hugh Northcote's *Christianity and Sex Problems* (1906) and the Roman Catholic layman Anomaly's *The Invert* (1927) as the first adaptations of Ellis's notion of inversion for Christian audiences. Jordan, *Recruiting Young Love*, 14.
33. H. R. White, *Reforming Sodom*, 4.
34. Herman, *Antigay Agenda*, 29. *Christianity Today* continues to be an influential platform for the Christian Right's policing of LGBTQ Christians and the so-called LGBTQ agenda.
35. Herman, *Antigay Agenda*, 50.
36. While the comparative study of Bible translations is beyond the scope of this project, a little context on the differences among Bible translations is necessary. Bible scholars usually recognize two approaches to translating the ancient texts from their original Hebrew, Greek, and Aramaic languages. Formal equivalency translations, like the RSV and the updated New Revised Standard Version (NRSV), attempt a literal "word for word" translation. By contrast, functional equivalency translations use a "thought for thought" approach, more freely paraphrasing the original language to capture cultural idiom and nuance or to translate obscure ancient concepts into equivalent contemporary ones. Among the functional equivalency translations, some Bible scholars also distinguish between dynamic (thought for thought) and free (paraphrase) translations. The New International Version (NIV), for example, is widely considered to be the best among dynamic translations, while translations like Eugene Peterson's *The Message* represent the latter. In general Bible scholars consider formal equivalency translations as better suited for serious academic study in that such translations are less prone to introducing cultural biases into the text. Even so, both formal and functional equivalency approaches are interpre-

tations, and interpretations are always political. As the history of the entrance of homosexuality into English-language Bibles demonstrates, the translational process is inevitably conditioned by politics and culture.

37. A recent study found that the KJV is still the most widely read Bible translation, with 55 percent of Americans who read Scripture using it. The NIV follows at 19 percent. Goff, Farnsley, and Thuesen, *Bible in American Life*, 7.

38. Gutjahr, "From Monarchy to Democracy," 164.

39. For a discussion of the evangelical reaction to what was perceived to be a liberal bias and acquiescence to liberalism and modernism in the RSV and the translation history of the NIV as a conservative Protestant response, see Thuesen, *In Discordance with the Scriptures*, 136. Some evangelicals criticized the 2011 revision of the NIV for incorporating more gender-neutral language in certain passages. Associated Press, "New Bible Draws Critics of Gender-Neutral Language," *Washington Post*, March 17, 2011, http://www.washingtonpost.com/wp-dyn/content/article/2011/03/17/AR201103 1703434.html.

40. Michael Gryboski, "NIV Bible Translation Clearer on Homosexual Sins, Says Theologian," *Christian Post*, January 4, 2012, http://www.christianpost.com/news/latest-niv-bible-translation-clearer-on-homosexual-sins-says-theologian-66393/.

41. The 2011 NIV translates *arsenekoitais* in a similar vice list in 1 Tim. 1:10 as "those practicing homosexuality."

42. "For this cause God gave them up unto vile affections: for even their women did change the natural use into that which is against nature: And likewise also the men, leaving the natural use of the woman, burned in their lust one toward another; men with men working that which is unseemly, and receiving in themselves that recompense of their error which was meet" (Rom. 1:26–27 KJV).

43. The Conservative Bible Project might be considered an extreme dynamic translation. It's hosted and written by a group of editors—including Andrew Schlafly, the son of Phyllis Schlafly—on a very conservative wiki-style online encyclopedia designed to be a conservative alternative to Wikipedia. "Conservative Bible Project," Conservapedia.com, http://www.conservapedia.com/Conservative_Bible_Project, accessed October 19, 2017.

44. "Romans 1–8 (Translated)," Conservapedia.com, http://www.conservapedia.com/Romans_1–8_(Translated), accessed October 19, 2017.

45. Peterson, *The Message*, 308.

46. Herman, *Antigay Agenda*, 69.

47. The presentation was recorded on March 8 and posted on March 10, 2012. Vines, "The Gay Debate."

48. Douglas Quenqua, "Turned Away, He Turned to the Bible," *New York Times*, September 14, 2012, http://www.nytimes.com/2012/09/16/fashion /matthew-vines-wont-rest-in-defending-gay-christians.html?_r=1; Mark Sandlin, "I'm Not Saying You're Homophobic; I'm Just Saying You're Homophobic," *Huffington Post*, July 10, 2012, http://www.huffingtonpost .com/mark-sandlin/im-not-saying-youre-homophobic-im-just-saying -youre-homophobic_b_1656240.html; Dan Savage, "The Gay Debate: The Bible and Homosexuality," *Savage Love* (blog), May 29, 2012, http://slog .thestranger.com/slog/archives/2012/03/29/the-gay-debate-the-bible -and-homosexuality.

49. See also Kathy Baldock, "The Bible and Homosexuality, a Biblical Presen-tation with Matthew Vines," *LGBTQ Nation*, March 27, 2017, https://www .lgbtqnation.com/2012/03/the-bible-and-homosexuality-a-biblical -presentation-with-matthew-vines/; Chellew-Hodge, "God and the Gay Christian"; Roy Wenzl, "A Christian Family, a Gay Son, and a Wichita Father's Change of Heart," *Wichita Eagle*, June 7, 2014, http://www.kansas .com/news/article1145473.html.

50. See chapter 3 for a discussion of ex-gay ministries.

51. Quoted in Chellew-Hodge, "God and the Gay Christian."

52. Vines, *God and the Gay Christian*, 2.

53. Jonathan Merritt, "Christian Bookstores Are the Next Gay-Marriage Bat-tleground," *The Week*, July 9, 2014, http://theweek.com/articles/445561 /christian-bookstores-are-next-gaymarriage-battleground.

54. "Blind Leading the Blind: Matthew Vines' Dime Store Gay Theology," *Gay Christian Movement Watch* (blog), March 29, 2013, https://gcmwatch .wordpress.com/.

55. Mohler, *God and the Gay Christian?*

56. Quoted in James A. Smith Sr., "Pro-Gay Book 'Exceedingly Dangerous,'" *Baptist News*, April 22, 2014, http://www.bpnews.net/42415/progay-book -exceedingly-dangerous.

57. Jordan, *Recruiting Young Love*, 56–57.

58. Bailey, *Homosexuality*, x–xi.

59. Bailey, *Homosexuality*, x; emphasis in original.

60. Jordan, *Recruiting Young Love*, 57.

61. Boswell, *Christianity*, 37.

62. See, for example, Boswell, *Christianity*, 12, 17. Boswell argues elsewhere, "If the categories 'homosexual/heterosexual' and 'gay/straight' are the inventions of particular societies rather than real aspects of the human psyche, there is no gay history" ("Revolutions," 93). For essays on Boswell's legacy in gay-affirming theology, church debates on homosexuality, and

debates in queer studies around social constructionism and essentialism, see Kuefler, *Boswell Thesis*.

63. For a brief biography of Wood, see "Profile: Rev. Robert W. Wood," LGBTran.org; Jordan, *Recruiting Young Love*, 75; and H. R. White, *Reforming Sodom*, 96.

64. Wood, *Christ and the Homosexual*, 154, 168. Wood also tentatively endorses same-sex marriage ceremonies (p. 200).

65. Vines, *God and the Gay Christian*, 3; emphasis in original.

66. Vines, *God and the Gay Christian*, 18.

67. Vines, *God and the Gay Christian*, 137.

68. Vines, *God and the Gay Christian*, 10.

69. Some Christians believe that the new covenant wholly renders the old covenant obsolete, and therefore even Jewish people will have to convert to Christianity to be saved. Some also believe that widespread Jewish conversion to Christianity will be a sign of the end of times.

70. Vines, *God and the Gay Christian*, 79.

71. Vines, *God and the Gay Christian*, 67–68, 137–47. See also Drake, *Slandering the Jew*.

72. Vines, *God and the Gay Christian*, 1. In a footnote to chapter 6—during a discussion of a passage in Romans where Vines argues that the Apostle Paul's language about God giving people over to shameful lusts and unnatural sexual relations refers not to committed, same-sex relationships but to excess passion—Vines suggests, "My argument is not limited to the same-sex relationships of gay people. Long-term, monogamous same-sex unions—whether the partners identify as gay, bisexual, pan, queer, or whether they eschew sexual identity labels altogether—are significantly different from the lustful, self-centered behavior Paul has in view in Romans 1:26–27" (*God and the Gay Christian*, 206n36).

73. Vines, *God and the Gay Christian*, 40.

74. Vines, *God and the Gay Christian*, 3.

75. "The Reformation Project: Training Christians to Eradicate Homophobia from the Church," *Huffington Post*, March 5, 2013, http:// www .huffingtonpost.com/matthew-vines/the-reformation-project-christians -homophobia_b_2790039.html.

76. "The Reformation Project: Training Christians to Eradicate Homophobia from the Church," *Huffington Post*, March 5, 2013, http:// www .huffingtonpost.com/matthew-vines/the-reformation-project-christians -homophobia_b_2790039.html.

77. Ehrman, *How Jesus Became God*, 172.

78. Coley, *Gay on God's Campus*, 32.

79. Isaac, Jacobs, Kucinskas, and McGrath, "Social Movement Schools."
80. As of mid-2018 Vines had directed five of these leadership-development programs: Kansas City in October 2013; Washington DC in April 2015; Atlanta in April 2016; Los Angeles in April 2017; and Chicago in April 2018.
81. "Statement of Faith," ReformationProject.org, https://www.reformation project.org/statement-of-faith/, accessed October 19, 2017.
82. Vines also referred to them as ambassadors at one point.
83. As of mid-2018 TRP had organized five regional training conferences: Washington DC in November 2014; Atlanta in June 2015; Kansas City in November 2015; Los Angeles in October 2016; and Chicago in October 2017.
84. The Reformation Project, 2015 Atlanta conference program, 14. See also chapter 3.
85. The conversations I describe from the Bible-breakout sessions are reconstructions based on my fieldnotes. The names of Bible-breakout moderators and participants are pseudonyms. There were two of these afternoon sessions, lasting from seventy-five to ninety minutes, at each of the three conferences I attended. Therefore, I do not claim that my impressions of the Bible breakouts are representative of the experience of every conference attendee but are limited to my experience participating in the small groups to which I happened to be assigned.
86. See chapter 4 for a brief discussion of gender complementarianism.
87. Rom. 1:26–29 NRSV.
88. Vines, *God and the Gay Christian*, 93.
89. Vines, *God and the Gay Christian*, 143.
90. Webb, *Slaves, Women and Homosexuals*, 30.
91. I have in mind here Foucault's body of work on various technologies of the self, including the "care of the self." See, for example, Foucault, *Hermeneutics of the Subject*.
92. Webb, *Slaves, Women and Homosexuals*, 13.
93. Webb, *Slaves, Women and Homosexuals*, 22.
94. Webb, *Slaves, Women and Homosexuals*, 37.
95. Webb, *Slaves, Women and Homosexuals*, 252; emphasis in original.
96. Piper and Grudem, *Recovering Biblical Manhood and Womanhood*.
97. Webb, *Slaves, Women and Homosexuals*, 243.
98. Martin, *Sex and the Single Savior*, 50.
99. See chapter 3 for a discussion of Side A/Side B.
100. Jakobsen and Pellegrini, *Love the Sin*, 89.
101. Luhrmann, *When God Talks Back*.

3. *The Sexual Self and Spiritual Health*

1. Nauffts, *Next Fall*.
2. Nauffts, *Next Fall*, 60–61.
3. Nauffts, *Next Fall*, 61–62.
4. Nauffts, *Next Fall*, 62.
5. Cregan, "Queer Spirituality," 153.
6. Throughout this chapter I use "gay Christian," inclusive of both lesbians and gay men, in that my discussion pertains to sexuality and same-sex sexual desire rather than gender identity. When talking about specific individuals, I try to use the language with which they described themselves.
7. On sexuality and the sexual body as sites for the production and negotiation of evangelical belief, see DeRogatis, *Saving Sex*; Erzen, *Straight to Jesus*; and Gerber, *Seeking the Straight and Narrow*. For a brief history of sexuality in religious studies and the role of sexuality in shaping religious beliefs, see Griffith, "Sexing Religion." On the role of sexuality in the formation of Christian belief and identity during the early formative centuries of Christianity, see P. Brown, *Body and Society*. For the role of sex and sexuality in shaping Puritan America, see Godbeer, *Sexual Revolution*.
8. DeRogatis, *Saving Sex*, 1.
9. DeRogatis, *Saving Sex*, 3.
10. Foucault, *History of Sexuality*, 15–49.
11. See 2 Cor. 12:7.
12. H. R. White, *Reforming Sodom*, 4.
13. Tim, "Why I Cannot Identify as a Gay Christian," *Liberum Servus* (blog), October 11, 2014, https://liberumservus.wordpress.com/2014/10/11/why-i-cannot-identify-as-a-gay-christian/.
14. Sedgwick, *Epistemology of the Closet*, 17, 25.
15. Lee, *Torn*, 37–38.
16. Jordan, *Recruiting Young Love*, xx.
17. A 2012 Pew Research Center study found that slightly more than half of white evangelicals believe homosexuality is a choice, compared to less than 20 percent of white mainline Protestants. Pew Research Center, "Obama Endorsement Has Limited Impact: Two-Thirds of Democrats Now Support Gay Marriage," PewForum.org, http://www.pewforum.org/2012/07/31/2012-opinions-on-for-gay-marriage-unchanged-after-obamas-announcement/, last modified July 31, 2012.
18. For ethnographies of ex-gay ministries, see Erzen, *Straight to Jesus*; and Wolkomir, *"Be Not Deceived."* See also M. White, *Stranger at the Gate*.

19. For a concise history of conversion and reparative therapies, see Drescher, "I'm Your Handyman."

20. See, for example, Katz, *Gay American History*, 129–207.

21. Bieber et al., *Homosexuality*; Moberly, *Homosexuality*; and Nicolosi, *Reparative Therapy*. See also LeVay, *Queer Science*, 74–77.

22. Moberly, *Homosexuality*, 9.

23. Jordan, *Recruiting Young Love*, 159.

24. For examinations of compulsory heterosexuality, see Pascoe, *Dude, You're a Fag*; and Rich, "Compulsory Heterosexuality."

25. One pivotal moment was when the American Psychiatric Association removed "homosexuality" from the *Diagnostic and Statistical Manual of Mental Disorders* in 1973, which effectively delegitimized and marginalized proponents of conversion therapy among the scientific and therapeutic professional communities. Drescher, "I'm Your Handyman," 15–16.

26. Perhaps the first ex-gay ministry was Frank Worthen's Love in Action. Renamed New Hope in 1995, Love in Action grew out of Worthen's handmade tape ministry promoting his personal testimony of "stepping out of homosexuality." The organization, which opened its first live-in residential program in 1979, began in 1973 in the San Francisco Bay Area as a small Bible-study group and ministry to help Christians manage their same-sex attractions. Worthen, who died in early 2017, was also instrumental in helping to organize Exodus International in 1976.

27. Nicolosi, along with Charles Socarides and Benjamin Kaufman, founded the NARTH Institute in 1992. Those interested in policing gay Christians will often uphold NARTH as an example of the successes of conversion therapy. See, for example, Gagnon, *The Bible and Homosexual Practice*, 421; and Peter Sprigg, "Gay Christians Should Change or Remain Celibate: A Response to Matthew Vines," *Christian Post*, June 27, 2014, http://www.christianpost.com/news/gay-christians-should-change-or-remain-celibate-a-response-to-matthew-vines-122359/.

28. Herman, *Antigay Agenda*, 61.

29. LaHaye's *The Unhappy Gays* was later retitled *What Everyone Should Know about Homosexuality*. See also LaHaye and Jenkins, *Left Behind*.

30. Jordan, *Recruiting Young Love*, 167.

31. Herman, *Antigay Agenda*, 81–82. *The Gay Agenda* was produced for a weekly cable television talk show called *The Report*, a project of Ty and Jeannette Beeson's Springs of Life Church in California. The video was circulated in Congress and the Pentagon during the early 1990s debates over gay people in the military. David Colker, "Anti-Gay Video Highlights Church's Agenda," *Los Angeles Times*, February 22, 1993, http://articles.latimes.com/1993

-02-22/news/mn-444_1_gay-agenda. John Paulk founded Love Won Out. Like Chambers, Paulk later distanced himself from the ex-gay movement and announced that he no longer believed that reparative therapy could change sexual orientation. Byron Beck, "Is John Paulk Ready to Renounce His Ex-Gay Gospel?" *PQ Monthly*, April 18, 2013, http://www.pqmonthly .com/is-john-paulk-ready-to-renounce-his-ex-gay-gospel-2/13867.

32. Gagnon, *The Bible and Homosexual Practice*, 408–9, 422–23.

33. Erzen, *Straight to Jesus*, 18.

34. Erzen, *Straight to Jesus*, 18. See also p. 186. Beginning in 2012 a number of cities and states began passing legislation banning conversion therapy for minors. Amy B. Wang, "Supreme Court Upholds California's Ban on Gay 'Conversion Therapy,'" *Washington Post*, May 2, 2017, https://www .washingtonpost.com/news/post-nation/wp/2017/04/27/lgbtq-people -were-born-perfect-a-new-bill-would-ban-conversion-therapy-nationwide /?utm_term=.1047f2bc278d.

35. Jordan, *Recruiting Young Love*, 150–59; Jonathan Merritt, "The Downfall of the Ex-Gay Movement: What Went Wrong with the Conversion Ministry, According to Alan Chambers, Who Once Led Its Largest Organization," *The Atlantic*, October 6, 2015, https://www.theatlantic.com/politics/archive /2015/10/the-man-who-dismantled-the-ex-gay-ministry/408970/.

36. Mary Slosson, "Gay 'Conversion Therapy' Proponents Seek to Halt California Ban," Reuters, November 30, 2012, https://www.reuters.com/article /us-usa-california-gaytherapy/gay-conversion-therapy-proponents-seek -to-halt-california-ban-idUSBRE8B000020121201.

37. As reported to me during my fieldwork.

38. Jakobsen and Pellegrini, *Love the Sin*, 1.

39. See, for example, VanderWal-Gritter, *Generous Spaciousness*, 23.

40. For more on Side A/Side B, as well as a discussion about the management of desire among Side B gay Christians, see Creek, "'Not Getting Any.'"

41. Lee, *Torn*, 219–23. GCN was incorporated as a nonprofit in 2004. While the organization's focus initially was mostly limited to gay men, early on Lee expanded the mission to the LGBTQ community more generally, and the organization now seeks to reflect and meet the social and spiritual needs of a more diverse queer religious community. Lee parted ways with GCN in June 2017 for undisclosed reasons.

42. Nearly 1,500 people attended GCN's conference in 2016. Betsy Shirley, "The Gay Christian Network Conference Just Met in Houston. Here's Why That's Significant," *Sojourners*, January 11, 2016, https://sojo.net/articles /gay-christian-network-conference-just-met-houston-heres-why-thats -significant. GCN is now known as Q Christian Fellowship.

43. Fraser, "Rethinking the Public Sphere," 123.

44. Lee, *Torn*, 221.

45. PFLAG is an organization comprised of LGBTQ people, their families, and allies.

46. While the website no longer exists, some of the history of the website is preserved elsewhere online. Heather Elizabeth Peterson, "Pro-Gay and Ex-Gay: Is There Room for Dialogue?" *Greenbelt Interfaith News*, December 1997, http://www.greenbelt.com/news/97/12/03.htm; Maggie Heineman and Steve Calverley, "Bridges across the Divide: Journeys, Faith, and Science," *Whosoever*, July–August 1997, http://www.whosoever.org/Issue7/bridges.html.

47. Lee, *Torn*, 222.

48. Perhaps 95 percent of GCN's participants are Side A or undecided while the remaining 5 percent are Side B. VanderWal-Gritter, *Generous Spaciousness*, 50.

49. Lee, *Torn*, 223.

50. For one gay Christian's perspective on celibacy and spiritual friendships, see Hill, *Washed and Waiting*.

51. See, for example, Kimberly Knight's critique of Side B theology on her blog, hosted on the Patheos website. Kimberly Knight, "Why This Christian Lesbian Was Not at the Gay Christian Network Conference," *Coming Out Christian* (blog), January 11, 2016, http://www.patheos.com/blogs/kimberlyknight/2016/01/why-this-christian-lesbian-was-not-at-the-gay-christian-network-conference/.

52. My analysis of the social and political work of reconciliation narratives is indebted to Lynn Davidman's study of narratives of leaving Hasidic Judaism and, in particular, her emphasis on the role of the body in religious conversion. Davidman, *Becoming Un-Orthodox*.

53. See, for example, Susan Harding's discussion of conversion narratives in *Jerry Falwell*, 33–60, and Kenneth Plummer's discussion of what he calls "sexual stories," including coming-out narratives, in *Telling Sexual Stories*, 126.

54. Seidman, *Beyond the Closet*, 87.

55. Plummer, *Telling Sexual Stories*, 87.

56. There is a vast body of scholarship on conversion. For an extensive historical and theoretical overview of the study of religious conversion, see Rambo and Farhadian, *Oxford Handbook of Religious Conversion*.

57. Harding, *Jerry Falwell*, 33–60.

58. Harding, *Jerry Falwell*, 35.

59. Robbins, "Continuity Thinking," 11.

60. Bender, *New Metaphysicals*, 58.

61. Foucault argues that mysticism itself is a form of counter-conduct: "A third form of counter-conduct is mysticism, that is to say, the privileged status of an experience that by definition escapes pastoral power." Foucault, *Security, Territory, Population*, 212–13.

62. David Shallenberger, *Reclaiming the Spirit*, analyzes similar narratives—he calls them "spiritual journeys"—of how multi-faith lesbians and gay men seek to integrate their sexuality with their spirituality. Many of Shallenberger's interviewees describe the rejection of religion as part of the coming-out process and integration into the gay and lesbian community, only later to rediscover and redefine religion and spirituality.

63. Interview with Paul Creekmore, Kansas City, April 7, 2015. Unless otherwise stated, all quotes are from this interview.

64. Luhrmann, *When God Talks Back*, 132.

65. Bender, *New Metaphysicals*, 66.

66. Bender, *New Metaphysicals*, 66.

67. Matt. 7:15–20 and Luke 6:43–45.

68. The test verse individuals often cite is Gal. 5:22–23: "The fruit of the Spirit is love, joy, peace, patience, kindness, generosity, faithfulness, gentleness, and self-control" (NRSV).

69. Foucault, "Technologies of the Self," 225.

70. Interview with Jonah, Kansas City, September 16, 2015. Unless otherwise stated, all quotes are from this interview.

71. Phil. 4:13.

72. Luke 1:37.

73. *Blueprints to Freedom: An Ode to Bayard Rustin*, written by and starring Michael Benjamin Washington as Rustin, had opened a month before at the La Jolla Playhouse in California.

74. D'Emilio, *Lost Prophet*, 349.

75. Among others: "I cry to you and you do not answer me; I stand, and you merely look at me. You have turned cruel to me; with the might of your hand you persecute me" (Job 30:20–21 NRSV).

76. Sedgwick, *Epistemology of the Closet*, xvi.

77. Gen. 2:18 NRSV.

78. Rubin, "Thinking Sex," 149.

79. On the linkages between the management of sexuality and salvation in Christian traditions, see Foucault, "Sexuality and Solitude," 182.

80. DeRogatis, *Saving Sex*, 151.

81. Vines, *God and the Gay Christian*, 54.

82. Vines, *God and the Gay Christian*, 137, 47.

83. Vines, *God and the Gay Christian*, 155.

84. Vines, *God and the Gay Christian*, 155–56.

85. Vines, *God and the Gay Christian*, 158.

86. Rubin, "Thinking Sex," 153.

87. Moon, Tobin, and Sumerau, "Alpha, Omega, and the Letters in Between," 584; emphasis added. See also Moon and Tobin, "Sunsets and Solidarity." On homonormativity, see Duggan, *Twilight of Equality?*; Stryker, "Transgender History"; and Warner, *Trouble with Normal*.

88. Moon, Tobin, and Sumerau, "Alpha, Omega, and the Letters in Between," 587. I discuss gender complementarianism more at length in chapter 4.

89. Mark Jordan argues that even progressive churches have failed "to provide a Christian poetics of queer desire" (*Recruiting Young Love*, 209).

90. For a history of purity culture in the United States, see Moslener, *Virgin Nation*.

91. Fahs, "Daddy's Little Girls," 117. See also DeRogatis, *Saving Sex*, 41.

92. Based on my fieldnotes at the Atlanta conference, June 13, 2015, and supplemented with TRP's recording of the conference.

93. Schneider, "Homosexuality, Queer Theory, and Christian Theology," 3–4.

94. Jakobsen and Pellegrini, *Love the Sin*, 96; emphasis added.

4. Transgender Figures and Trans Inclusion

1. I use "transgender" throughout as an umbrella term for people whose gender expression or gender identity differs from that which they were assigned at birth. When referring to specific individuals, I try to use the pronouns and terms with which they describe themselves.

2. There is a substantial body of scholarship from queer, feminist, and trans theologians who are rethinking Christian theology through a transgender lens. See, for example, McLaughlin, "Feminist Christologies"; Mollenkott, *Omnigender*; Mollenkott and Sheridan, *Transgender Journeys*; Tanis, *Trans-Gendered*; Tigert and Tirabassi, *Transgendering Faith*; and Althaus-Reid and Isherwood, *Trans/Formations*.

3. See, for example, the opening of chapter 2.

4. Jonathan Capehart, "Obama Comes Out against 'Conversion Therapy' to Support 'Leelah's Law,'" *Washington Post*, April 10, 2015, https://www .washingtonpost.com/blogs/post-partisan/wp/2015/04/10/obama-comes -out-against-conversion-therapy-to-support-leelahs-law/?utm_term= .bb93e6b2a247.

5. Caitlin Emma, "Obama Administration Releases Directive on Transgender Rights to School Bathrooms," *Politico*, May 12, 2016, http://www.politico .com/story/2016/05/obama-administration-title-ix-transgender-student -rights-223149. The Trump administration later rescinded these protec-

tions. Sandhya Somashekhar, Emma Brown, and Moriah Balingit, "Trump Administration Rolls Back Protections for Transgender Students," *Washington Post*, February 22, 2017, https://www.washingtonpost.com/local/education/trump-administration-rolls-back-protections-for-transgender-students/2017/02/22/550a83b4-f913–11e6-bf01-d47f8cf9b643_story.html?utm_term=.be927cef8734.

6. Such legislation was introduced in at least twenty-four state legislatures between 2013 and 2016. Joellen Kralik and Jennifer Palmer, "'Bathroom Bill' Legislative Tracking," NCSL.org, http://www.ncsl.org/research/education/-bathroom-bill-legislative-tracking635951130.aspx#3, last modified July 28, 2017.

7. Katie Zezima, "'Not about Bathrooms': Critics Decry North Carolina Law's Lesser-Known Elements," *Washington Post*, May 14, 2016, https://www.washingtonpost.com/national/not-about-bathrooms-critics-decry-north-carolina-laws-lesser-known-elements/2016/05/14/387946ec-186b-11e6–924d-838753295f9a_story.html?utm_term=.86c32215a693. Compare Herdt, *Moral Panics, Sex Panics*.

8. According to Pew Research Center polling in October 2016, 76 percent of white evangelicals say that transgender people should be required to use the public restrooms corresponding with the gender they were assigned at birth. Michael Lipka, "Americans Are Divided over Which Public Bathrooms Transgender People Should Use," PewResearch.org, http://www.pewresearch.org/fact-tank/2016/10/03/americans-are-divided-over-which-public-bathrooms-transgender-people-should-use/, last modified October 3, 2016.

9. Jordan, *Recruiting Young Love*, 194.

10. Valentine, *Imagining Transgender*, 14–15.

11. O'Donovan, *Transsexualism and Christian Marriage* and *Begotten or Made?*

12. Recent monographs include Anderson, *When Harry Became Sally*; Mohler, *We Cannot Be Silent*; Walker, *God and the Transgender Debate*; and Yarhouse, *Understanding Gender Dysphoria*.

13. Mark Narankevicius Jr., "Transgender People Need As Much Help As the 'Human Ken Doll' Does," *The Federalist*, March 1, 2017, http://thefederalist.com/2017/03/01/transgender-people-need-much-help-human-ken-doll/.

14. Heather Clark, "California Man Undergoes over 100 Procedures in Quest to Transition into 'Genderless' Alien," *Christian News Network*, March 3, 2017, http://christiannews.net/2017/03/03/california-man-undergoes-over-100-procedures-in-quest-to-transition-into-genderless-alien/.

15. Michael L. Brown, "The Father of 7 Who Believes He's a 6-Year-Old Girl," *Charisma News*, December 14, 2015, https://www.charismanews.com

/opinion/in-the-line-of-fire/53811-the-father-of-7-who-believes-he-s-a-6
-year-old-girl. See also "If You Can Be Transgender Why Can't You Be Transracial?" *Christian Post*, June 15, 2015, http://www.christianpost.com/news
/if-you-can-be-transgender-why-cant-you-be-transracial-140396/. People
who identify as furries differ widely, from those who participate in furry
fandom to those who identify as part human and part animal or Otherkin.

16. Cynthia Burack, "Politics of a Praying Nation," documents, for example,
how the Christian Right weaponized "LGBTQ" in its opposition to the
Obama administration.

17. Jordan, *Recruiting Young Love*, xviii; Rudy, *Sex and the Church*, xi.

18. Bethany Blankley, "What the Bible Really Says about 'Transgender,'" *Charisma News*, June 16, 2016, https://www.charismanews.com/opinion
/57835-what-the-bible-really-says-about-transgender.

19. Quoted in "Questions for President Obama: A Town Hall Special," PBS.org,
http://www.pbs.org/newshour/bb/questions-for-president-obama-a-town
-hall-special/, last modified June 1, 2016 (10:09 p.m.).

20. Blankley, "What the Bible Really Says."

21. Deut. 22:5.

22. De La Torre, *Liberating Sexuality*, 161.

23. See, for example, Bruce, *New International Bible Commentary*, 273; Walton, Matthews, and Chavalas, *IVP Bible Background Commentary*, 194;
Barker, *Zondervan NIV Study Bible*, 272. The NIV Study Bible reads transvestism and homosexuality into the verse. The prohibition is "probably
intended to prohibit such perversions as transvestism and homosexual
practices, especially under religious auspices. The God-created differences
between men and women are not to be disregarded." The word "transvestism," coined in 1910, made its way into Bible commentaries by the 1970s
and perhaps earlier.

24. Blankley, "What the Bible Really Says."

25. Blankley, "What the Bible Really Says." See, in contrast, Stevie Borrello,
"Sexual Assault and Domestic Violence Organizations Debunk 'Bathroom
Predator Myth,'" ABC News, April 22, 2016, http://abcnews.go.com/US
/sexual-assault-domestic-violence-organizations-debunk-bathroom
-predator/story?id=38604019.

26. See Moon, Tobin, and Sumerau, "Alpha, Omega, and the Letters in
Between," for a discussion on how TRP and related organizations work to
undo gender by undoing the narrative of gender complementarianism.

27. See, for example, Piper and Grudem, *Recovering Biblical Manhood and
Womanhood*.

28. O'Donovan, *Begotten or Made?*, 29.

29. O'Donovan, *Begotten or Made?*, 66.
30. See, for example, Yarhouse, *Understanding Gender Dysphoria*, 43.
31. The book was published just after the Supreme Court's *Obergefell* decision. Mohler speaks positively of the dissenting opinions in his postscript.
32. Jakobsen and Pellegrini, *Love the Sin*, 13.
33. Mohler, *We Cannot Be Silent*, 69.
34. Mohler, *We Cannot Be Silent*, 75.
35. Mohler, *We Cannot Be Silent*, 35.
36. Mohler, *We Cannot Be Silent*, 39. While Mohler credits *After the Ball* with the strategies and successes of the gay rights movement, in reality the book has arguably been more influential in the antigay rhetoric of the Christian Right. Responding to a blog post in 2006 about his and Kirk's book, Madsen reflected upon the legacy of *After the Ball*: "While the book was widely read (and, in most cases, excoriated) by gay activists when it was first published, in 1989, and while a great many of its techniques have obviously been employed by activists since then, I see no evidence that the book itself serves as any kind of reference for the movement today." Quoted in Jonathan Rowe, "Hunter Madsen Stops By," *The Jon Rowe Archives* (blog), June 23, 2006, http://jonrowe.blogspot.com/2006/06/hunter-madsen -stops-by-who-is-he.html. As part of the prolonged campaign to shore up conservative Christian hegemony, a 2003 book, *The Homosexual Agenda*, by Alan Sears and Craig Osten, both of whom are associated with the conservative Christian and virulently anti-LGBTQ nonprofit Alliance Defending Freedom, similarly used Kirk and Madsen's book to characterize the gay rights movement as a coordinated threat to religious freedom. Alliance Defending Freedom has been working with the Trump administration to advance so-called religious liberty legislation, which enables, among other things, Christians to discriminate against LGBTQ people as an exercise of their "religious freedom." Laura Jarrett, "Sessions Reveals in Closed-Door Speech New Protections for Religious Liberty on the Way," CNN.com, July 13, 2017, http://www.cnn.com/2017/07/13/politics/jeff-sessions-alliance -defending-freedom-speech-released/index.html.
37. For more on the figure of the adolescent as a rhetorical strategy in Christian discourse about same-sex desire, see Jordan, *Recruiting Young Love*.
38. For more on demonology discourse in the Christian Right's antigay rhetoric, see Herman, *Antigay Agenda*, 6, 41.
39. Mohler, *We Cannot Be Silent*, 81.
40. The language of principalities and powers can be found in some translations of Rom. 8:38–39 and Eph. 6:12. Mohler's language closely mirrors the latter: "For we do not wrestle against flesh and blood, but against prin-

cipalities, against powers, against the rulers of the darkness of this age, against spiritual *hosts* of wickedness in heavenly *places*" (New King James Version [NKJV]); emphasis in original.

41. Mohler, *We Cannot Be Silent*, 81.

42. Mohler, *We Cannot Be Silent*, 79.

43. "For it was you who formed my inward parts; you knit me together in my mother's womb" (Ps. 139:13 NRSV).

44. Mohler, *We Cannot Be Silent*, 83.

45. Mohler, *We Cannot Be Silent*, 71.

46. Mohler, *We Cannot Be Silent*, 79.

47. Mohler, *We Cannot Be Silent*, 82.

48. Mohler, *We Cannot Be Silent*, 82.

49. Valentine, *Imagining Transgender*, 14; emphasis in original.

50. Mohler, *We Cannot Be Silent*, 79.

51. Elliot, *Debates*, 36.

52. Wheaton College asks students and staff to sign a "Community Covenant," which declares that only sex that takes place in the context of monogamous, heterosexual marriage is appropriate. Wheaton administrators objected to Rodgers's openly identifying as gay rather than "same-sex attracted" because doing so conflicted with their championing of sexual orientation change and opposition to marriage equality. Julie Rodgers, "How a Leading Christian College Turned against Its Gay Leader," *Time*, February 23, 2016, http://time.com/4233666/wheaton-college-gay-leader/.

53. See figure 3 for a version of the talking points on display at Kansas City PrideFest.

54. Paige, who uses the pronouns they/them, is an ordained elder in the Presbyterian Church (USA) and the executive director of Transfaith, a nonprofit whose mission is to support transgender and gender-nonconforming people through public education and working with faith communities.

55. Ahmed, *On Being Included*, 117.

56. Although taking place before *Obergefell v. Hodges*, by the time of the conference in November 2014, same-sex marriages were legal or recognized in thirty-one states.

57. Jonathan Shorman, "Gov. Sam Brownback Issues Order on Religious Liberty in Wake of Gay Marriage Decision as State Agencies Change Stance," *Topeka Capital-Journal*, July 7, 2015, http://cjonline.com/news-local-state /2015–07–07/gov-sam-brownback-issues-order-religious-liberty-wake -gay-marriage.

58. The conference was held just across the state line in Missouri, but given that the Kansas City metropolitan area straddles the state line, both Kan-

sas and Missouri state politics often shaped conversations at steering committee meetings.

59. Fetner, *How Religious Right Shaped Lesbian and Gay Activism*, 45.

60. My discussion of Christian Scripture and trans identities is not meant to be exhaustive but to call attention to some of the strategies I encountered during my fieldwork. For an in-depth discussion of transgender theology, see Mollenkott, *Omnigender*.

61. "Then God said, 'Let us make humankind in our image, according to our likeness.' . . . So God created humankind in his image, in the image of God he created them; male and female he created them" (Gen. 1:26–27 NRSV). Other feminist and queer theologians have made related arguments about other passages in Scripture. See, for example, Cheng, *Radical Love*, 58, 85.

62. McNeill, *Freedom*, 211. Gaiser, "A New Word on Homosexuality?" makes a similar argument using Isa. 56:1–8.

63. One frequently cited verse is: "There is no longer Jew or Greek, there is no longer slave or free, there is no longer male and female; for all of you are one in Christ Jesus" (Gal. 3:28 NRSV).

64. See also chapter 2. Harding defines "witnessing" as a practice of conversion (*Jerry Falwell*, 35).

65. "Conduct yourselves honorably among the Gentiles, so that, though they malign you as evildoers, they may see your honorable deeds and glorify God when he comes to judge" (1 Pet. 2:12 NRSV). Some versions translate the Greek *epopteuontes*—rendered here as "see," from *epopteo*, meaning "to watch" or "inspect"—as "witness."

66. Toward the end of *God and the Gay Christian*, Vines raises the issue of "witness" in the context of when reasoned argument fails. Drawing on and quoting John Boswell, Vines writes: "Gay Christians, Boswell continued, can follow in Christ's footsteps. While they should engage the scriptural concerns of their brothers and sisters, reasoned argument has its limits. Ultimately, the most powerful case gay Christians can offer is the witness of their own lives. 'It is much harder for most people to remain hostile to and unmoved by a living brother than it is to rail against an abstraction,' Boswell concluded. 'Gay Christians are *logoi* in this sense, arguments incarnated in persons'" (*God and the Gay Christian*, 178; Vines quotes from Boswell, "Logos and Biography").

67. Alex McNeill, "Guest Post: Why I Tell My Story: Putting It All on the Line," GLAAD.org, November 19, 2012, https://www.glaad.org/blog/guest-post -why-i-tell-my-story-putting-it-all-line?response_type=embed.

68. For debates in transgender studies over intelligibility and unintelligibility, see Elliot, *Debates*, 61–83. See also Cornwall, "Apophasis and Ambiguity."

69. Austen Hartke was also one of the discussants on this panel. I introduce the other participants farther on.

70. Greer, Broderick, (@BroderickGreer), April 21, 2015, 7:47 p.m. Tweet.

71. "I affirm, by the boasting in you which I have in Christ Jesus our Lord, I die daily" (1 Cor. 15:31 NKJV).

5. Academies of Racial Justice

1. Megan Rohrer, ordained in 2006, is the first openly transgender person to be ordained by the ELCA.

2. This practice is known as deadnaming.

3. Matt Campbell, "Murder Charge Filed in Kansas City Transgender Death," *Kansas City Star*, June 20, 2016, http://www.kansascity.com/news/local /crime/article84922117.html.

4. Homa Khaleeli, "#SayHerName: Why Kimberlé Crenshaw Is Fighting for Forgotten Women," *The Guardian*, May 30, 2016, https://www.theguardian .com/lifeandstyle/2016/may/30/sayhername-why-kimberle-crenshaw -is-fighting-for-forgotten-women.

5. See Mbembe, "Necropolitics"; and Puar, *Terrorist Assemblages*, 36. Compare Snorton and Haritaworn, "Trans Necropolitics."

6. Amelia Markham, "Why The Reformation Project's Atlanta Conference Will Start with a Racial Justice Institute," *Believe Outloud* (blog), May 27, 2015, https://www.believeoutloud.com/latest/why-reformation-project %e2%80%99s-atlanta-conference-will-start-racial-justice-institute.

7. Jordan, *Convulsing Bodies*, 10.

8. Alexander, *Pedagogies of Crossing*, 324.

9. Ahmed, "Affective Economies," 119; emphasis in original. See also Ahmed, *Cultural Politics of Emotion*. Compare Pellegrini, "'Signaling through the Flames.'"

10. Foucault, "Technologies of the Self," 225.

11. Foucault, *Security, Territory, Population*, 205.

12. Emily Waters, "Lesbian, Gay, Bisexual, Transgender, Queer, and HIV-Affected Hate Violence in 2016" (New York: National Coalition of Anti-Violence Programs, 2016), http://avp.org/wp-content/uploads/2017/06 /NCAVP_2016hateViolence_REPORT.pdf.

13. These figures are according to a 2016 study by the Pew Research Center. Hannah Fingerhut, "Support Steady for Same-Sex Marriage and Acceptance of Homosexuality," Pew Research Center, May 12, 2016, http://www .pewresearch.org/fact-tank/2016/05/12/support-steady-for-same-sex -marriage-and-acceptance-of-homosexuality/.

14. Stephanie Russell-Kraft, "#SorryNotSorry: What U.S. Christian Denominations Teach about Homosexuality," *Religion Dispatches*, June 28, 2016, http://religiondispatches.org/sorrynotsorry-what-u-s-christian-denominations-teach-about-homosexuality/.

15. Barrett-Fox, *God Hates*, 115.

16. The basic structure and content were roughly the same at both workshops.

17. This is not even to mention the deeply concerning close relationship between various alt-right groups and some groups on the Christian Right. For the connections between white Christian fundamentalism and the protection of whiteness, see Harding, "Representing Fundamentalism"; and Jones, *The End of White Christian America*.

18. "Religious Landscape Study: Evangelical Protestants," Pew Research Center, https://www.pewforum.org/religious-landscape-study/religious-tradition/evangelical-protestant/, accessed April 8, 2020.

19. Gasaway, *Progressive Evangelicals*, 77.

20. Gasaway, *Progressive Evangelicals*, 76.

21. Bartkowski, *Promise Keepers*, 62–63.

22. In fact evangelicalism's historical relationship to white nationalism helps explain the broad white evangelical support of Trump's presidential campaign. According to exit polls, 81 percent of white evangelicals voted for Trump, a higher percentage than those who in 2000 and 2004 voted for George W. Bush, whose religious and moral values ostensibly aligned more consistently with the evangelical community. Gregory A. Smith and Jessica Martínez, "How the Faithful Voted: A Preliminary 2016 Analysis," PewResearch.org, http://www.pewresearch.org/fact-tank/2016/11/09/how-the-faithful-voted-a-preliminary-2016-analysis/, last modified November 9, 2016.

23. David Weigel, "Glenn Beck Got 20,000 People to Turn Out for an 'All Lives Matter' Rally," *Washington Post*, August 31, 2015, https://www.washingtonpost.com/news/post-politics/wp/2015/08/31/glenn-beck-got-20000-people-to-turn-out-for-an-all-lives-matter-rally/; John Inazu, "Do Black Lives Matter to Evangelicals?" *Washington Post*, January 6, 2016, https://www.washingtonpost.com/news/acts-of-faith/wp/2016/01/05/do-black-lives-matter-to-evangelicals/.

24. Wallis, *America's Original Sin*.

25. Duggan, *Twilight of Equality?*; and Roediger, "Making Solidarity Uneasy."

26. Shirley, "The Gay Christian Network Conference Just Met in Houston. Here's Why That's Significant," *Sojourners*, January 11, 2016, https://sojo.net/articles/gay-christian-network-conference-just-met-houston-heres-why-thats-significant.

27. The figure of "roughly a third" comes from a 2012 Gallup poll. Gary J. Gates and Frank Newport, "Special Report: 3.4% of U.S. Adults Identify as LGBT," Gallup.com, http://www.gallup.com/poll/158066/special-report-adults-identify-lgbt.aspx, last modified October 18, 2012.

28. Keone, Kenji, (@Afreshmind), June 11, 2015, 5:36 p.m. Tweet.

29. According to the National LGBTQ Task Force's website, the Racial Justice Institute at the 2015 Denver conference marked the eighth year the day-long institute had opened the annual conferences. "Building an Anti-Racist LGBT Movement at Creating Change," TheTaskForce.org, http://www.thetaskforce.org/building-an-anti-racist-lgbt-movement-at-creating-change/, accessed October 18, 2017.

30. Markham, "Why The Reformation Project's Atlanta Conference Will Start with a Racial Justice Institute."

31. I use pseudonyms throughout for the facilitators and participants in the Academy for Racial Justice workshops.

32. Roestone Collective, "Safe Space," 110–11. See also Collins, *Black Feminist Thought*, 110–11.

33. Quoted in Eliel Cruz, "Gay Christian Network Gathering Models What the Church Could Be," *Religion News Service*, January 13, 2015, http://religionnews.com/2015/01/13/together-table-time-feasting/.

34. Justin Massey, "Special Report: Gay Christian Conference Shows Hope for a New Era of Evangelicalism," *Bedlam Magazine*, January 13, 2015, http://www.bedlammag.com/special-report-gay-christian-conference-shows-hope-for-a-new-era-of-evangelicalism/.

35. Ahmed, "Affective Economies," 119.

36. "Uniting Communities," WesternStatesCenter.org, http://www.westernstatescenter.org/our-work/uniting_communities, accessed October 18, 2017.

37. Landsberg, *Prosthetic Memory*, 2.

38. Landsberg, *Prosthetic Memory*, 2.

39. "Queer spawn" is a phrase that refers to a child of LGBTQ parents. Nikkei are Japanese people in diaspora.

40. He was paraphrasing Ps. 46:1: "God is our refuge and strength, a very present help in trouble" (NRSV).

41. The idiom comes from Ezek. 22:30: "So I sought for a man among them who would make a wall, and stand in the gap before Me on behalf of the land, that I should not destroy it; but I found no one" (NKJV).

42. Butler, *Precarious Life*, 30.

43. Puar, *Terrorist Assemblages*, 28.

44. Foucault, "The Subject and Power," 330.

45. Foucault, *Hermeneutics of the Subject*, 208.

Conclusion

1. Davidson, "In Praise of Counter-Conduct," 33–39.
2. Asad, "Thinking about Religion, Belief, and Politics," 56; emphasis in original.
3. Asad, "Thinking about Religion, Belief, and Politics," 56; emphasis in original.
4. Butler, *Precarious Life*, 23.
5. Asad, *Formations of the Secular*, 183; Jakobsen and Pellegrini, *Love the Sin*, 4, and "Introduction to World Secularism at the Millennium," 15.
6. Jakobsen and Pellegrini, "Bodies-Politics," 147.
7. "Nashville Statement," CBMW.org, https://cbmw.org/nashville-statement, accessed September 15, 2017.
8. Sarah Jones, "The Nashville Statement Is the Religious Right's Death Rattle," *New Republic*, September 5, 2017, https://newrepublic.com/article/144679/nashville-statement-religious-rights-death-rattle; Eliel Cruz, "The Nashville Statement Is an Attack on LGBT Christians," *New York Times*, September 1, 2017, https://www.nytimes.com/2017/09/01/opinion/nashville-statement-lgbt-christians.html.
9. Henry Giroux, among others, has written about the authoritarian strain of the Christian Right: "What progressives and others need to acknowledge and make visible is that the . . . attempt to undo the separation between church and state is driven by a form of fundamentalism that discredits democratic values, public goods, the social state, and critical citizenship. . . . Religious fundamentalism poses a direct challenge to the secular traditions that inform the most basic foundations of American democracy, and it is the roots and heritage of this tradition that must become an object of historical recovery and pedagogical engagement" ("Rapture Politics," 81).
10. Greene, *Moral Tribes*; and Kahan, Jenkins-Smith, and Braman, "Cultural Cognition."
11. Feinberg and Willer, "From Gulf to Bridge," 1.

Bibliography

Abu-Lughod, Lila. "Writing against Culture." In *Recapturing Anthropology: Working in the Present*, edited by Richard Fox, 137–62. Santa Fe NM: School of American Research, 1991.

Agamben, Giorgio. *The Time That Remains: A Commentary on the Letter to the Romans*. Stanford CA: Stanford University Press, 2005.

Ahmed, Sara. "Affective Economies." *Social Text* 22, no. 2 (2004): 117–39.

———. *The Cultural Politics of Emotion*. New York: Routledge, 2004.

———. *On Being Included: Racism and Diversity in Institutional Life*. Durham NC: Duke University Press, 2012.

Alexander, M. Jacqui. *Pedagogies of Crossing: Meditations on Feminism, Sexual Politics, Memory, and the Sacred*. Durham NC: Duke University Press, 2005.

Althaus-Reid, Marcella, and Lisa Isherwood, eds. *Trans/Formations*. London: SCM, 2009.

Althusser, Louis. "Ideology and Ideological State Apparatuses: Notes towards an Investigation." In Louis Althusser, *Lenin and Philosophy and Other Essays*, 127–86. New York: Monthly Review Press, 1972.

Ammerman, Nancy T. *Bible Believers: Fundamentalism in the Modern World*. New Brunswick NJ: Rutgers University Press, 1987.

Anderson, Ryan T. *When Harry Became Sally: Responding to the Transgender Moment*. New York: Encounter Books, 2018.

Armstrong, Elizabeth A. *Forging Gay Identities: Organizing Sexuality in San Francisco, 1950–1994*. Chicago: University of Chicago Press, 2002.

Asad, Talal. *Formations of the Secular: Christianity, Islam, Modernity*. Stanford CA: Stanford University Press, 2003.

———. *Genealogies of Religion: Discipline and Reasons of Power in Christianity and Islam*. Baltimore: Johns Hopkins University Press, 1993.

———. *The Idea of an Anthropology of Islam*. Washington DC: Center for Contemporary Arab Studies, 1986.

———. "Religion and Politics: An Introduction." *Social Research* 59, no. 1 (1992): 3–16.

———. "Thinking about Religion, Belief, and Politics." In Orsi, *The Cambridge Companion to Religious Studies*, 36–57.

———. "Thinking about Tradition, Religion, and Politics in Egypt Today." *Critical Inquiry* 42, no. 1 (2015): 166–214.

Bailey, Derrick Sherwin. *Homosexuality and the Western Christian Tradition*. Hamden CT: Archon Books, 1975.

———. "The Problem of Sexual Inversion." *Theology* 55, no. 380 (1952): 47–52.

Balmer, Randall. *Encyclopedia of Evangelicalism*. Louisville: Westminster John Knox Press, 2002.

———. *Mine Eyes Have Seen the Glory: A Journey into the Evangelical Subculture in America*. New York: Oxford University Press, 1989.

Barker, Kenneth L. *Zondervan NIV Study Bible*. Rev. ed. Grand Rapids MI: Zondervan, 2002.

Barrett-Fox, Rebecca. *God Hates: Westboro Baptist Church, American Nationalism, and the Religious Right*. Lawrence: University Press of Kansas, 2016.

Bartkowski, John P. *The Promise Keepers: Servants, Soldiers, and Godly Men*. New Brunswick NJ: Rutgers University Press, 2004.

———. *Remaking the Godly Marriage: Gender Negotiation in Evangelical Families*. New Brunswick NJ: Rutgers University Press, 2001.

Bebbington, David W. *Evangelicalism in Modern Britain: A History from the 1730s to the 1980s*. New York: Routledge, 1989.

Behar, Ruth, and Deborah Gordon, eds. *Women Writing Culture*. Berkeley: University of California Press, 1995.

Bender, Courtney. *The New Metaphysicals: Spirituality and the American Religious Imagination*. Chicago: University of Chicago Press, 2010.

———. "Practicing Religions." In Orsi, *The Cambridge Companion to Religious Studies*, 273–95.

Berger, Peter L. *The Sacred Canopy: Elements of a Sociological Theory of Religion*. Garden City NY: Anchor Books, 1969.

Bernauer, James W., and Jeremy R. Carrette. *Foucault and Theology: The Politics of Religious Experience*. Aldershot: Ashgate, 2004.

Bialecki, Jon. "The Bones Restored to Life: Dialogue and Dissemination in the Vineyard's Dialectic of Text and Presence." In *The Social Life of Scriptures: Cross-Cultural Perspectives on Biblicism*, edited by James S. Bielo, 136–56. New Brunswick NJ: Rutgers University Press, 2009.

Bieber, Irving, et al. *Homosexuality: A Psychoanalytic Study*. New York: Basic Books, 1962.

Bielo, James S. "Introduction: Encountering Biblicism." In *The Social Life of Scriptures: Cross-Cultural Perspectives on Biblicism*, edited by James S. Bielo, 1–9. New Brunswick NJ: Rutgers University Press, 2009.

———. *Words upon the Word: An Ethnography of Evangelical Group Bible Study*. New York: New York University Press, 2009.

Binkley, Sam, and Barbara Cruikshank. "Counter-Conduct [Special Issue]." *Foucault Studies* 21 (2016).

———. "Introduction: Counter-Conduct." *Foucault Studies* 21 (2016): 3–6.

Boisvert, Donald L., and Jay Emerson Johnson, eds. *Queer Religion: Homosexuality in Modern Religious History*. Santa Barbara CA: ABC-CLIO, 2012.

Boswell, John. *Christianity, Social Tolerance, and Homosexuality: Gay People in Western Europe from the Beginning of the Christian Era to the Fourteenth Century*. Chicago: University of Chicago Press, 1980.

———. "Logos and Biography." In *Theology and Sexuality: Classic and Contemporary Readings*, edited by Eugene F. Rogers Jr., 356–61. Malden MA: Blackwell, 2002.

———. "Revolutions, Universals, Sexual Categories." *Salmagundi* 58–59 (1983): 89–113.

Bowen, John R. "Elaborating Scriptures: Cain and Abel in Gayo Society." *Man* 27 (1992): 495–516.

Brekus, Catherine A. *Sarah Osborn's World: The Rise of Evangelical Christianity in Early America*. New Haven CT: Yale University Press, 2013.

Brown, Brené. *Daring Greatly: How the Courage to Be Vulnerable Transforms the Way We Live, Love, Parent, and Lead*. New York: Gotham Books, 2012.

Brown, Peter. *The Body and Society: Men, Women, and Sexual Renunciation in Early Christianity*. New York: Columbia University Press, 2008.

Bruce, F. F., ed. *New International Bible Commentary*. Grand Rapids MI: Zondervan, 1979.

Bucke, Emory S., J. Wesley Hole, and John E. Proctor. *The Book of Discipline of the United Methodist Church*. Nashville: United Methodist Publishing House, 1973.

Burack, Cynthia. "The Politics of a Praying Nation: The Presidential Prayer Team and Christian Right Sexual Morality." *Journal of Religion and Popular Culture* 26, no. 2 (2014): 215–29.

Burrow-Branine, Jon. "Blogging While Gay and Christian: Andrew Sullivan and the Production of the Religious, Secular, and Sexual." *Culture and Religion* 16, no. 1 (2015): 66–86.

Butler, Judith. *Bodies That Matter: On the Discursive Limits of "Sex."* New York: Routledge, 1993.

———. *Gender Trouble: Feminism and the Subversion of Identity*. New York: Routledge, 1990.

———. *Precarious Life: The Powers of Mourning and Violence*. London: Verso, 2006.

Buzzell, Timothy. "Gay and Lesbian Activism in American Protestant Churches: Religion, Homosexuality, and the Politics of Inclusion." In *The Politics of Social Inequality*, edited by Betty A. Dobratz, Lisa K. Waldner, and Timothy Buzzell, 83–114. Kidlington, UK: Elsevier Science, 2001.

Cadge, Wendy. "Vital Conflicts: The Mainline Denominations Debate Homosexuality." In *The Quiet Hand of God: Faith-Based Activism and the Public Role of Mainline Protestantism*, edited by Robert Wuthnow and John Hyde Evans, 265–86. Berkeley: University of California Press, 2002.

Carter, Julian B. *The Heart of Whiteness: Normal Sexuality and Race in America, 1880–1940*. Durham NC: Duke University Press, 2007.

Casanova, José. *Public Religions in the Modern World*. Chicago: University of Chicago Press, 1994.

Cheng, Patrick S. *Radical Love: An Introduction to Queer Theology*. New York: Seabury Books, 2011.

Cho, Sumi, Kimberlé Crenshaw, and Leslie McCall. "Toward a Field of Intersectionality Studies: Theory, Applications, and Praxis." *Signs: Journal of Women in Culture and Society* 38, no. 4 (2013): 785–810.

Chrulew, Matthew. "Pastoral Counter-Conducts: Religious Resistance in Foucault's Genealogy of Christianity." *Critical Research on Religion* 2, no. 1 (2014): 55–65.

Chu, Jeff. *Does Jesus Really Love Me? A Gay Christian's Pilgrimage in Search of God in America*. New York: Harper, 2013.

Cobb, Michael. *God Hates Fags: The Rhetorics of Religious Violence*. New York: New York University Press, 2006.

Cody, Francis. "Publics and Politics." *Annual Review of Anthropology* 40 (2011): 37–52.

Coley, Jonathan S. *Gay on God's Campus: Mobilizing for LGBT Equality at Christian Colleges and Universities*. Chapel Hill: University of North Carolina Press, 2018.

Collins, Patricia Hill. *Black Feminist Thought: Knowledge, Consciousness, and the Politics of Empowerment*. Boston: UnwinHyman, 1990.

Comstock, Gary David. *A Whosoever Church: Welcoming Lesbians and Gay Men into African American Congregations*. Louisville: Westminster John Knox Press, 2001.

Comstock, Gary David, and Susan Henking, eds. *Que(e)rying Religion: A Critical Anthology*. New York: Continuum, 1999.

Conlon, Deirdre. "Hungering for Freedom: Asylum Seekers' Hunger Strikes—Rethinking Resistance as Counter-Conduct." In *Carceral Spaces: Mobility and Agency in Imprisonment and Migrant Detention*, edited by Dominique Moran, Nick Gill, and Deirdre Conlon, 133–48. New York: Routledge, 2013.

Cornwall, Susannah. "Apophasis and Ambiguity: The 'Unknowingness' of Transgender." In Althaus-Reid and Isherwood, *Trans/Formations*.

Creek, S. J. "'Not Getting Any Because of Jesus': The Centrality of Desire Management to the Identity Work of Gay, Celibate Christians." *Symbolic Interaction* 36, no. 2 (2013): 119–36.

Cregan, David. "Queer Spirituality and the Ethics of the Open Horizon in Geoffrey Nauffts's *Next Fall*." *Performing Ethos* 2, no. 2 (2011): 137–54.

Crenshaw, Kimberlé. "Demarginalizing the Intersection of Race and Sex: A Black Feminist Critique of Antidiscrimination Doctrine, Feminist Theory and Antiracist Politics." *University of Chicago Legal Forum*, no. 1 (1989): 139–67.

———. "Mapping the Margins: Intersectionality, Identity Politics, and Violence against Women of Color." *Stanford Law Review* 43, no. 6 (1991): 1241–99.

Csordas, Thomas J. "Embodiment as a Paradigm for Anthropology." *Ethos* 18, no. 1 (1990): 5–47.

Davidman, Lynn. *Becoming Un-Orthodox: Stories of Ex-Hasidic Jews*. Oxford: Oxford University Press, 2015.

———. *Tradition in a Rootless World: Women Turn to Orthodox Judaism*. Berkeley: University of California Press, 1991.

Davidson, Arnold I. "In Praise of Counter-Conduct." *History of the Human Sciences* 24, no. 4 (2011): 25–41.

Davie, Jodie Shapiro. *Women in the Presence: Constructing Community and Seeking Spirituality in Mainline Protestantism*. Philadelphia: University of Pennsylvania Press, 1995.

Davis, James Calvin. *In Defense of Civility: How Religion Can Unite America on Seven Moral Issues That Divide Us*. Louisville: Westminster John Knox Press, 2010.

Dean, Mitchell. *Governmentality: Power and Rule in Modern Society*. 2nd ed. Los Angeles: SAGE, 2010.

Death, Carl. "Counter-Conducts: A Foucauldian Analytics of Protest." *Social Movement Studies* 9, no. 3 (2010): 235–51.

DeFranza, Megan K. *Sex Difference in Christian Theology: Male, Female, and Intersex in the Image of God*. Grand Rapids MI: Eerdmans, 2015.

De La Torre, Miguel A. *Liberating Sexuality: Justice between the Sheets*. St. Louis MO: Chalice, 2016.

D'Emilio, John. *Lost Prophet: The Life and Times of Bayard Rustin*. Chicago: University of Chicago Press, 2003.

———. *Making Trouble: Essays on Gay History, Politics, and the University*. New York: Routledge, 1992.

————. *Sexual Politics, Sexual Communities: The Making of the Homosexual Minority in the United States, 1940–1970*. Chicago: University of Chicago Press, 1983.

D'Emilio, John, and Estelle B. Freedman. *Intimate Matters: A History of Sexuality in America*. 3rd ed. Chicago: University of Chicago Press, 2012.

DeRogatis, Amy. *Saving Sex: Sexuality and Salvation in American Evangelicalism*. New York: Oxford University Press, 2015.

Dochuck, Darren. *From Bible Belt to Sunbelt: Plain-Folk Religion, Grassroots Politics, and the Rise of Evangelical Conservatism*. New York: W. W. Norton, 2011.

Dowland, Seth. *Family Values and the Rise of the Christian Right*. Philadelphia: University of Pennsylvania Press, 2015.

Drake, Susanna. *Slandering the Jew: Sexuality and Difference in Early Christian Texts*. Philadelphia: University of Pennsylvania Press, 2013.

Drescher, Jack. "I'm Your Handyman: A History of Reparative Therapies." *Journal of Homosexuality* 36, no. 1 (1998): 5–24.

Duggan, Lisa. *The Twilight of Equality? Neoliberalism, Cultural Politics, and the Attack on Democracy*. Boston: Beacon Press, 2003.

Ehrman, Bart D. *How Jesus Became God: The Exaltation of a Jewish Preacher from Galilee*. New York: HarperCollins, 2014.

Elisha, Omri. *Moral Ambition: Mobilization and Social Outreach in Evangelical Megachurches*. Berkeley: University of California Press, 2011.

Elliot, Patricia. *Debates in Transgender, Queer, and Feminist Theory: Contested Sites*. Burlington VT: Ashgate, 2010.

Emerson, Robert M., Rachel I. Fretz, and Linda L. Shaw. *Writing Ethnographic Fieldnotes*. 2nd ed. Chicago: University of Chicago Press, 2011.

Engelke, Matthew. *God's Agents: Biblical Publicity in Contemporary England*. Berkeley: University of California Press, 2013.

Erzen, Tanya. *Straight to Jesus: Sexual and Christian Conversions in the Ex-Gay Movement*. Berkeley: University of California Press, 2006.

Faderman, Lillian. *The Gay Revolution: The Story of the Struggle*. New York: Simon and Schuster, 2015.

Fahs, Breanne. "Daddy's Little Girls: On the Perils of Chastity Clubs, Purity Balls, and Ritualized Abstinence." *Frontiers: A Journal of Women Studies* 31, no. 3 (2010): 116–42.

Feinberg, Matthew, and Robb Willer. "From Gulf to Bridge: When Do Moral Arguments Facilitate Political Influence?" *Personality and Social Psychology Bulletin* 41, no. 12 (2015): 1–17.

Fetner, Tina. "Ex-Gay Rhetoric and the Politics of Sexuality: The Christian Anti-gay/Pro-Family Movement's 'Truth in Love' Ad Campaign." *Journal of Homosexuality* 50, no. 1 (2005): 71–95.

———. *How the Religious Right Shaped Lesbian and Gay Activism*. Minneapolis: University of Minnesota Press, 2008.

Fletcher, John. *Preaching to Convert: Evangelical Outreach and Performance Activism in a Secular Age*. Ann Arbor: University of Michigan Press, 2013.

Foucault, Michel. *The Hermeneutics of the Subject: Lectures at the Collège de France, 1981–1982*. Translated by Graham Burchell. New York: Picador, 2005.

———. *The History of Sexuality*. Vol. 1, *An Introduction*. New York: Pantheon, 1978.

———. *Security, Territory, Population: Lectures at the Collège de France, 1977–1978*. Translated by Graham Burchell. New York: Picador, 2007.

———. "Sexuality and Solitude." In Michel Foucault, *Ethics: Subjectivity and Truth*, edited by Paul Rabinow, 175–84. New York: New Press, 1997.

———. "The Subject and Power." In Michel Foucault, *Power*, edited by James D. Faubion, 326–48. New York: New Press, 2000.

———. "Technologies of the Self." In Michel Foucault, *Ethics: Subjectivity and Truth*, edited by Paul Rabinow, 223–51. New York: New Press, 1997.

———. *The Use of Pleasure: The History of Sexuality*. Vol. 2. New York: Pantheon Books, 1985.

Frank, Thomas. *What's the Matter with Kansas? How Conservatives Won the Heart of America*. New York: Metropolitan Books, 2004.

Fraser, Nancy. "Rethinking the Public Sphere: A Contribution to the Critique of Actually Existing Democracy." In *Habermas and the Public Sphere*, edited by Craig Calhoun, 109–42. Cambridge MA: MIT Press, 1992.

Frei, Hans W. "Response to 'Narrative Theology: An Evangelical Appraisal.'" *Trinity Journal* 8 (1987): 21–24.

———. *Theology and Narrative: Selected Essays*. Edited by George Hunsinger and William C. Placher. New York: Oxford University Press, 1993.

Fuist, Todd Nicholas, Laurie Cooper Stoll, and Fred Kniss. "Beyond the Liberal-Conservative Divide." *Qualitative Sociology* 35, no. 1 (2012): 65–87.

Gagnon, Robert A. J. *The Bible and Homosexual Practice: Texts and Hermeneutics*. Nashville: Abingdon, 2001.

Gaiser, Frederick J. "A New Word on Homosexuality? Isaiah 56:1–8 as Case Study." *Word and World* 14, no. 3 (1994): 280–93.

Garriott, William, and Kevin Lewis O'Neill. "Who Is a Christian? Towards a Dialogic Approach in the Anthropology of Christianity." *Anthropological Theory* 8, no. 4 (2008): 381–98.

Gasaway, Brantley W. *Progressive Evangelicals and the Pursuit of Social Justice*. Chapel Hill: University of North Carolina Press, 2014.

Gerber, Lynne. *Seeking the Straight and Narrow: Weight Loss and Sexual Reorientation in Evangelical America*. Chicago: University of Chicago Press, 2011.

Giroux, Henry A. "Rapture Politics and the Passion of the Religious Right." In *America on the Edge: Henry Giroux on Politics, Culture, and Education*, 71–87. New York: Palgrave Macmillan, 2006.

Gloege, Timothy E. W. *Guaranteed Pure: The Moody Bible Institute, Business, and the Making of Modern Evangelicalism*. Chapel Hill: University of North Carolina Press, 2015.

Godbeer, Richard. *Sexual Revolution in Early America*. Baltimore: Johns Hopkins University Press, 2004.

Goff, Philip, Arthur E. Farnsley II, and Peter J. Thuesen. *The Bible in American Life*. Indianapolis: Center for the Study of Religion and American Culture, 2014.

Greene, Joshua David. *Moral Tribes: Emotion, Reason, and the Gap between Us and Them*. New York: Penguin Press, 2013.

Grenz, Stanley J. *Renewing the Center: Evangelical Theology in a Post-Theological Era*. Grand Rapids MI: Baker Academic, 2000.

———. *Welcoming but Not Affirming: An Evangelical Response to Homosexuality*. Louisville: Westminster John Knox Press, 1998.

Griffith, R. Marie. *Born Again Bodies: Flesh and Spirit in American Christianity*. Berkeley: University of California Press, 2004.

———. "Sexing Religion." In Orsi, *The Cambridge Companion to Religious Studies*, 338–59.

Gutjahr, Paul C. "From Monarchy to Democracy: The Dethroning of the King James Bible in the United States." In *The King James Bible after 400 Years: Literary, Linguistic, and Cultural Influences*, edited by Hannibal Hamlin and Norman W. Jones, 164–78. Cambridge: Cambridge University Press, 2010.

Habermas, Jürgen. *The Structural Transformation of the Public Sphere: An Inquiry into a Category of Bourgeois Society*. Translated by Thomas Burger. Cambridge MA: MIT Press, 1989.

Harding, Susan Friend. *The Book of Jerry Falwell: Fundamentalist Language and Politics*. Princeton NJ: Princeton University Press, 2000.

———. "Representing Fundamentalism: The Problem of the Repugnant Cultural Other." *Social Research* 58, no. 2 (1991): 373–93.

Harris, Joshua. *I Kissed Dating Goodbye*. Colorado Springs CO: Multnomah, 1997.

Herbst, Susan. *Rude Democracy: Civility and Incivility in American Politics*. Philadelphia: Temple University Press, 2010.

Herdt, Gilbert, ed. *Moral Panics, Sex Panics: Fear and the Fight over Sexual Rights*. New York: New York University Press, 2009.

Herman, Didi. *The Antigay Agenda: Orthodox Vision and the Christian Right*. Chicago: University of Chicago Press, 1997.

Hill, Wesley. *Washed and Waiting: Reflections on Christian Faithfulness and Homo-sexuality*. Grand Rapids MI: Zondervan, 2010.

Hirschkind, Charles. *The Ethical Soundscape: Cassette Sermons and Islamic Coun-terpublics*. New York: Columbia University Press, 2006.

Hornsby, Teresa J. "Heteronormativity/Heterosexism." In *The Oxford Encyclo-pedia of the Bible and Gender Studies*, edited by Julia M. O'Brien, 321–27. Oxford: Oxford University Press, 2014.

Hulsether, Mark. *Building a Protestant Left: Christianity and Crisis Magazine, 1941–1993*. Knoxville: University of Tennessee Press, 1999.

———. *Religion, Culture, and Politics in the Twentieth-Century United States*. New York: Columbia University Press, 2007.

Hunter, James Davison. *Culture Wars: The Struggle to Define America*. New York: Basic Books, 1991.

Isaac, Larry W., Anna W. Jacobs, Jaime Kucinskas, and Allison R. McGrath. "Social Movement Schools: Sites for Consciousness Transformation, Train-ing, and Prefigurative Social Development." *Social Movement Studies* 19, no. 2 (2020): 1–23.

Jakobsen, Janet R. "Sex + Freedom = Regulation: Why?" *Social Text* 23, nos. 3–4 (2005): 285–308.

Jakobsen, Janet R., and Ann Pellegrini. "Bodies-Politics: Christian Secularism and the Gendering of U.S. Policy." In *Religion, the Secular, and the Politics of Sexual Difference*, edited by Linell E. Cady and Tracy Fessenden, 139–74. New York: Columbia University Press, 2013.

———. "Introduction to World Secularisms at the Millennium." *Social Text* 64 (2000): 1–28.

———. *Love the Sin: Sexual Regulation and the Limits of Religious Tolerance*. New York: New York University Press, 2003.

Jasper, James M. *The Art of Moral Protest: Culture, Biography, and Creativity in Social Movements*. Chicago: University of Chicago Press, 1997.

Jones, Robert P. *The End of White Christian America*. New York: Simon and Schuster, 2016.

Jordan, Mark D. *Convulsing Bodies: Religion and Resistance in Foucault*. Stanford CA: Stanford University Press, 2015.

———. *The Invention of Sodomy in Christian Theology*. Chicago: University of Chicago Press, 1997.

———. *Recruiting Young Love: How Christians Talk about Homosexuality*. Chi-cago: University of Chicago Press, 2011.

Kahan, Dan M., Hank Jenkins-Smith, and Donald Braman. "Cultural Cognition of Scientific Consensus." *Journal of Risk Research* 14, no. 2 (2010): 147–74.

Katz, Jonathan Ned. *Gay American History: Lesbians and Gay Men in the USA*. New York: Meridian, 1992.

———. *The Invention of Heterosexuality*. New York: Dutton, 1995.

Kirk, Marshall, and Hunter Madsen. *After the Ball: How America Will Conquer Its Fear and Hatred of Gays in the '90s*. New York: Doubleday, 1989.

Kniss, Fred. "Mapping the Moral Order: Depicting the Terrain of Religious Conflict and Change." In *Handbook of the Sociology of Religion*, edited by Michele Dillon, 331–47. New York: Cambridge University Press.

Kuefler, Mathew, ed. *The Boswell Thesis: Essays on Christianity, Social Tolerance, and Homosexuality*. Chicago: University of Chicago Press, 2006.

LaHaye, Tim F. *What Everyone Should Know about Homosexuality*. Carol Stream IL: Tyndale House, 1978.

LaHaye, Tim F., and Jerry B. Jenkins. *Left Behind: A Novel of the Earth's Last Days*. Carol Stream IL: Tyndale House, 1995.

Landsberg, Alison. *Prosthetic Memory: The Transformation of American Remembrance in the Age of Mass Culture*. New York: Columbia University Press, 2004.

Latour, Bruno. "From Realpolitik to Dingpolitik." In *Making Things Public: Atmospheres of Democracy*, edited by Bruno Latour and Peter Weibel, 4–31. Cambridge MA: MIT Press, 2005.

Lee, Justin. *Torn: Rescuing the Gospel from the Gays-vs.-Christians Debate*. New York: Jericho Books, 2012.

LeVay, Simon. *Queer Science: The Use and Abuse of Research into Homosexuality*. Cambridge MA: MIT Press, 1996.

Lorenzini, Daniele. "From Counter-Conduct to Critical Attitude: Michel Foucault and the Art of Not Being Governed Quite So Much." *Foucault Studies* 21 (2016): 7–21.

Luhrmann, Tanya M. *When God Talks Back: Understanding the American Evangelical Relationship with God*. New York: Alfred A. Knopf, 2012.

Madison, D. Soyini. *Critical Ethnography: Method, Ethics, and Performance*. 2nd ed. Thousand Oaks CA: SAGE, 2012.

Marsden, George M. *Fundamentalism and American Culture*. 2nd ed. New York: Oxford University Press, 2006.

———. *Understanding Fundamentalism and Evangelicalism*. Grand Rapids MI: Eerdmans, 1991.

Martin, Dale B. *Sex and the Single Savior*. Louisville: Westminster John Knox Press, 2006.

Marty, Martin E. *Pilgrims in Their Own Land: 500 Years of Religion in America*. Boston: Little, Brown, 1984.

Mauss, Marcel. *The Gift: Forms and Functions of Exchange in Archaic Societies*. London: Cohen and West, 1966.

Mbembe, Achille. "Necropolitics." *Public Culture* 15, no. 1 (2003): 11–40.

McGuire, Meredith B. "Religion and the Body: Rematerializing the Human Body in the Social Sciences of Religion." *Journal for the Scientific Study of Religion* 29 (1990): 283–96.

McKanan, Dan. *Prophetic Encounters: Religion and the American Radical Tradition*. Boston: Beacon Press, 2011.

McLaren, Brian D. *A Generous Orthodoxy: Why I Am a Missional, Evangelical, Post/Protestant, Liberal/Conservative, Mystic/Poetic, Biblical, Charismatic/ Contemplative, Fundamentalist/Calvinist, Anabaptist/Anglican, Methodist, Catholic, Green, Incarnational, Depressed-Yet-Hopeful, Emergent, Unfinished Christian*. Grand Rapids MI: Zondervan, 2004.

McLaughlin, Eleanor. "Feminist Christologies: Re-Dressing the Tradition." In *Reconstructing the Christ Symbol: Essays in Feminist Christology*, edited by Maryanne Stevens, 118–49. Eugene OR: Wipf and Stock, 1993.

McNeill, John J. *Freedom, Glorious Freedom: The Spiritual Journey to the Fullness of Life for Gays, Lesbians, and Everybody Else*. Maple Shade NJ: Lethe, 1995.

McQueeney, Krista. "'We Are God's Children, Y'all': Race, Gender, and Sexuality in Lesbian- and Gay-Affirming Congregations." *Social Problems* 56, no. 1 (2009): 151–73.

Moberly, Elizabeth R. *Homosexuality: A New Christian Ethic*. Cambridge: James Clark, 1983.

Mohler, R. Albert, Jr., ed. *God and the Gay Christian? A Response to Matthew Vines*. Louisville: SBTS, 2014.

———. *We Cannot Be Silent: Speaking Truth to a Culture Redefining Sex, Marriage, and the Very Meaning of Right and Wrong*. Nashville: Nelson Books, 2015.

Mollenkott, Virginia Ramey. *Omnigender: A Trans-Religious Approach*. Cleveland: Pilgrim, 2001.

Mollenkott, Virginia Ramey, and Vanessa Sheridan. *Transgender Journeys*. Eugene OR: Resource, 2003.

Moon, Dawne. "Difficult Dialogues: The Technologies and Limits of Reconciliation." In *Religion on the Edge: De-centering and Re-centering the Sociology of Religion*, edited by Courtney Bender, Wendy Cadge, Peggy Levitt, and David Smilde, 179–99. New York: Oxford University Press, 2012.

———. *God, Sex, and Politics: Homosexuality and Everyday Theologies*. Chicago: University of Chicago Press, 2004.

Moon, Dawne, and Theresa W. Tobin. "Humility: Rooted in Relationship, Reaching for Justice." *Political Power and Social Theory* 36 (2019): 101–21.

———. "The Politics of Shame in the Motivation to Virtue: Lessons from the Shame, Pride, and Humility Experiences of LGBT Conservative Christians and Their Allies." *Journal of Moral Education* 48 no. 1 (2018): 109–25.

———. "Sunsets and Solidarity: Overcoming Sacramental Shame in Conservative Christian Churches to Forge a Queer Vision of Love and Justice." *Hypatia* 33, no. 3 (2018): 451–68.

Moon, Dawne, Theresa W. Tobin, and J. E. Sumerau. "Alpha, Omega, and the Letters in Between: LGBTQI Conservative Christians Undoing Gender." *Gender & Society* 33, no. 4 (2019): 583–606.

Moore, R. Laurence. *Religious Outsiders and the Making of Americans*. New York: Oxford University Press, 1986.

Moslener, Sara. *Virgin Nation: Sexual Purity and American Adolescence*. New York: Oxford University Press, 2015.

Nauffts, Geoffrey. *Next Fall*. New York: Dramatists Play Service, 2010.

Nicolosi, Joseph. *Reparative Therapy of Male Homosexuality: A New Clinical Approach*. Lanham MD: Rowman and Littlefield, 1991.

Niebuhr, H. Richard. *The Social Sources of Denominationalism*. New York: Holt, 1929.

O'Donovan, Oliver. *Begotten or Made? Human Procreation and Medical Technique*. Oxford: Clarendon, 1984.

———. *Transsexualism and Christian Marriage*. Bramcote, UK: Grove Books, 1982.

Okely, Judith. *Anthropological Practice: Fieldwork and Ethnographic Method*. New York: Bloomsbury, 2012.

Orsi, Robert A. *Between Heaven and Earth*. Princeton NJ: Princeton University Press, 2005.

———, ed. *The Cambridge Companion to Religious Studies*. Cambridge: Cambridge University Press, 2012.

———. *History and Presence*. Cambridge MA: Harvard University Press, 2016.

Pascoe, C. J. *Dude, You're a Fag: Masculinity and Sexuality in High School*. Berkeley: University of California Press, 2007.

Pellegrini, Ann. "'Signaling through the Flames': Hell House Performance and Structures of Religious Feeling." *American Quarterly* 59, no. 3 (2007): 911–35.

———. "Testimonial Sexuality; or, Queer Structures of Religious Feeling: Notes towards an Investigation." *Journal of Dramatic Theory and Criticism* 20, no. 1 (2005): 93–102.

Peterson, Eugene H. *The Message: The New Testament, Psalms, and Proverbs in Contemporary Language*. Colorado Springs CO: NavPress, 1995.

Petro, Anthony. *After the Wrath of God: AIDS, Sexuality, and American Religion*. New York: Oxford University Press, 2015.

Piper, John, and Wayne Grudem, eds. *Recovering Biblical Manhood and Womanhood: A Response to Evangelical Feminism*. Wheaton IL: Crossway, 2012. First published in 1991.

Plummer, Kenneth. *Telling Sexual Stories: Power, Change and Social Worlds*. New York: Routledge, 1995.

Porterfield, Amanda. *Conceived in Doubt: Religion and Politics in the New American Nation*. Chicago: University of Chicago Press, 2012.

"Position Statement on Therapies Focused on Attempts to Change Sexual Orientation (Reparative or Conversion Therapies)." *American Journal of Psychiatry* 157, no. 10 (2000): 1719–21.

Puar, Jasbir K. "Reading Religion Back into *Terrorist Assemblages*: Author's Response." *Culture and Religion* 15, no. 2 (2014): 198–210.

———. *Terrorist Assemblages: Homonationalism in Queer Times*. Durham NC: Duke University Press, 2007.

Rambo, Lewis R., and Charles E. Farhadian, eds. *The Oxford Handbook of Religious Conversion*. Oxford: Oxford University Press, 2014.

Rich, Adrienne. "Compulsory Heterosexuality and Lesbian Existence." *Signs* 5, no. 4 (1980): 631–60.

Robbins, Joel. "Continuity Thinking and the Problem of Christian Culture: Belief, Time, and the Anthropology of Christianity." *Current Anthropology* 48, no. 1 (2007): 5–38.

———. "What Is a Christian? Notes toward an Anthropology of Christianity." *Religion* 33, no. 3 (2003): 191–99.

Rochon, Thomas R. *Culture Moves: Ideas, Activism, and Changing Values*. Princeton NJ: Princeton University Press, 1998.

Roediger, David R. "Making Solidarity Uneasy: Cautions on a Keyword from Black Lives Matter to the Past." *American Quarterly* 68, no. 2 (2016): 223–48.

Roestone Collective. "Safe Space: Towards a Reconceptualization." *Antipode* 46, no. 5 (2014): 1346–65.

Rubin, Gayle S. "Thinking Sex: Notes for a Radical Theory of the Politics of Sexuality." In *Pleasure and Danger: Exploring Female Sexuality*, edited by Carol Vance, 143–78. New York: Routledge, 1984.

Rudy, Kathy. *Sex and the Church: Gender, Homosexuality, and the Transformation of Christian Ethics*. Boston: Beacon Press, 1997.

Schneider, Laurel. "Homosexuality, Queer Theory, and Christian Theology." *Religious Studies Review* 26, no. 1 (2000): 3–12.

Sears, Alan, and Craig Osten. *The Homosexual Agenda: Exposing the Principal Threat to Religious Freedom Today*. Nashville: Broadman and Holman, 2003.

Sedgwick, Eve Kosofsky. *Epistemology of the Closet*. Berkeley: University of California Press, 1990.

Seidman, Steven. *Beyond the Closet: The Transformation of Gay and Lesbian Life*. New York: Routledge, 2002.

Shallenberger, David. *Reclaiming the Spirit: Gay Men and Lesbians Come to Terms with Religion*. New Brunswick NJ: Rutgers University Press, 1998.

Smith, Christian. *The Bible Made Impossible: Why Biblicism Is Not a Truly Evangelical Reading of Scripture*. Grand Rapids MI: Brazos, 2011.

Snorton, C. Riley, and Jin Haritaworn. "Trans Necropolitics: A Transnational Reflection on Violence, Death, and the Trans of Color Afterlife." In *The Transgender Studies Reader 2*, edited by Susan Stryker and Aren Z. Aizura, 66–76. New York: Routledge, 2013.

Springs, Jason A. *Generous Orthodoxy: Prospects for Hans Frei's Postliberal Theology*. Cambridge: Oxford University Press, 2010.

Stein, Arlene. *The Stranger Next Door: The Story of a Small Community's Battle over Sex, Faith, and Civil Rights*. Boston: Beacon Press, 2001.

Streenland, Brian, and Philip Goff, eds. *The New Evangelical Social Engagement*. New York: Oxford University Press, 2014.

Stryker, Susan. "Transgender History, Homornormativity, and Disciplinarity." *Radical History Review* 100 (2008): 145–57.

Sumerau, J. E. "'That's What a Man Is Supposed to Do': Compensatory Manhood Acts in an LGBT Christian Church." *Gender & Society* 26, no. 3 (2012): 461–87.

Sutton, Matthew Avery. *American Apocalypse: A History of Modern Evangelicalism*. Cambridge MA: Belknap, 2014.

Swartz, David R. *Moral Minority: The Evangelical Left in an Age of Conservatism*. Philadelphia: University of Pennsylvania Press, 2012.

Talvacchia, Kathleen T., Michael F. Pettinger, and Mark Larrimore, eds. *Queer Christianities: Lived Religion in Transgressive Forms*. New York: New York University Press, 2015.

Tanis, Justin Edward. *Trans-Gendered: Theology, Ministry, and Communities of Faith*. Cleveland: Pilgrim, 2003.

Taylor, Charles. *A Secular Age*. Cambridge MA: Belknap, 2007.

Thomas, Jim. *Doing Critical Ethnography*. Newbury Park CA: SAGE, 1993.

Thuesen, Peter J. *In Discordance with the Scriptures: American Protestant Battles over Translating the Bible*. Oxford: Oxford University Press, 1999.

Thumma, Scott. "Negotiating a Religious Identity: The Case of the Gay Evangelical." *Sociological Analysis* 52, no. 4 (1991): 333–47.

Thumma, Scott, and Edward R. Gray, eds. *Gay Religion*. Walnut Creek CA: AltaMira, 2005.

Tigert, Leanne McCall, and Maren C. Tirabassi, eds. *Transgendering Faith: Identity, Sexuality, and Spirituality*. Cleveland: Pilgrim, 2004.

Troeltsch, Ernst. *The Social Teachings of the Christian Churches*. New York: Macmillan, 1931.

Turner, Bryan S. *Religion and Modern Society: Citizenship, Secularisation, and the State*. Cambridge: Cambridge University Press, 2011.

Udis-Kessler, Amanda. *Queer Inclusion in the United Methodist Church*. New York: Routledge, 2008.

Valentine, David. *Imagining Transgender: An Ethnography of a Category*. Durham NC: Duke University Press, 2007.

VanderWal-Gritter, Wendy. *Generous Spaciousness: Responding to Gay Christians in the Church*. Grand Rapids MI: Brazos, 2014.

Vickers, Jason E., ed. *The Cambridge Companion to American Methodism*. Cambridge: Cambridge University Press, 2013.

Vines, Matthew. *God and the Gay Christian: The Biblical Case in Support of Same-Sex Relationships*. New York: Convergent Books, 2014.

Walker, Andrew T. *God and the Transgender Debate: What Does the Bible Actually Say about Gender Identity?* Centralia WA: Good Book Company, 2017.

Wallis, Jim. *America's Original Sin: Racism, White Privilege, and the Bridge to a New America*. Grand Rapids MI: Brazos, 2016.

Walton, John H., Victor H. Matthews, and Mark W. Chavalas. *The IVP Bible Background Commentary: Old Testament*. Downers Grove IL: InterVarsity, 2000.

Warner, Michael. *The Trouble with Normal: Sex, Politics, and the Ethics of Queer Life*. Cambridge MA: Harvard University Press, 1999.

Webb, William J. *Slaves, Women and Homosexuals: Exploring the Hermeneutics of Cultural Analysis*. Downers Grove IL: InterVarsity, 2001.

Weber, Max. "On Church, Sect, and Mysticism." *Sociological Analysis* 34 (1973): 140–49.

Weston, Kath. "The Virtual Anthropologist." In *Anthropological Locations: Boundaries and Grounds of a Field Science*, edited by Akhil Gupta and James Ferguson, 163–84. Berkeley: University of California Press, 1997.

White, Heather R. "Proclaiming Liberation: The Historical Roots of LGBT Religious Organizing, 1946–1976." *Nova Religio* 11, no. 4 (2008): 102–19.

———. *Reforming Sodom: Protestants and the Rise of Gay Rights*. Chapel Hill: University of North Carolina Press, 2015.

White, Mel. *Stranger at the Gate: To Be Gay and Christian in America*. New York: Plume, 1994.

Wilcox, Melissa M. *Coming Out in Christianity: Religion, Identity, and Community*. Bloomington: Indiana University Press, 2003.

———. "Outlaws or In-Laws?" *Journal of Homosexuality* 52, nos. 1–2 (2006): 73–100.

———. "When Sheila's a Lesbian: Religious Individualism among Lesbian, Gay, Bisexual, and Transgender Christians." *Sociology of Religion* 63, no. 4 (2002): 497–513.

Williams, Daniel K. *God's Own Party: The Making of the Christian Right*. New York: Oxford University Press, 2010.

Wilson, Ken. *A Letter to My Congregation: An Evangelical Pastor's Path to Embracing People Who Are Gay, Lesbian and Transgender into the Company of Jesus*. Canton MI: Read the Spirit Books, 2014.

Wolkomir, Michelle. *"Be Not Deceived": The Sacred and Sexual Struggles of Gay and Ex-Gay Christian Men*. New Brunswick NJ: Rutgers University Press, 2006.

Wood, Robert W. *Christ and the Homosexual: Some Observations*. New York: Vantage, 1960.

Worthen, Molly. *Apostles of Reason: The Crisis of Authority in American Evangelicalism*. New York: Oxford University Press, 2013.

Wuthnow, Robert. *Red State Religion: Faith and Politics in America's Heartland*. Princeton NJ: Princeton University Press, 2012.

———. *The Restructuring of American Religion: Society and Faith since World War II*. Princeton NJ: Princeton University Press, 1988.

Yarhouse, Mark A. *Understanding Gender Dysphoria: Navigating Transgender Issues in a Changing Culture*. Downers Grove IL: IVP Academic, 2015.

Young, Neil J. *We Gather Together: The Religious Right and the Problem of Interfaith Politics*. New York: Oxford University Press, 2015.

Index

academic study of American religion. *See* American religious studies

academic study of LGBTQ people. *See* LGBTQ studies

Academy for Racial Justice: activities and practices of, 185–99; and affective economies, 179, 188; and counter-conduct, 177; and evangelical racial politics, 177–79, 181; and prosthetic memories, 192; purpose and inspiration of, 177, 186

activism: antigay, 11–12, 54, 67, 118–19, 152–53, 156–59; antitransgender, 150–62, 168; conservative evangelical, 10–12; definition of, 17–21; and ethnography, 28–29; as an evangelical ethos, 17; and LGBTQ organizations, 8, 13; progressive evangelical, 18. *See also* counter-conduct; LGBTQ Christian activism

affect, 176, 179, 188

affirming Christians, 15–16, 18, 123, 164–65

Agamben, Giorgio, 63

Ahmed, Sara, 164, 177, 188

allyship, 16, 87, 197

American religious studies, 9

Anderson, Carmarion, 172–74

Anderson, Matthew Lee, 59–60

apologia, 80–81, 87

Asad, Talal, 37, 202–3

attentional learning, 53

authoritarianism, 203–4

authority: biblical, 5, 69, 70, 82, 85, 89, 97–98, 103, 107–9; challenges to, 46; moral, 45; pastoral, 36, 68; patriarchal, 102; of religious experience, 127; white evangelical culture of, 21

Bailey, Derrick Sherwin, 79–81

bathroom bills, 151, 157

Bebbington quadrilateral, 68–69

belief, 9, 17, 96, 113–15, 126–40, 204–5

Bender, Courtney, 127, 129

Bible: as authoritative, 5, 69, 70, 82, 85, 89, 97–98, 100, 103, 107–9; and counter-conduct, 68; and experience, 69, 99, 104–5, 108–9; and heteronormativity, 71, 74–76; inclusive message of, 99–103, 169–70; and inerrancy, 69; interpretation of, 48–49, 68–69, 93, 100, 226n36; politics of, 26–27, 70, 109; as presence, 69; and training at TRP conferences, 86–97; and transgender issues,

Martin, Dale, 103

matters of concern, 38–39, 42, 46

McLaren, Brian, 55

McNeill, Alex, 169, 171–72, 174

McNeill, John, 169

Mere Orthodoxy, 59

The Message (Bible translation), 76

Metropolitan Community Church
(MCC), 13–14

microaggressions, 64

Moberly, Elizabeth, 117, 119

Mohler, R. Albert, Jr., 59, 79, 158–62

Moo, Douglas, 75

Moon, Dawne, 36, 42

moral panics, 151

narrative theology. *See* postliberal
theology

NARTH Institute, 118–19

Nashville Statement, 203–4

National City Christian Church, 33

National LGBTQ Task Force, 186

Neo Sandja, 172

New Direction Ministries, 54

New International Version (NIV),
74–75

New Revised Standard Version
(NRSV), 74

Next Fall (play), 111–13

Nicolosi, Joseph, 117, 119

nonaffirming Christians. *See* affirming
Christians

nondenominationalism, 12, 40, 44. *See
also* denominationalism

Obama, Barack, 155

Obama administration, 150, 156

Obergefell v. Hodges, 67, 150, 166. *See
also* marriage equality

objects of concern, 3, 68, 113, 153

O'Donovan, Oliver, 152–53, 157–58

Orsi, Robert, 69

Paige, Chris, 164–65, 170

parachurch organizations, 10–15,
45–46, 59

pastoral power, 19, 36, 68

patriarchy, 83, 85, 97, 100–103, 143,
146, 157

Perry, Troy, 13–14

Plummer, Kenneth, 126

politics: of the Bible, 26–27, 70, 109;
and conservative evangelicals,
16–18, 21, 35–39, 114, 119, 146, 152,
154, 176–82; definition of, 37;
Kansas, 5, 166; and LGBTQ
Christian activism, 42–43, 47, 58,
62–63, 164, 166, 172, 198–99,
202–4; as making things public,
37–39; and religion, 10, 21, 37

postevangelicalism, 18

postliberal theology, 55

postmodernism, 158, 160

power: academic study of, 7–8; in
Christian discourse, 34–35, 159,
169, 180, 189–90; and counter-
conduct, 19–21; cultural and
political, of conservative evangelicals, 85, 204; and religion, 37, 177;
and resistance, 21

progressive evangelicals, 18

prosthetic memories, 192

Puar, Jasbir, 7, 199

publics, 37–39, 42, 47, 62–63, 122. *See
also* counterpublics

purity culture, 144

queer secularity, 7–8, 13, 112

Racial Justice Institute, 186

Springs, Jason A., 55
Strachan, Owen, 59, 60
strategic essentialism, 75, 147
subaltern counterpublics. *See* counterpublics; publics
Sullivan, Andrew, 5
supersessionism, 84–85
Supreme Court, U.S. See *Obergefell v. Hodges*

Taylor, Vivian, 169–70
technologies of the self, 131, 177, 199
Teetsel, Eric, 59, 60
theodicy, 198
theology, 3–4, 34, 55, 86, 201
Third Way churches, 56–60
Thomas, Jim, 25
transgender: and antitransgender activism, 149–62; and the Bible, 151–52, 155–56, 160, 169–70, 173; Christians, experiences of, 149–51, 168–74, 175–76; and LGBTQ Christian activism, 162–68. *See also* gender
Transgender Day of Remembrance, 1–2
Tree and Its Fruits (Bible parable), 89–90, 131
Trump, Donald J., 181, 197, 204

United Church of Christ (UCC) Gay Caucus, 15
United Methodist Church, 36, 40, 60
United Methodist Gay Caucus, 41

VanderWal-Gritter, Wendy, 53–56
Vines, Matthew, 4–6, 22–23, 58–61, 76–91, 98–103, 142–46, 167. *See also* The Reformation Project (TRP)
viscerality, 70, 176
vulnerability, 63, 178, 187, 195, 198–99, 203

Wallis, Jim, 181
Washington, Shae, 98–99, 100, 132–33
Webb, William J., 100–102
welcoming churches, 14–16, 164–65, 170
Westboro Baptist Church, 178
Westphal, Karl Friedrich Otto, 72
White, Heather, 71
whiteness, 20, 73, 176, 179, 181–82. *See also* racism and LGBTQ Christian activism
Wilson, Ken, 56, 165
witnessing, 127, 170–74
Wood, Robert, 81
Wuthnow, Robert, 10

In the Anthropology of Contemporary North America series:

To order or obtain more information on these or other
University of Nebraska Press titles, visit nebraskapress.unl.edu.